D0208764

The AGEING & DEVELOPMENT *Report*

Poverty, Independence & the World's Older People

HelpAge INTERNATIONAL

EARTHSCAN

The Ageing and Development Report

The Ageing and Development Report
Poverty, Independence and the World's Older People

Edited by Judith Randel, Tony German and
Deborah Ewing of Development Initiatives

Earthscan Publications Ltd, London

Help the Aged

The Ageing and Development Report is funded by Help the Aged

First published in the UK in 1999 by
Earthscan Publications Limited

A catalogue record for this book is available from the British Library

ISBN: 1 85383 648 6

Typesetting and page design by PCS Mapping & DTP, Newcastle upon Tyne
Printed and bound by Thanet Press Ltd, Margate, Kent   .
Cover design by Andrew Corbett
Cover photo © Barry Lewis/Network

For a full list of publications please contact:

Earthscan Publications Limited
120 Pentonville Road
London N1 9JN
Tel: +44 (0)171 278 0433
Fax: +44 (0)171 278 1142
Email: earthinfo@earthscan.co.uk
http://www.earthscan.co.uk

Earthscan is an editorially independent subsidiary of Kogan Page Limited and publishes in association
with WWF-UK and the International Institute for Environment and Development.

Ths book is printed on elemental chlorine free paper.

Contents

Part I: An Introduction to Ageing and Development

Part II: The State of the World's Older People

Part III: Ageing and Development Data

Part IV: Reference Section

List of Figures, Boxes and Tables

Figures

Boxes

Tables

Foreword

A global demographic revolution is underway. At its heart is the growth in the number and proportion of older people, and the worldwide transition from high death and birth rates to low mortality and fertility. One of the great achievements of our century has been the significant growth of life expectancy at birth in almost every country of the world. Public health advances in both rich and poor countries mean that for the first time in human history the majority of people can expect to survive into old age. Given that the proportion of the world's population over 60 years is increasing more rapidly than in any previous era, it is timely and appropriate that the United Nations (UN) has chosen the closing year of the century to celebrate the contribution of older people to social well-being by declaring 1999 as the International Year of Older Persons.

As we celebrate we also need to remind ourselves that poverty and exclusion remain the greatest threats to the well-being of older people all over the world. Far too many older people remain on the margins of their societies. Too many older people spend the later years of their lives in poverty, beyond the reach of even the most basic provision for social well-being and health. The majority of older people are women, often widows, who suffer multiple disadvantages on the basis of their gender, ranging from abandonment to failing health. Yet the evidence is that most older people are not only resourceful survivors, but are supporting the fabric and well-being of their families and communities.

The challenge for policy makers is to make the extra years worth living.
© Sean Sprague/ Panos Pictures

The productive contribution of older people to their families and communities goes largely unrecognized and unnoticed by policy makers across the globe. To add to the burden they carry, many older people have to work into very old age – not by choice but from the sheer necessity to survive. This is so especially in developing countries, often despite chronic and disabling diseases.

Fifty years on from the United Nations Declaration of Universal Human Rights, and eight years since the UN adopted specific principles for older persons covering the fields of independence, care, participation, self-fulfilment and dignity, we find that basic and recognized rights of older citizens are still denied or restricted. Many older people face insidious age discrimination in the provision of services and access to support; many face discrimination and abuse; many are forgotten and invisible in emergencies; our social support systems are inadequate for their needs; too often their voice goes unheard or is silenced.

This not only represents a denial of rights to a significant and growing proportion of the world's people. It is also a waste of a resource which needs to be seen as a precious asset. Older people have skills and experience which if better recognized could be of enormous value to their communities and societies. In some countries governments have begun to recognize their responsibility to ensure that the rights of older persons are not violated, that they get opportunities to contribute and that they receive an equitable share in development benefits. Measures which benefit older people are not only an expression of their social inclusion, but can also assist other disadvantaged social groups. Now, more than ever before, there is a global need for affirmative action in favour of older people.

To help this process the World Health Organization (WHO) is launching within this International Year the Global Movement on Active Ageing. Our contribution is fundamental to ensuring that a majority of older persons will enjoy the highest possible quality of life in older age. For rich or poor, in the North or the South, men or women, in any culture, health is regarded as the most important asset for active ageing. This was the theme of our World Health Day earlier this year. And this is my personal pledge – to strengthen WHO action in this field.

As we celebrate the millennium it is most appropriate to reflect on the situation of older people in the developed and developing world and resolve to remedy their hardship by adopting attitudes, policies and programmes that protect and support their rights and contributions. This timely report by HelpAge International sets out to establish some of the key social and political issues affecting older people's lives. It also poses challenges, and puts forward to policy and programme makers ideas based on sound experience. The report highlights a number of priority themes, including the factors relating to the health and well-being of older people, the role of family and community in their lives, and the importance of material support, especially for the poorest. *The Ageing and Development Report* marks the first documentation of this information, and I feel sure that it will be an important contribution to the growing debate on issues affecting the lives of the world's oldest and poorest citizens – a debate with which WHO feels proud to be associated.

Gro Harlem Brundtland, MD, MPH
Director-General
World Health Organization

Ageing and Development:
The Message

The ageing of the global population is a triumph of the 20th century and presents unprecedented opportunities. But for the majority of older people, who live on or below the poverty line, the future also carries great uncertainties.

This report reviews the state of our knowledge of the situation of older people in developing and transitional countries. It seeks to examine the impact which social and economic development policies have had – and could have – on older people struggling to overcome poverty and disadvantage.

Unlike other major social and economic changes, it is possible to predict ageing with a considerable degree of confidence. If old age is not to be synonymous with endemic poverty then policies and resources need to be redirected now to support the rights of older people.

Paying residents and fundraising subsidize care for poorer people in this home in Belize.
© Adam Platt/ HelpAge International

Executive Summary

A global demographic revolution is underway

- The rapid, large-scale and widespread growth in the numbers of older people has never before been seen in the history of the planet.
- The proportion of the world's population over 60 years is increasing more rapidly than in any previous era.
- In 1950 there were about 200 million people over 60 throughout the world. In the year 2000 there will be about 550 million, and by 2025 there will be about 1.2 billion.
- The 20th century is witnessing a rapid demographic transition from high birth and death rates to low fertility and mortality.

The speed of change is without precedent

- It took France 115 years to increase the proportion of its older population from 7 per cent to 14 per cent.
- In Japan the same process has occurred in the quarter century between 1970 and 1996.
- In many developing countries it will take 20 years or less and it will have happened by 2040.

This demographic shift is certain, and its main outlines can be discerned

- All those who will be over 65 in the first half of the 21st century are alive today.
- For the first time in history, the majority of those who have survived childhood in all countries can expect to live past 50 years of age.

Most of the world's older people live in developing countries

- The myth that older populations do not exist in the developing world because life expectancy is low does not stand up. Those who survive the diseases of infancy and childhood even in the world's poorest countries have a very good chance of living to be grandparents.
- 61 per cent of the global population of people over 60 live in developing countries now; that will be 70 per cent by 2025.
- The number of older people in developing countries will more than double over the next quarter century, reaching 850 million by 2025 – 12 per cent of the population.
- By 2020, countries like Cuba, Argentina, Thailand and Sri Lanka will have higher proportions of over-65s than the US does today.

Older people are consistently among the poorest people. Poverty and exclusion remain the greatest threats to their well being

- People who have lived their lives in poverty cannot accumulate savings.
- Older people's cash incomes are a fraction of minimum earnings and material assets are typically of very little value.
- In developing countries, older age is associated with problems of poor diet, ill health and inadequate housing.
- Older people are often isolated, living on the margins of families and communities and deeply vulnerable. The extent to which they are reached by services and support is a litmus test of the development process.

Ageing is an increasingly female experience

- women outlive men in nearly all countries, rich and poor. In developed countries older women account for more than 10 per cent of the total population.
- The number of older women in Asia currently exceeds the total for all older women in developed countries and will increase from 144 million today to 355 million by 2025.
- Sub-Saharan Africa's 15 million older women are projected to more than double to 33 million by 2025.
- Older women are more likely than not to be widows, with this likelihood increasing with age. In 1990 there were 21.5 million widows in China, greater than the combined total for Europe.
- Older women often suffer multiple disadvantages arising from biases of gender, widowhood and old age.

Many older people are resourceful survivors, and contribute to the well being of their families and communities

- The substantial productive contribution of older people to their families and communities is largely unrecognized by policy makers.
- Too often older people are stereotyped as passive or helpless – the realities of their lives unobserved.
- Ageing is often perceived as a burden for countries and communities. But channelling resources to enable older people is an investment in society.

The great enemy of independence and autonomy in old age is not changing family or community values, but poverty

- The majority of older people in most countries live in their own homes, in connection to their own families and communities. The remarkable feature of family support is its durability, not its fragility.
- But rapid urbanization and migration for work in many countries have significantly altered family and community relations, especially where changing living conditions and lack of income stretch family capacities to provide for the more vulnerable members.
- Demographic change will increase strains on hard-pressed family support structures, as falling fertility rates combine with increasing longevity.
- Care of older, dependent parents will fall on fewer children, and the impact will be greatest on those with the least material resources.

Many people enter old age in a poor state of health resulting from life-long deprivations

- A 40 year old woman with a history from childhood of poor nutrition, multiple pregnancies and punishing physical labour is already on the threshold of old age.
- Chronic illness is endemic among many older people in the developing world, where technical advances in medicine have far outrun the social and economic development which in industrialized countries have enabled relatively disease-free living.

The ageing world is a world of work, especially in developing countries

- In developing countries the majority of old people continue to work into very old age, often despite chronic and disabling illness. Work encompasses not only paid labour, but also the full range of livelihoods on which older people, in common with other age groups, rely.
- In most developing countries older people are concentrated in rural areas, but they are also small traders, traditional healers, providers of domestic help, and involved in countless other pursuits.
- Only a small proportion of countries in either the developed or developing world provide comprehensive social security or pension programmes. These have no impact on the great majority of people who work in the informal sectors of their countries' economies.

Fifty years on from the United Nations Declaration of Universal Human Rights the rights of older citizens are still denied or restricted

- Older people face insidious age discrimination in the provision of services and access to support.
- Some governments have begun to recognize their responsibility to ensure that the rights of older persons are not violated, that they get opportunities to contribute and an equitable share in development benefits.
- The requirement for affirmative action in favour of older people needs to be assessed.
- Special attention needs to be paid to older women so that they do not become victims of triple neglect and discrimination on account of gender, widowhood and age.

Recommendations and Action Points

The far-reaching economic and social implications of global ageing during the next century are beginning to be recognized in countries throughout the South and the North. Much of the focus, however, is on the 'crisis', rather than the challenge of ageing. Action is needed to avert the negative consequences associated with major demographic change. However, there also needs to be a fundamental shift in policy and opinion on ageing. Firstly, we must acknowledge the contribution to economic and social development made by older people. Secondly, we must address the situation and needs of older people in the context of their basic human rights.

Despite the unprecedented growth in the numbers and proportions of older people in the developing world, they remain neglected, on the margins of the development process. The price of this neglect is increasing poverty – not only for those who are now old, but for future generations of older people. This will be an opportunity lost to all of us to manage our own future unless determined action is taken now. Individual and collective initiatives, by donor countries, international agencies and NGOs, and by national governments in the South, could be taken at once in the following priority areas.

Working and caring – older people throughout the world make an important contribution to community and family life.
© Tawach Malila/ HelpAge International

The United Nations Principles for Older Persons should be given much greater global prominence

- *Key action point:* adopt the UN Principles for Older Persons as a legally binding charter of rights, to which all governments are accountable.

National and international action to address the situation of older people needs to be based on an integrated approach within the context of broader social policy

- *Key action point:* develop integrated strategies to enable older people's basic needs to be met in the areas of income, health, housing, and community support, as well as social attitudes, addressing isolation, fear, discrimination, disability and abuse.

The profile of ageing and the policy issues it raises in the South need priority attention

- *Key action point:* increase research, data collection and analysis relating to the special needs and capacities of older people.

Policy makers need to acknowledge, measure and support the contributions of older people to their societies

- *Key action point:* set and measure development targets – together with appropriate indicators – which relate to older people, particularly in areas such as health status, income and poverty.

Policy making for older citizens should actively involve them in identifying key problems and their solutions. The experience of older people needs to be recognized as a major resource in the development process

- *Key action point:* ensure that policy research, planning exercises, programme design and monitoring directly involve older people, especially the most disadvantaged, in the consultation process.

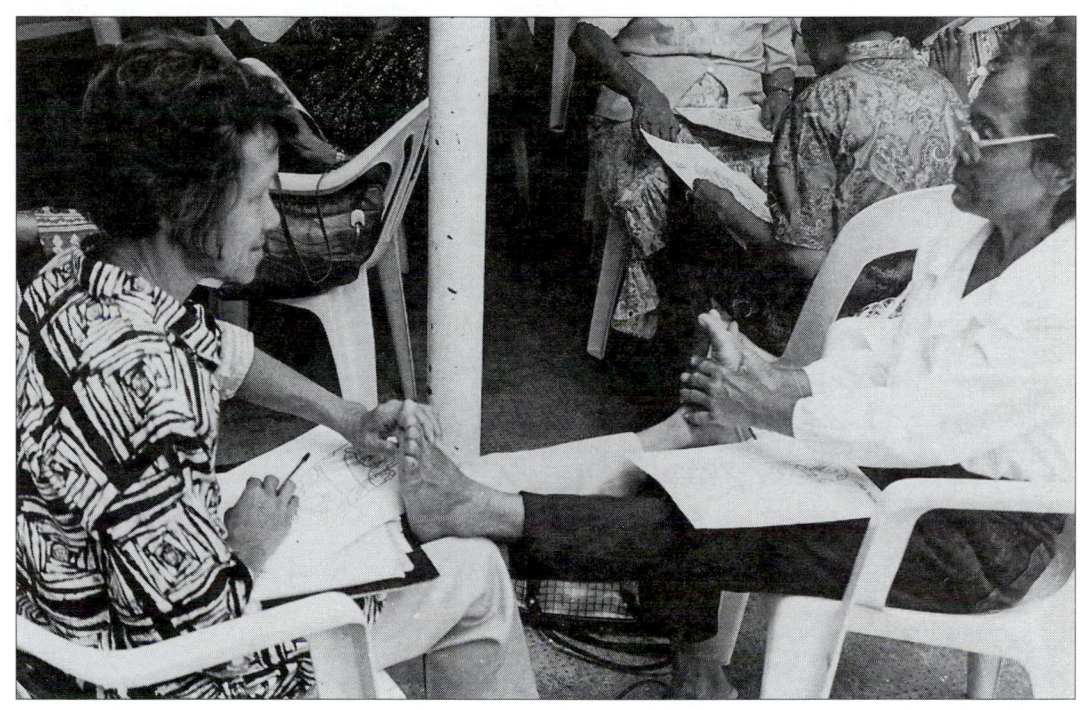

Part I

An Introduction to Ageing and Development

1

Development and the Rights of Older People

Mark Gorman[1]

Including older people in development

For the past fifty years, older people have been all but invisible in international development policy and practice. Now, in the midst of an ageing revolution, which will have its primary impact in developing countries, the needs and capacities of older people are starting to appear on the global development agenda.

A growing concern about demographic change in the South has begun to drive a new attitude towards ageing. Governments are engaged for the first time in considering policy options to meet the challenges of older populations. In some parts of the world – particularly where population ageing is happening most quickly – international agencies, such as the UN's Economic and Social Commission for Asia and the Pacific, have played a leading role in stimulating debate. The number of studies on ageing issues, though still extremely small, is growing and some donor governments are starting to build up their understanding of ageing and poverty reduction.

For the past fifty years, development policy has been focused on achieving economic growth and increased productivity. Older people, typically characterized as economically unproductive, dependent and passive, have been considered at best as irrelevant to development and at worst as a threat to the prospects for increased prosperity. As a result, development policy in the post-war era has excluded and marginalized people purely on the basis of their age.

> *'Older people, typically characterized as economically unproductive, dependent and passive, have been considered at best as irrelevant to development and at worst as a threat to the prospects for increased prosperity.'*

Older people's great capacity for productivity, independence and active involvement in the development of their communities and countries has been all too frequently overlooked. The benefits of older populations – the wealth of skill and experience that older people bring to the workplace, to public life and the family – are hardly noticed.

> *'When we're united, they listen to us'*
> Don Esteban, older people's day centre, Huari, Bolivia

Even within the human development priorities – health, education, water and sanitation – there has been little room to consider the rights of older citizens.

Older people are excluded – often systematically – from access to services and support and the inevitable restrictions which old age brings are used as a justification for their social exclusion. At the same time the neglect of older people in policy is rationalized by an appeal to traditional values, which are alleged to safeguard the position of older people in their families and communities.

Good development practice starts with the perspective of those most affected. When older people are consulted they make clear their awareness of the major forces of change that are impacting on their lives. Institutions such as kinship and marriage are becoming less important than the labour market for economic survival. Social and economic change is exacerbating the processes which, in most societies, push older people to the margins.[2]

Change has also created opportunities for older people. Older women in some communities now have much greater scope to participate in life outside the household. Older people are helping to absorb the shocks of change, by making significant material and psychological contributions to family well being. The failure to recognize or understand these contributions in times of rapid and disruptive change not only marginalizes older people. It also discounts a resource whose real value therefore remains unknown. For countries seeking to reduce the burden of poverty and disadvantage this is hugely wasteful.

The need for informed international debate on ageing

In contrast to the North, the absence of informed debate on ageing in the South is striking. In the countries of the developed world where population ageing has been acknowledged as a policy issue, deep foundations of knowledge have been established which inform both policy and practice in relation to older people. In developing countries, the dearth of even the most basic information on older people and the lack of informed research has fuelled misconceptions and led to a neglect of the rights of older people in policy and in practice. Too often the discussion is laden with warnings of looming economic and social crises combined with regret for lost traditional values. It is based far too little on the facts about older people or the structural inequalities that result in their poverty and exclusion.

Older people and modernization

The polarization of 'traditional' and 'modern' societies has compounded negative attitudes towards older people. As they have not always been visible actors in the 'modernization' process, they have come to be associated with traditional ways and the past. Indeed, as attention finally begins to turn to older people, modernization is often seen as the cause of their vulnerability as a group. Features of this process, such as urbanization, increased social and geographical mobility, changes in family and social structures as well as social and cultural values are said to have undermined 'traditional' arrangements providing security and status to older people. Typically, the 'breakdown of the extended family' and loss of respect for older people are ascribed to modernization.

The appeal of modernization theory is that it exposes some of the ways in which older people are vulnerable to change. The danger of this analysis is that it overlooks the part played by structural inequalities in the exclusion and impoverishment of older people.

Inequalities experienced in earlier life, for example in access to education, employment and health care, as well as those based on gender, have a critical bearing on status and well being in old age. For older people in poverty, such inequalities culminate in exclusion from decision-making processes and from access to services and support.

Development programmes also exclude older people; the rules of most credit schemes, for example, effectively make it impossible for older people to join. Thus it has been suggested that 'impoverishment in old age may be a common cross-cultural experience of the ageing process rather than simply resulting from 'modernization''.[3]

Resources and livelihoods

The late 20th century is the first time in human history when significant numbers of people worldwide can reasonably expect to enjoy an old age in which a secure income means that work can be put behind them and personal concerns take precedence. Even in developing countries there are small but growing numbers of older people with access to pension income. However, the reality for the great majority of older people in the developing world is that, in the absence of affordable, accessible social security or social insurance provision, earning a living remains their primary task.

> 'the reality for the great majority of older people in the developing world is that, in the absence of affordable, accessible social security or social insurance provision, earning a living remains their primary task.'

Although nearly every country has some form of social security or insurance coverage for older people, in practice these benefits are often limited to certain occupational groups, typically retired government officers and employees of large-scale private enterprises. Even for those people who do have a pension, it may be far from adequate for their needs. In China, where until recently those retiring from state enterprises received a non-contributory pension, inflation is eroding the value of their income, a situation that is causing protests by pensioners.[4] The great majority in developing countries, who make their living in the informal sector as farm-workers, day labourers, the self-employed and family workers, are excluded from any state provision.

The assurance of an adequate income thus remains a critical issue for older people in the developing world and the transitional countries of East and Central Europe. The debate over the respective merits of publicly funded programmes for income security and private provision is increasingly engaging policy makers in both the developed and developing worlds. From the 1940s the welfarist approach taken by the International Labour Office advocated a universal, state-provided social security system. The ILO continues to promote this on the grounds that economic activity in old age is falling in most parts of the world and that socio-economic change is reducing the ability and willingness of children to care for their parents. This approach came under increasing criticism

Progress on the ageing agenda

Attempts to include older people's issues on the international development agenda date back to 1948. At the initiative of Argentina a draft 'Declaration on Old Age Rights' was proposed at the United Nations General Assembly. However, it was not until 1982 that a major international conference addressed the subject, when the UN hosted a 'World Assembly on Ageing' in Vienna and adopted an International Plan of Action on Ageing. Despite this initiative, and the designation of both a UN Day and an International Year for Older Persons, it has proved extremely difficult to capture the interest of the wider international community. This is reflected in their priorities, which typically put ageing well down the agenda. Crude formulas regarding low life expectancies at birth and the existence of comprehensive informal support systems are often used to justify this lack of interest. The response of international agencies in the first decade after the Vienna conference was minimal. Despite the establishment of programmes on ageing by agencies such as the World Health Organization and within the Division for Social Policy and Development, as well as the work of the International Labour Organization and the UN Population Fund, questions of ageing scarcely featured on the development agenda.

In the 1990s, international conferences such as the International Conference on Population and Development (1994) and the World Summit for Social Development (1995) began to respond to the call in the Vienna Plan of Action to make a distinction between the humanitarian and the developmental aspects of ageing.

The 1999 International Year of Older Persons, with its theme of 'A Society for All Ages' provides the best opportunity so far for establishing an agenda for ageing in the developing world.

during the 1980s, culminating in the publication by the World Bank of its report 'Averting the Old Age Crisis' (1994). Concentrating on pension systems, the report queries the value of public schemes on the grounds, amongst other things, of low rates of return, inadequate protection from inflation, and the incentive to evade the consequent taxes required. The World Bank opposed the ILO's argument that social welfare is required to offset falling support for older people from their families; in the World Bank's view, pensions and other public social welfare programmes *cause* reduced support by children for their elderly parents.[5]

The World Bank's approach, with its argument for the primacy of the market (in this case in the provision of pensions), its assumption that most people are able to save for their old age, and its belief that the key determinant of older people's welfare is the performance of the whole economy, has had a powerful influence on governments. A number of transitional countries are seeking a reform of universal state pension

'We can't walk alone, but always together'
Doña Severa, President, older people's day centre, Huari, Bolivia

systems in line with the World Bank model. Drastic reductions in government expenditures and rampant inflation have made private contributory schemes very attractive. In Latin America there has also been a move towards privatization of public systems, with Chile providing the lead in 1980. State pension provision in Latin American countries was far from universal, and high inflation during the 1980s eroded the value of such state pensions as did exist. For the great majority of older people in the region other income strategies, such as continued employment or family support, remain important.

The Asia-Pacific region, with its diversity of development paths, has a wide range of systems, but (with exceptions such as Singapore) state welfare provision has generally been minimal. Given the difficulty of achieving adequate lifetime savings, informal support and continued work remain the most viable options for most older people. This is even more the case in sub-Saharan Africa, where, with the notable exceptions of South Africa and Namibia, universal

Defining old

The ageing process is of course a biological reality which (despite medical interventions) has its own dynamic, largely beyond human control. However, it is also subject to the constructions by which each society makes sense of old age.

In the developed world chronological time (the age of education, working age, retirement age) plays a paramount role. The age of 60 or 65, roughly equivalent to retirement ages in most developed countries, is said to be the beginning of old age.

In many parts of the developing world, chronological time has little or no importance in the meaning of old age. Other socially constructed meanings of age are more significant such as the roles assigned to older people; in some cases it is the loss of roles accompanying physical decline which is significant in defining old age. Thus, in contrast to the chronological milestones which mark life stages in the developed world (school age, working age, retirement age), old age in many developing countries is seen to begin at the point when active contribution is no longer possible.

---

pension provision is unknown.

China provides an example of the scale of old-age insurance systems with comprehensive coverage. A pilot scheme begun in rural areas of Shandong province in 1991 had by 1995 achieved coverage in rural districts of all 30 of China's provinces. Despite a coverage of more than 60 million rural workers between the ages of 20 and 60, this still represented a participation rate of only just over 14 per cent.[6] Even in those countries with more developed systems, there tend to be large sections of the work force who are not covered. Indeed, in the case of Chile the proportion of the work force covered by social insurance has fallen significantly since privatization of the system, reflecting the preference of private insurers for contributors with regular and reliable incomes.[7]

Thus, for the millions of workers in the informal sector, for whom pension provision and retirement remain unattainable aspirations, other means of material support need to be identified. The most rational form of old-age security seems to remain family support, which is reflected in the importance still attached to family ties in the developing world. Family support facilitates the pooling of risks when incomes are irregular and uncertain, and helps to reduce the cost of support of older family members by enabling them to take

'We mustn't become faint hearted. We've always got to work together'
Simón Ocza, older people's day centre, Huari, Bolivia

on productive roles within the household.[8]

But family is only one of the assets deployed by older people in gaining a livelihood. Their participation in the wider economic life of developing countries is surprisingly pervasive. Although data on the economic activity of those over the age of 60 is almost entirely absent, available information indicates that significant social capital is created by older people's activity. In rural Cambodia almost half of those over 65 continue to work, and do so until ill health forces them to stop.[9] This is a pattern repeated in many developing countries. In these communities, and in other rural areas of the developing world, agricultural work remains of primary importance. When land and water are available and accessible, even frailer people are able to manage small-scale agricultural activity.[10] Farming, whether for subsistence or for a cash income, is complemented by other income-earning activities, such as small-scale trading and production of handmade goods. Indeed, farm-based income in some situations becomes effectively a substitute for retirement, as well as providing other material and psychological supports. A study of older Jamaican farmers found that the farm 'serves as a social nexus for the economic activities of rural households, as well as a place to be born, raised, and buried. It provides important and often overlooked sources of food

The remarkable feature of family support is its durability, not its fragility.
© Giacomo Pirozzi/ Panos Pictures

for household members. It serves as a safety net and occupies a specific and critical place in the domestic cycle'.[11] However, the study also notes the low status of farming as an occupation, and the lack of recognition given to the contribution made by older farmers. An FAO report on Jamaica, noting the 'relatively advanced age' of many farmers, states that this has 'important implications for development, since it could be expected that there would be greater resistance to change among older farmers'.[12]

'Younger people must be made aware that they are living a biological process of ageing' Graciela Gonzalez, Caritas Chile

Change, family life and coping strategies

In all societies the demographic transition is having a profound effect on family structures. Changes in life expectancy, economic opportunity, social and geographical mobility are all impacting on family relationships.

The trend to smaller families, visible in nearly all societies, implies an increasing number and proportion of older family members. At the same time the reduction of extended family networks means that while the need for caregiving (particularly to very old relatives) may be increasing, the number of available family members able to offer care is declining. Rapid demographic transition, accompanied by other changes such as migration, urbanization and the increasing numbers of women entering formal workforces, is likely to affect the capacity of families to provide effective old age care.

'We're independent. Even those of us who have husbands are independent. That's the strength that older people have. We have nothing to lose, and everything to gain' Doly Quijada, President, National Association for Older People, Bolivia

Poverty also remains a significant intergenerational risk factor. In a family trapped in endemic poverty the capacity of younger adults to assist older relatives is severely impaired. The developing world is also beginning to experience the phenomenon of sizeable numbers of older people living alone, the result of a rise in divorces, increasing numbers of people who remain unmarried or who are childless. There is a significant gender issue, since throughout the developing world women's greater longevity and earlier age at marriage mean that widowhood is becoming their characteristic experience in old age.

In the face of this rapid socio-economic change there remains a strong consensus on the importance of the family as a basic component of the social structure, and a key role assigned to families is that of providing care at every stage of life.

'Family support systems for the overwhelming majority of older people in the developing world, whether in the context of extended families, co-residence of parents with their adult children or otherwise, remain in place.'

Care in old age is still perceived as a special family responsibility, particularly where alternatives, in the form of public support structures, are absent. Family support systems for the overwhelming majority of older people in the developing world, whether in the context of extended families, co-residence of parents with their adult children or otherwise, remain in place.

'the most unfortunate are either those who live utterly alone or with young, dependent grandchildren and no middle generation.'

Indeed in many developing countries, family care is the most widely used survival strategy for older people. This durability of family support exists in the face of the reduced number of older people who are living with their adult children in a number

of countries. Noting these changes in societies as diverse as Thailand, Singapore and Taiwan, a study of living arrangements of older people in south-east Asia nevertheless concludes that co-residence of elders with children should remain viable at least for the next generation.[13] It is therefore important to recognise the diverse paths which different societies are taking through the demographic transition:

'Each country or culture seems likely to climb onto the higher ageing plateau with its own traditional familial forms, modified by demography but still in being'.[14]

Care of older relatives by younger family members by no means describes the full extent of family living arrangements and different types of intergenerational support. Older people are also active contributors to household economies, not only passive recipients of care. Cash transfers and in-kind contributions such as child-minding and domestic chores play a significant, if unacknowledged, part in family survival. This is a feature of the integration between family life and work where contributions starting from early childhood continue into very old age, characterized by shifts from more to less demanding work. In contrast to the chronological milestones which western societies attach to the ageing process, old age in many developing countries is seen to begin only at the point when active contribution is no longer possible.

Consideration of family support systems begs the question of the quality of support available to older people without family resources. Older people themselves attach great significance to the existence or otherwise of family support as an indicator of relative poverty. A study in a rural South African community found that, irrespective of material resources 'the most unfortunate are either those who live utterly alone or with young, dependent grandchildren and no middle generation'.[15] It is important not to equate this lack of support with helplessness. There is for example growing evidence of the critical roles played by older people in giving care to family members with HIV/AIDs and to orphaned grandchildren. This is often undertaken with no external support, and in the face of many difficulties. Financial stress, community discrimination, lack of information and support from health services, as well as their own illness and frailty were some of the problems identified by older people responding to a survey in Mumbai, India.[16]

'I lost my house and almost everything I possess but I got no support from anyone in the village'
Older person, Tanzania

Health and well-being

Changing health status is arguably the single most important factor in the fertility decline and increased longevity which mark the demographic transition. However, the ways in which improved health has been achieved differ radically between the developed and developing worlds.

While developed countries have experienced substantial health gains through rising affluence, better nutrition, sanitation and housing, in the developing world socio-economic change has had significantly less impact than technological innovations such as mass vaccination campaigns. 'Powerful interventions to control birth and death' have been made against a backdrop of continuing poverty in the developing world.[17]

The biological ageing process does expose individuals to greater risks from disability and chronic illness, a process exacerbated by lifetime exposure to health problems. For many in developing countries old age will be accompanied by chronic

'For many in developing countries old age will be accompanied by chronic illness and disability, the result of lives lived in poverty, with little or no access to adequate health care facilities.'

illness and disability, the result of lives lived in poverty, with little or no access to adequate health care facilities. Many such people are functionally 'old' in their forties and fifties, calling into question the relevance of chronological definitions of old age. This is particularly so for women who, after years of hard physical labour, poor nutrition and multiple pregnancies, are on the threshold of old age by the end of their reproductive years.[18]

For older individuals in the developing world personal health consistently ranks alongside material security as a priority concern. Physical health is significantly bound up with the ability to work and maintain a reasonable standard of living. Illness in old age is thus an ever-present threat, carrying with it the potential loss of the means for self-support. For those without family or other assets this can be catastrophic.[19] First and foremost, access to health care is problematic for older people. Health care facilities tend to be concentrated in cities and towns, while the majority of older people in many developing countries live in rural areas. Older people in rural Africa, for example, regularly identify distance and transport costs as barriers to their using health facilities.[20] Even where facilities are relatively accessible, older people find it difficult to reach them on foot, and cannot afford transport costs. Treatment costs are also high, even in public institutions where invariably drugs have to be purchased. Older people also encounter strongly negative attitudes from medical personnel, who give them a low priority for treatment.[21]

In these circumstances it is not surprising that older people rely heavily on self-treatment, by buying drugs without prescription, or on traditional healers, or a combination of both. Whichever method is used, costs are high. Older people consistently identify medical treatment as their most significant expense. There is evidence that those who can make provision to meet medical costs do so, through cash savings or setting aside assets such as land. However, for the great majority the decision regarding medical treatment is a balance between the apparent seriousness of the illness against the risk to their livelihoods – and those of their children – involved in selling off assets or incurring debt.[22]

'I worked for my country for over 30 years but now I am retired and need money for an operation they do not want to know me'
Older Man, Tanzania

A significant factor here is that care or self-care in old age will take place at home. Long-term care for older people in most developing countries and those of East and Central Europe is available only to a very small proportion of older people, and in most cases is provided by private and non-profit organizations rather than governments. Strong social norms rejecting the idea of long-term care outside the family mean that institutions for frail older people are populated mainly by those without families, and their low status means that the quality of care offered (particularly in public facilities) is often low.

Older people are acknowledged health care providers. Skills in home remedies and herbal treatments usually come with experience, and most herbalists tend to be older men and women. In parts of Latin America and South East Asia, older people have set up local projects in which they use their skills and knowledge to cultivate herbs, and to develop and use herbal treatments. The unique role of older women as birth attendants is recognized in many communities and they are increasingly utilized within public sector and non-governmental health care services. Older practitioners in many parts of the world have played an important role in retaining health knowledge and practices.

'Men have about seven hours rest during the day whereas in that time women will be occupied with tasks even if they say they are resting'
HelpAge International Tanzania Research Team

However, these individual issues for older people have relatively little impact on health policy and planning in developing countries. Given the intensity of competi-tion for scarce resources, it is not surprising that responding to the problems of older age is not a high priority for health planners. Indeed, overall health budgets are being increasingly squeezed in the difficult economic climates affecting many developing countries. Even in countries with a tradition of substantial state provision, public investment in basic health care is lagging severely behind demand. In India by 1990, 75 per cent of health care expenditure was made by individuals, with consequent impact on household disposable incomes.[23]

Poverty and exclusion

The 1995 World Summit on Social Development called for a re-orientation of objectives so that 'human well-being', rather than economic growth, became the highest development priority. The Summit Declaration 'puts people at the centre of development' and sets an agenda for the substantial reduction of overall poverty. This agenda for action is both a response to the perceived failures of development efforts in the past, and a reaction to the increasing forces of change which are destabi-lizing many societies. The impact of these forces on the vulnerable groups at the social margins is particularly severe, and the declaration of the Summit therefore has a special relevance to older people in the developing world.

Poverty and social exclusion still impose formidable barriers against the participation of older people in their societies. Material poverty is the first limiting factor, and there is clear evidence that the majority of older people in the developing world are poor. Many experience the same lack of physical necessities, assets and income felt by other poor people, but without the resources which younger, fitter and more active adults can deploy as some compensation. In consequence, older people are characteristically among the poorest members of their society. In Zimbabwe, the income older people generate is only about one-third of the formal sector minimum wage – and for rural widows it is half that.[24] In Cambodia people continue to rely on themselves or their families for support because poverty has prevented them accumulating savings.[25] A recent study of older Tanzanians found that not only were cash incomes low, but other material assets such as land were of little value. Although most respondents owned land, their lack of capital created a vicious circle of inability to invest in land maintenance, or to pay for labour to work it. Low crop prices and declining fertility meant that land ownership was a rapidly dwindling asset for older farmers. Their own capacity to farm the land was reduced, and their children were tending to leave the rural areas in search of wage labour.[26]

> **'Social exclusion, the effective distancing of older people from the mainstream of their societies, carries with it impacts which go beyond income and wealth into poor housing, ill-health and personal insecurity.'**

Thus poverty, narrowly defined as a lack of material means, is a serious impediment, but it is the consequent inability to participate effectively in economic, social and political life that profoundly disadvantages older people. Social exclusion, the effective distancing of older people from the mainstream of their societies, carries with it impacts which go beyond income and wealth into poor housing, ill-health and personal insecurity.[27]

It is often argued that social exclusion is mitigated for older people in many developing countries by the informal networks of family and community, which provide them with an assured place and clear social roles. But this has always been contingent on factors such as gender and material means rather than age. Rapid social and economic

> *'With modern medicine, many older people are living longer than they are prepared for'*
> Zdenek Placher, Zivot 90 Czech Republic

> *'No one thought I would live when I was ill but the community health worker had me taken to the health centre and she is still doing follow-up'* Older man, South Africa

change has further undermined the capacity of these informal structures to provide support. A study of the impact of socio-economic forces on intergenerational relations in South Asian extended families concluded that:

> *'Given the already difficult choice facing sons regarding the allocation of their meagre income…and given the inability of poor third world governments…to mount substantial social service programs, it is likely that more and more elderly people will be unable to live their latter years in a secure and dignified setting'.*[28]

Social inferiority, isolation, physical weakness and vulnerability, all of which form part of the experience of poverty, thus combine for many older people to make old age itself a form of social exclusion. Rather than using a chronological definition, old age is defined in many societies as a state of dependence and incapacity. In Bosnia, for example, old age is identified with the concept of loss of health and social status leading to a state of dependence. 'People are able to 'explain' old age in Bosnia by this one notion which defines the point at which full adult status starts to be lost'.[29]

Gender

The differing roles and needs of women and men grow more diverse in old age. Older men and women play important, but different roles in contributing to their families and communities, though the part played by older women is least often recognized or valued. The support needs of older people are also to a large extent gender-

Women outlive men in nearly all countries, rich and poor. In this harsh, arid area of Bolivia most young people have migrated to the cities. Left behind, the older people have set up health and agricultural projects.
© Pat Stocker/ HelpAge International

specific. Yet it is equally unusual for these requirements to be acknowledged, and 'older people' tend to be seen as an undifferentiated mass.

Throughout the life cycle, women and men experience the impact of social and economic structures differently, beginning with differential life expectancy. Although more boys than girls are born each year throughout the world, by late life excess male mortality rates have moved the differential in favour of women in all but a few countries. Though in the developing world the female advantage is not generally as great as in the developed countries, the number and diversity of women produces differing trends. India, Bangladesh and Egypt, for example, report more men than women in most older groups. However, countries with a relatively high proportion of older people (for example Argentina and South Korea) have a higher proportion of women at older ages than some European countries.[30]

Marriage experience differs very greatly, with women's greater longevity and earlier age of marriage contributing to the preponderance of widowhood in old age in many developing countries. The problems confronted by older people in the developing world are in most countries likely to be those of older women, a likelihood which increases at older ages.[31]

The experience of poverty likewise has a gender dimension. Where systems of social welfare or social insurance exist, women are less likely to receive the full benefits due to factors such as the lack of a record of continuous paid employment. Where people have to rely on their own material resources, women are again less likely to have property or other assets of their own. Even where women's labour has created assets, the property is controlled by the male household head. A report from Tanzania notes that farm income generated by women accrues to the husband when crops are sold, a situation common elsewhere too.[32] The risk in either case of a fall into absolute poverty (due, for instance, to the death of a husband) is great.

> *'We are the reflection of your future'*
> Campaign slogan in Bolivia

> *'Power to Older People'*
> Needs Assessment Project,
> South Africa

What counts as work for older women?

Dependency ratios in the developing world typically assume that older people withdraw from the work force at 'normal' retirement ages, despite the evidence that people continue to work while they are physically able. Even where older people's work is counted, assumptions are made as to what counts as 'work'. Older people, particularly older women, tend to accept these assumptions. Thus it may well be that labour force participation rates for developing countries are severely under-valuing the contribution of older people, with the help of the attitudes of older people themselves, as these extracts show:

'Frequently an elderly woman, when asked if she "works", will reply "no", even though she spends most of her day selling vegetables or fruit in the market, or selling home prepared food in the street...this is a problem in society that this kind of informal work is not given the value it deserves and is not seen as "work".'[33]

'The two women taking part in interviews did not initially perceive their comparatively heavy workload in terms of a contribution to the household. Both of them however, described spending half or more of the day on their mashambas (farms) during 'normal' or non-drought years...The second woman is the first of two wives, and is the main supporter of the household...Her daily routine consists of rising before sunrise, collecting water, cleaning the house, working in the mashamba, grinding millet or looking for firewood and cooking. When she can obtain ingredients, she also makes cakes for the family and for sale.'[34]

The disadvantage suffered by women in developing countries through lack of access to educational opportunities is felt particularly by older women, with consequent restrictions such as a reduced ability to enter the labour market. The unpaid work done by older women in support of household economies, such as caring for older or younger dependants, provides no guarantee of future material security. In these ways, the life pattern of women's dependency is a function of role changes due not to age but to family events, such as the death or remarriage of the household head.[35]

Health issues in old age show further gender-specific variations. Poor nutrition, endemic communicable disease, arduous, often dangerous, working conditions and violence are the shared experience of older women and men in the developing world. Women however are more likely to have experienced greater disadvantage. The life-cycle differential in nutrition is an example, starting with the relative disadvantage of

*'Who you are, we were;
Who we are, you will be!'*
Appeal message in Latvia

girl children and continuing into old age, with similar discrimination experienced by older women. Yet 'behind most food security policies lies the assumption that, once a household obtains sufficient food, all its individual members will be adequately nourished'.[36] Reproductive health problems also disadvantage older women, with numerous full-term pregnancies taking their toll on those entering the post-menopausal stage.

The differing impact of rapid socio-economic change on older men and women is another issue which has been insufficiently recognized. Yet these impacts can differ radically.

Migration

The 20th century has seen greater mass movements of people, whether as individuals or whole populations, than any other era in history. People migrated in unprecedented numbers, not only across international frontiers, but also from the country to cities, and between regions within the same national state. Alongside economic migration the century has seen the forced movement of refugees and displaced people, victims of natural and human disasters, some on a massive scale. Migration, along with reduced fertility and greater longevity, has been one of the three critical variables for demographic change this century.[37]

'Thank you for opening our brains again. Before my brain was just going down, down, down. My grandchildren laugh at me because I can't do spellings. Now I tell them I am going to school again to open my brain'
Older woman, Republic of South Africa

Many features of these migrations have had an impact on the lives of older people, both for those who were migrants and those who remained behind. In the earlier part of the century, migration, notably from Europe to the Americas, represented the search for a new life, and was expected to be permanent. These migrants, as well as their children and grandchildren, have grown old as citizens of their new homelands. More recent migrations, for example from ex-colonies to the former colonizer, or from poorer to more affluent areas of developing countries, have often been seen, in theory or practice, as temporary, with the aim of amassing wealth or remitting funds, before an eventual return home. In fact rural–urban migration in many developing countries has been a 'circular' process, with (generally single male) migrants going to seek work, but maintaining close links with their home villages, and aspiring to return after retirement. Indeed poor living conditions in Indian cities have been partly ascribed to the tendency of migrants to invest their earnings in the home community, either in housing or land ownership.[38] The return, from the UK and North America to their home countries, of significant numbers of Caribbean emigrants on retirement is a further demonstration of

'Before I was like a thrown away item. Now after sitting for 2 weeks in this workshop alongside government officers and respected people, I am rising up'
Older woman, Ethiopia

the attraction of circular migration – even after a working lifetime away from 'home'. The availability of fast and cheap communications makes such migration increasingly viable.

The speed of urbanization in the 20th century has affected older people along with other age groups. Urban growth is most rapid in developing countries, and, given that it is driven mainly by the migration of younger people, it influences the age distribution in both urban and rural areas. In developing countries, which are still predominantly rural, a little over one-third of older people live in urban areas. This is expected to be more than one-half by 2015. There are, however, significant regional variations. In Latin America and the Caribbean, urban migrants usually remain in the cities in old age; hence these older populations are already substantially urbanized.[39]

The movement of younger workers from rural to urban areas has significant consequences for the older people left behind and for those who return. For example, the economic viability of small-scale rural enterprise and semi-subsistence farm units, denied the labour of younger workers, is questionable. In Thailand, the departure of workers from the rice-cultivation areas has led to reduced household and allotment productivity.[40]

As people age in rural areas, they rely increasingly on the support of others, particularly children. In rural Cambodia, this support is likely to be from a distance, given the very high rates of migration. About two-thirds of older people in rural areas of Cambodia may have children living in another area. Although remittances from them still seem to be an important source of support, in most cases this is inadequate to cover older people's needs.[41]

'We are older people with rights' – older people everywhere are pushing for change.
© Valerie Mealla/ HelpAge International

For the migrants who have swelled the size of cities throughout the developing world, ageing presents other challenges. For many of those who came to the city in their youth, the aspiration of a return to their home community to retire is not fulfilled and their old age is spent in the city. However, even in the face of the harsh conditions of city slum life, many have maintained family and community ties, which provide essential support mechanisms in old age. The majority continue to support themselves and, though paid labour declines with advancing age, contributions to household economies remain important.

Poverty remains a major risk factor as work opportunities become increasingly scarce and irregular, and the support of hard-pressed families or neighbours is insufficient.[42] For those who come to the city in

'I never believed these poor older people had anything to say. Now I have changed my mind and will always consult them'
Government officer, Ethiopia

old age these problems multiply. A recent study of older people in Lima, Peru, found that those brought to the city in old age felt isolated and lost, afraid to go out and feeling themselves a burden to their children. They typically underrated their own contribution to the household economy through childminding or looking after the home for their working relatives, believing that they had no useful role in the family.[43]

Forced migration: older people in emergencies

The chronic problems faced daily by older people in the developing world become acute in emergency situations. While crises have impacts on whole communities, older people are among those whose capacity to respond is most seriously compromised, as the shock of the emergency breaks down the limited support systems available to them.

Isolation is perhaps the most important factor creating vulnerability. Older people find that the problems they face are compounded by the destruction of their families and communities, and with them the support mechanisms on which they had relied. Isolated older people are often left to fend for themselves as those around them struggle for their own survival and that of their families. In the chaos of the early stages of emergencies older people are physically less able than most other adults to struggle for food and other resources, to travel long distances, and to endure even relatively short periods without shelter.

> *'If I can read and write my eyes are open...'*
> Older Woman, Republic of South Africa

The capacity of the community to take on the care of its vulnerable members is seriously compromised by the lack of food, medical, material and human resources associated with emergencies. Many older people find themselves looking after young dependants whose parents are missing. Others live alone or with an equally vulnerable spouse, relying on hard-pressed neighbours and the support services for essentials. The very limited livelihood opportunities for younger adults are rarely available to the most vulnerable older people.

> *'Reducing vulnerability and promoting inclusion for older people is therefore not so much about creating special services for older people but rather ensuring that they have equal access to mainstream services along with other vulnerable groups.'*

Discrimination against older people in emergency situations can occur in subtle ways. For example, basic organizational priorities can effectively exclude them. Distribution programmes tend to require the attendance of, rather than delivery to, refugees; medical programmes tend to focus on acute rather than chronic illness, while health facilities tend to be walk-in clinics rather than community-based interventions.

> *'I don't even know how to read... I only go out if my children take me'*
> Older Woman, Lima, Peru

At the rehabilitation stage, agencies find it difficult to envisage income-generating activities in which it is possible for older people to participate. This happens despite the fact that almost invariably older people had been economically active to some extent before they were forced into flight from their home communities. The result of these attitudes 'is that older people continue to be perceived as aid dependent victims within a refugee situation, rather than participants in more durable solutions to the common problems of refugee environments'.[44] Reducing vulnerability and promoting inclusion for older people is therefore not so much about creating special services for older people but rather ensuring that they have equal access to mainstream services along with other vulnerable groups. Ensuring this access relies on raising the awareness of service providers to the obstacles faced by older people.

It is also important to understand that older people are not simply vulnerable victims in emergency situations. Knowledge of traditional coping strategies, alternative technical or health knowledge, a sense of history and continuity all have a special role to play in preserving the identity of communities in crisis. Older people may still have control of material assets and decision-making processes at family and community level. They may also be able to influence younger generations in peace-building and community regeneration. This is not to deny that older people may also play a more negative role; their memories of past conflict and perceptions of long-lasting discrimination may keep alive a sense of injustice and lay the foundation for further instability.

In either case an understanding of their role needs to go beyond the stereotype of vulnerability. Older people in emergency situations are far more likely to be givers than receivers of support. They are caregivers for young and disabled family members in the absence of other able adults. Since older people are characteristically eager to make an effective contribution to household survival, support with basic needs items, health care, credit, skills training and other assistance given to them is by extension support to their families and communities.

> *'The elderly themselves are the best people who can articulate accurately issues that impact on them negatively, and through their voices and actions the public will be able to respond accordingly'*
> Rachel Mukwaya, Uganda Reach the Aged Association

Finally it needs to be remembered that many older people never become refugees at all but remain behind because of their inability or unwillingness to leave their homes when younger people flee. In extreme cases, such as that of Croatia after the refugee movements of August 1995, older people can be left isolated in scattered villages, their homes severely damaged, in poor health and lacking even basic services. Large-scale relief efforts in such situations can provide only temporary support, with few guarantees of longer term viability.

Reinforcing capability or dependency: an agenda for action

The lives of older people, in common with those of other age groups, are subject to the social and cultural constraints of the societies in which they live. The difference for older people is that in

> *'The workshop was very enriching and educative, especially in my job which involves mass communication in the media of television. I realize that there is need to involve the elderly themselves to participate in the process of awareness creation about themselves'*
> Rachel Mukwaya, Uganda Reach the Aged Association

many societies, including those that profess to respect their elders, negative stereotypes of ageing are common. Development thinking, dominated by the concept of economic progress, has focused on the most economically active adult populations and assigned older people – along with children – to a marginal role. Being able-bodied has come to be equated with normality, and to the degree that older people are not able to conform to this ideal they are viewed in negative terms.

Ageing brings inevitable decline in capacity, and greater vulnerability to sudden change. But, older people are heterogeneous, with widely varying capacities. Older people do not live in isolation from the social environment. Relationships with family, community and the wider society play key roles in their lives. In these relationships there are three interacting factors – physical independence, autonomy and interdependence. These are not separate but exist along a spectrum;

- *Physical independence* may mean both being able to look after yourself and being able to contribute to a family economy.
- *Autonomy* exists when an older person, though physically dependent, still retains the ability to make free choices.
- *Interdependence* recognizes the fact of relationships – in family and community – in which older people give as well as receive support.[45]

For policy-making relating to older people this understanding is critical. The goals of policy for older people in developing countries should be to enable independence for as long as possible, to reinforce interdependent relationships between the generations in family and community, and to support the autonomy of physically dependent older people. An agenda for action for older people in the developing world therefore needs to address these issues.

Supporting independence   implies far greater attention to the income needs of older people. Income security is, for all older people, the critical factor in their material well-being. For those with access to insurance programmes, whether privately or publicly provided, there needs to be adequate protection of their savings. It should not be acceptable to allow the real value of pensions to lag behind inflationary economies, as has happened in the transitional countries of East and Central Europe. If it is accepted that saving for retirement is unrealistic for the major-ity of older people in the developing world, other means of providing for some degree of material security are needed.

'Poor from the parents down to the grandchildren'
Older woman, Doun Lai, Cambodia

Informal systems of self-support and mutual assistance need to be fostered. The capacity of older people to work, often in spite of great physical frailty, needs to be recognized and supported. Since older people in most developing countries live and work in rural areas, policies favouring agriculture and rural development would assist them. Protective tariffs and subsidized credit in sectors which draw resources and labour away from rural areas indirectly disadvan-tage older people. On an individual level, the opening of credit programmes to access by older people would have a significant impact on their ability to be self-supporting.

'Of course we always help our neigh-bours – in the future we will need their help!'
Older man, Cambodia

Family and other voluntary sources of support are likely to remain the key survival mechanism for most older people in most developing countries for the foreseeable future. Public services should, therefore, aim to complement, not replace, these informal systems. Nor should appeal to family support be used as a justification for reducing public services.

Family and wider collective support depend on each other for their viability. Thus such programmes as Singapore's tax deductions and preferred housing assignments to families caring for older relatives provide

'Nowadays young people know more than old people. They listen to the radio, watch TV. Old people are ignorant. We used to ask wise old people for advice, but now it is different'
Older woman, Kampong Cham, Cambodia

important support to informal systems. South Africa's universal pension system provides the most important (often sole) income for many families. Despite the potential for abuse, the South African pension means that older people (particularly older women) continue to play an important role in the maintenance of household economies.

Public assistance to collective support mechanisms operated for and by older people would be an important strategic development. Older people are involved in a wide range of collective activity, including community groups, centres and clubs, religious societies and the like. Many of these groups provide important mater-ial and psychological support for their members, but remain fragile because of the lack of continuity which external subsidy, even on a small scale, could provide.

Strategies for improving the health of older people will be linked to improved access to lifelong primary health care. However a much greater effort has to be made to target the needs of the many people who reach old age in chronic ill health. For example, while national policies to exempt older people from health service fees exist in a number of countries, in practice they have very limited impact because severely limited health budgets cannot contain the cost of implementation. It may be more feasible to target programmes to reach the most vulnerable, with adequate subsidy for implementation. This would have to include elements such as drug supply and information campaigns to raise aware-ness, both among potential users and health service staff.

Training for health staff offers substan-tial scope to improve the quality of health for older people. The importance of understanding the specific health needs of older people is beginning to be reflected by the inclusion of modules on basic gerontology in health staff training curricula, for example in Ghana, India and Zanzibar. There is significant scope within existing bilateral and international agency health programmes to include measures for training, improving access and service provision, and for supporting community-based initiatives. The programme in age care for community health workers from the Caribbean region offered by the University of the West Indies, and the geriatric nursing training course pioneered by the Asia Training Centre on Ageing are examples of regional initiatives in a still undeveloped field.

Also largely unrealized is the potential for links between formal public health systems and the informal sector. There are a number of examples of successful non-governmental and community-based health programmes – such as home visiting schemes and training for family carers – that also preserve the role of older people as health providers.

The gender dimension of ageing must be a prominent feature of all agendas for policy action. This means that the different needs and the contributions of older women and men need to be to the fore. Our older world is increasingly a female world. Policies need, therefore, to address the particular vulnerabilities that derive from women's lifetime disadvantages due to health and nutrition, limitations in labour force participation, and discrimination in property and inheritance, with consequent long-term poverty in old age.

> *'They only tell the young people about [development] projects, not the old people'*
> Older man, Cambodia

> *'I worry. I think a lot because I have no money and am often sick. I have no children except an adopted grandchild, but the grandchild is also poor. I don't know what to think every day – I think this way, think that way, like a cat with its head caught in a coconut shell'*
> Older woman, Kampong Cham, Cambodia

> *'Young people make rice, old people make merit'*
> Older man, Kampot, Cambodia

The gender dimension of old age is not only described in the disadvantage of women. It is also important for policy makers to recognize the disadvantage older men experience through loss of their established adult roles at retirement and the relatively greater problems faced by men in maintaining social support networks beyond the family in old age.

The lack of research data is a formidable barrier to the development of policy addressing any issue of ageing and development. Despite the efforts of a small number of institutions, research in the field has been severely hampered by the lack of resources to support it. High on any future policy agenda should therefore be the promotion of research that helps to address some of the key issues outlined above. In particular, research that enables the effective participation of older people themselves needs to be given adequate support.

Political will is the crucial factor These initiatives will meet with only partial success until the pervasive attitudes that support discrimination against older people are addressed. Despite frequent assertions about the dignity and respect with which old age is viewed in the developing world, older people often experience indignity and disrespect. In every society, gender and material wealth remain powerful determinants of the treatment which individuals can expect to receive in old age. So strongly linked are the concepts of old age, frailty and dependence in all societies that older people themselves assent to this negative imagery, feeling themselves to be passive burdens to their families, and ignoring their own contributions. A crucial overall goal of policy development must therefore be to challenge and overcome the invisible barriers of age prejudice that prevent older people playing a full and valued part in the development of their societies.

Notes

1 Mark Gorman is Deputy Chief Executive and Director of Development for HelpAge International.
2 Vincent, J, *Inequality and Old Age*, UCL Press, London, 1995 p52.
3 Sen K, *Ageing*, Zed Books, London, 1994.
4 *Far Eastern Economic Review*, October 1997, p83.
5 Lloyd-Sherlock, P & Johnson, P (eds), *Ageing and Social Policy: Global Comparisons*, STICERD, LSE, London, 1996, pp24–27.
6 Zeng Yi, *Population Ageing in China: Policy Trade-offs and Challenges*, paper for UNFPA Technical Meeting on Ageing, October 1998.
7 Lloyd-Sherlock, P, *Old Age and Urban Poverty in the Developing World*, Macmillan, London, 1997 p20.
8 World Bank Policy Research Report, *Averting the old age crisis: policies to protect the old and promote growth*, Oxford University Press, New York, 1994, p56.
9 HelpAge International/Ministry of Labour, Social Affairs Labour and Veterans Affairs (MSALVA), *Summary report on the Situation of Older People in Cambodia*, Phnom Penh, 1998.
10 Whiteside, M, *Evaluation of HelpAge International Cambodia Programme*, unpublished report, 1998.
11 Woodsong, C, 'Old Farmers, Invisible Farmers: Age & Agriculture in Jamaica', *Journal of Cross-Cultural Gerontology* 9:3, July 1994, pp277–300.
12 Food & Agriculture Organization of the United Nations, *Integrated development of Small-Scale Farms in the Upper Rio-Minho Watershed District*, Jamaica 1989, quoted in Woodsong, 1994, op cit.
13 Asis, M M B et al, 'Living Arrangements in Four Asian Countries: A Comparative Perspective', *Journal of Cross-Cultural Gerontology* 10:1&2, April 1995, pp145–62.
14 Laslett, P, *A Fresh Map of Life*, Macmillan, London, 1996, p153.
15 HelpAge International, unpublished report, 1996, p18.
16 Committed Communities Development Trust, 'Coping with HIV/AIDS & Ageing in the Family', unpublished report, Mumbai, India, no date.
17 Kalache, A & Sen, K, 'Ageing in Developing Countries', in M S J Pathy (ed) *Principles and Practice of Geriatric Medicine*, John Wiley and Sons, Chichester, 1998.
18 Kalache & Sen, 1998, op cit, p1570.
19 HelpAge International/MSALVA, 1998, op cit, p19.
20 As reported in participatory needs assessments conducted by HelpAge International in eg Ghana, South Africa, Tanzania (1997/8)
21 HelpAge International, *Older people in Tanzania – a Research Report*, Dar es Salaam, 1998 pp45–8.
22 HelpAge International/MSALVA, 1998, op cit, p19.
23 Kalache, A & Sen, K, 1998, op cit, p1570.
24 Adamchak, D J, Nyanguru, A C, Hampson, J & Wilson, A O, 'Family Support for the Elderly in Zimbabwe', *Southern African Journal of Gerontology* 3:1, 1994, pp22–6.
25 HelpAge International/MSALVA, 1998, op cit.
26 HelpAge International, 1998, op cit.
27 Quoted in Maltby, A, 'Poverty & Social Exclusion', *Working with Older People*, July 1997.
28 Goldstein, M C, Schuler, S & Ross, J L, 'Social & Economic Forces affecting Intergenerational Relations in Extended Families in a Third World Country: A Cautionary Tale from South Asia' *Journal of Gerontology* 38:6, 1983.
29 Vincent, J & Mudrovcic, Z, 'Lifestyles & Perceptions of Elderly People & Old Age in Bosnia & Hercegovina', in Arber, S & Evandrou, M, *Ageing, Independence & the Life Course*, Jessica Kingsley, London, 1993.
30 Kinsella, A & Taeuber, C, *An Aging World II*, Washington, US Bureau of the Census, 1993, p46.
31 Ibid, p48.
32 Massengo S, 'SAWATA Karagwe Older People's Programme', unpublished report, HelpAge International, 1998.
33 Clark, F C, 'Old Age, Gender & Exclusion: A Case Study of Lima, Peru', unpublished MA thesis, July 1998.
34 HelpAge International, London, unpublished report, 1996.
35 Gonnot, J P, 'Integration of Women in Development: Choice or Necessity?' unpublished paper, UN Office at Vienna, 1991, p3.
36 Bonita, R, *Women, Aging & Health*, World Health Organization, Geneva, 1996, p36.
37 Kinsella, K, presentation at International Federation on Ageing Conference, Durban, South Africa, September 1997.
38 De Haan, A, 'Rural–Urban Migration & Poverty: The Case of India', *IDS Bulletin* 28:2, April 1997, pp35–47.
39 Kinsella, K, 1997, op cit, pp40–41.
40 Warnes, A, 'Social Welfare Policies & Old Age Incomes in Thailand', in Lloyd-Sherlock & Johnson, 1996, op cit, pp61–79.
41 HelpAge International/MSALVA, 1998, op cit, p26.
42 Ara, S, *Old Age among Slum Dwellers*, HelpAge India, New Delhi, 1994, pp34 et seq.
43 Clark, F C, 'Old Age, Gender & Exclusion: A Case Study of Lima, Peru', unpublished MA thesis, 1998.
44 Peart, S, 'The situation of older refugees in Iran', unpublished report, HelpAge International, August 1998.
45 Arber & Evandrou, 1993, op cit, p19.

2

Poverty and Livelihoods in an Ageing World

Amanda Heslop[1]

Poverty is the problem

Understanding poverty has dominated much thinking and debate on development over recent years, but the poverty experienced by large numbers of older people in developing countries has been largely ignored. Older people, often regarded as economically unproductive, have been excluded by development analysts and policy makers. This affects both the human rights of older people and the possibilities for eradicating poverty because it ignores the actual and potential contributions of older people to the well being and survival of their families and communities.

The exclusion and impoverishment of older people is a product of structural inequalities.[2] Inequalities experienced in earlier life – for example in access to education, employment, and health care, as well as those based on gender – have a critical bearing on status and well being in old age. For older people, especially those who are poor, the consequences of such inequalities are worsened through their further exclusion, for example from decision-making processes, and access to services and support. This applies even to development initiatives, such as literacy programmes or credit schemes. Too often, programme managers believe that older people are unable to participate and have no productive role.

> *'This affects both the human rights of older people and the possibilities for eradicating poverty because it ignores the actual and potential contributions of older people to the well being and survival of their families and communities.'*

Structural inequalities affecting older people are not confined to developing countries. Social and economic factors that affect the status and security of older people in both the developed and developing world include relative wealth and poverty, gender, control of resources and ownership of assets. It is rather that the nature and impact of these forces differ within and between countries. In Britain for example, Vincent[3] suggests that work and ownership of property are key factors affecting social status in old age, and that:

> *'Inequalities resulting from low pay, unemployment, disability and sex and race discrimination are carried into old age.'*

In developing countries, any loss of status is more likely to have been:

> *'linked to ingrained structural inequalities experienced by most older people in most developing countries in earlier life. Impoverishment in old age may be a common cross cultural experience of the ageing process rather than simply resulting from modernization.'[4]*

> *'A poverty perspective is central to social development practice and policy on ageing.'*

A poverty perspective is central to social development practice and policy on ageing. Much of the literature on broadening conventional definitions of poverty[5] and on social exclusion[6] – so far overlooked in the field of ageing – provides a significant contribution to the development of a research and policy framework on ageing and development. The poverty perspective, which provides the link between actors in ageing and in development, has been very much neglected. Some of the reasons are discussed in the next section.

Ageing is a cross cutting issue and of critical significance to wider poverty alleviation strategies. The number of older people in poor countries is growing very fast. Older people are consistently and disproportionately among the poorest of the poor. Any credible anti-poverty strategy must therefore address the ways in which the capacity of older people to maintain themselves and to make a productive contribution to their families and communities can be enhanced as well as the ways in which frail older people living in poverty can be supported.

Multi-disciplinary approaches to funding, research on ageing, and policy development are necessary to increase awareness of issues as they relate across sectors. The health status of many older people, for example, is intimately related to access to transportation, livelihood strategies that affect ability to pay medical fees and even the time of year. Research among older people in Ghana found that disease prevalence increases in the rainy and the cold seasons when labour demands are greatest. For farmers, the rainy season is the period of planting, increased farm expenses and food insecurity. Yet older people must put up with ill health in order to get the farm work done. Harvest periods mark the beginning of improved nutrition, income and better health, when more families can afford to pay for health care. In short, the periods when demand for health services is most critical coincide with periods when poor people are least able to afford them. The development of more flexible payment structures in public health delivery, based on a knowledge and understanding of livelihoods, is clearly a key aspect of policy aimed at improving the long-term health status of resource-poor older people.

> *'Aspects of vulnerability such as physical weakness, isolation, powerlessness and low self-esteem are all factors that are often profoundly interconnected with age.'*

The linking of research to policy development implies the adoption of different and complementary research methodologies to address the needs of older people in the light of the potential and actual contributions they make within their families and communities.

Poverty and the exclusion of older people

Poverty of the community and in the family remains the greatest threat to the security of older people. Even co-residency is no guarantee of effective care for older people, since many of them stay with their families in a state of material and emotional neglect. For families trapped in endemic poverty the capacity of younger generations to assist their older relatives is severely impaired.

Participatory poverty research of the last decade has provided a broader understanding of dimensions of poverty that go beyond the lack of physical necessities, income and material assets.[7] Aspects of vulnerability such as physical weakness, isolation, powerlessness and low self-esteem are all factors that are often profoundly interconnected with age. In many communities age is a factor in local definitions of poverty. Older people, especially older women, are amongst the poorest as described by poor people themselves. In Ghana for example:

> *'the combination for women of age, widowhood and lack of adult children was frequently … associated with chronic vulnerability.'*[8]

Older people are amongst the poorest because of their diminished capacity for labour: most younger people in poverty lack assets and income but are able to rely on their own labour. In such communities, the significance of this may even be reflected through indigenous definitions of old age. Throughout the developing world, cultural norms consistently identify diminishing ability to work as the key criterion in defining old age for both older women and men.

Lack of assets, isolation and physical weakness are elements of the multi-dimensional disadvantages to which older people are vulnerable. These are closely related to processes and institutional arrangements that exclude older people from full participation in the economic, social and political life of their communities.[9] It is this social exclusion, the effective distancing of older people from the mainstream of their communities, that most profoundly disadvantages older people. In some parts of Northern India for instance and in some countries in Africa there is evidence that widowhood for older women involves not only loss of status but loss of property. In extreme cases older women are ejected from their deceased husbands' homes by the family.

In the public domain, even where rights exist, for example over property or access to free health care, older people frequently remain deprived through lack of information, and structures through which to pursue these claims. Public and private service delivery

> *'Older people face barriers accessing the most basic health and sanitation facilities, and are frequently denied access to bank loans and credit schemes as well as appropriate education and information.'*

structures commonly militate against the potential of older people to participate as valued and active members of their societies. Older people face barriers accessing the most basic health and sanitation facilities, and are frequently denied access to bank loans and credit schemes as well as appropriate education and information. Practice in age care has tended to focus on specific aspects of exclusion, resulting in

There is a need to develop new perspectives on ageing from the viewpoint and experience of older people. In this HelpAge International workshop in Rwanda, older people discuss their contributions and position in society, as well as their requirements as they age.
© Jane Thomas/ HelpAge International

localized, limited, micro projects for older people rather than broader strategies for inclusion at all levels.

It is often assumed that informal social networks and extended families provide protection for older people, and social roles and responsibilities through which to express their full participation in the social life of the community. The available evidence suggests that for the vast majority of older people, family support, whether in the context of co-residence with adult children or not, still provides the main source of care in old age.

A study of children on the street in Tamale, Ghana, found a significant number of girl children living with isolated female relatives or grandmothers 'who were not themselves capable of generating their own subsistence'. While the girls collected grains fallen from sacks as they were being loaded in the lorry parks, their older relatives sold items such as cigarettes from the room in which they lived.

> *'Both the child and the grandmother contribute equally to a household of fragile sustainability.'*

The result of long term poverty and insecurity affects more than one generation; in extreme cases both parties are at risk. This and other examples illustrate the importance of maintaining family support systems through mechanisms that support intergenerational reciprocity in the context of wider strategies for structural change.

Understanding the coping mechanisms of older people

Livelihood strategies in old age remain complex and diverse. They include capability to engage in productive activities such as farming, trading, and engaging in small-scale enterprises. They also include assets such as good health, knowledge, skills, and access to family and community support networks. In maintaining their livelihoods older people contribute to the well being and livelihood of the household and family. Factors that reduce these assets and limit the capacity of older people to provide for themselves include diminished physical strength, poor health, low status, landlessness, absence of or limited family or

> *'The result of long term poverty and insecurity affects more than one generation; in extreme cases both parties are at risk.'*

Poverty, a lifetime of overwork and ill health make older people deeply vulnerable.
© Jeremy Hartley/ HtA/Panos Pictures

community support, lack of capital, and lack of education or training opportunities.

In most developing countries, centrally developed systems for income security in old age are extremely limited. In practice eligibility is restricted to a small minority of workers previously employed in the formal sector in urban areas, such as government staff and employees of large-scale public or private enterprises. The livelihoods of most older people are based on multiple activities and sources of income and security outside the formal economy. The World Bank estimates that over 70 per cent of the world's older population rely on such 'informal' systems of security[10] and this percentage is certainly higher among older populations in the South.

Despite this awareness, much of the debate regarding income security for older people builds on the assumptions that old age is synonymous with dependency and that the economic welfare of the older population is largely determined by the performance of the economy as a whole.

Too often development of formal pension and social security programmes is taken as the single reform agenda for older people. This is problematic. Firstly, the prospect of poorer informal workers contributing to private pensions or savings schemes has not been adequately assessed. Secondly, in many less developed economies the preconditions for secure, long-term private savings, such as stable markets and sound regulatory structures, do not exist. As the World Bank recommends therefore, such reforms must be seen as complementary to programmes designed to protect the informal systems, which are the mainstay of old age security in most developing countries.

Where national provision for old age security exists, as in South Africa, the impact of this on older people and the wider community can inform development of policy elsewhere. The South African government currently spends three quarters of the welfare bill on old age pensions. Observers agree that this is well targeted to reach poorer households; that it is the major source of income for many extended families and that it has a development impact. A government review of the working of the pension system noted that '(p)eople are fed and sent to school out of this pension money, it enables investments in farming activities, and in general it is crucial for the very survival of these communities.'[11]

Due to high unemployment and the absence of other forms of social security, the pension in South Africa has been described as 'an imperative for the very survival of many urban poor.' The effect of this on older people needs further research. One study with older people in a Durban township,[12] found that older people were highly vulnerable to physical and psychological abuse because of the pressure on this income. Other main issues were access to health care, housing and transport services. In responding to these issues older people spoke consistently about their perceived lack of education and their feelings of inadequacy because of this. This raises questions about the relationship between pensions and well being for older people, particularly in relation to issues of self-esteem and adequate healthcare. It cannot be assumed that guaranteed income is enough to provide social security in old age.

Old age security can be substantially enhanced by measures aimed at strengthening the capacities of older people to contribute to and be included in the process of development. Governments have a role in supporting indigenous institutions and forms of social security as well as developing new ones.

Religious societies, traditional councils, savings groups and burial societies are among the institutions identified by older people as part of their support networks in many societies. It has been suggested that the fostering of relations between the state and these informal networks can create an environment of civic engagement, facilitate collective action and also strengthen state institutions. The gap between public and traditional or community based institutions is not as wide as is commonly supposed. Informal networks span both the public and private domains. In Ghana for example, members of local government unit committees and traditional councils are of the same community and work together with shared responsibility for community development. While the unit committees represent community concerns at district level, they recognize that decisions must be made in agreement with traditional councils. The development of partnerships between public and private institutions also implies the inclusion of the business sector, especially in the development of more accessible and flexible savings or pension schemes.

Older people's human rights

There are a growing number of examples at community and national levels that demonstrate the value of a rights-based approach in relation to older people.

Participatory approaches employed with older people enable them to express their concerns and participate in activities to address them. These processes can raise awareness within communities regarding rights and social exclusion issues and be an empowering experience for older people. Further work is required to develop these processes, establish good practice and develop advocacy work around them. If such approaches to programme development enable older people and their communities to recognize their rights it is more likely that they will develop ways of voicing these and participating actively in civil society. This implies encouraging partnerships with other groups and organizations and skills training to enable older people to fully participate at all levels of advocacy work.

Lessons can be learned from the experiences of NGOs working with people with HIV and AIDS. In fighting discriminatory practices, such as isolation and stigmatization of sufferers, agencies have successfully developed and promoted the notion that people with AIDS have a right to the support of their community. This principle is being upheld by innovative education programmes at community level. In East Africa, older midwives have received HIV/AIDS awareness training to enable them to continue to operate safely but also to demonstrate to other groups in society an important human rights principle. The rights of older people to the support of their community can be promoted by networking with other issue-based institutions and across sectors. There is a strong case for reversing the often-held view that older people, particularly those who are poor or frail, are a burden to their communities.

It makes economic sense too to recognize and respond to the legitimate demands of older people. By supporting the rights of older people to good health, to work and

maintain an adequate standard of living, household, family and community members gain both economically and socially. Across the world older people, especially women, contribute to their own welfare, provide child care, and protect the security of the home while other household members are at work.

For rights based approaches at community level to take hold and have significant impact, they must be supported at all levels. The United Nations Principles on Older People, published in 1992, outline the ten fundamental areas of social, political, cultural and economic rights of older people. This document has been used to promote awareness of the needs of older people through advocacy work worldwide. Further work is required to establish these principles as a Convention or Charter that is legally binding on all governments.

National and regional efforts are being made to lobby governments to establish national legislation protecting the rights of older people. In 1996 local groups networking in Bolivia helped to achieve the passing of a law recognizing older people's rights and the launching of a national programme of support for and protection of older people.

Whilst national and international laws and charters can uphold rights and promote good practice, resources will continue to be contested at various levels. National policies already exist in some countries, such as free medical care for older people, that fail to have effect because of poor communication, implementation and enforcement structures. A human rights approach implies a responsibility for groups at all levels and across sectors to promote these rights, and to develop effective legislation to protect them. Enabling older people to participate fully in this process, through training and awareness raising programmes, is a priority.

A checklist for action on age and poverty

Solutions to the problems faced by older people require broad and inclusive poverty

Graduates of a literacy programme in the Republic of South Africa – lack of formal education makes older people feel inadequate and vulnerable to abuse.
© Mandy Heslop/ HelpAge International

focused policy and development frameworks that deliberately seek to include older people in broader and holistic strategies for poverty amelioration.

Poor health, abandonment and exclusion are problems suffered in old age, but they are often the culmination of inequalities experienced throughout life. Older people, many of whom are older women, are increasingly involved in the care of the younger generation, often at a time when their own health and means of social support is precarious. To address poverty, age care strategies need to avoid the trap of narrow definitions of care, which tend to result in micro solutions. Strategies need to acknowledge the challenges that poverty poses to old and young alike and the importance of intergenerational links.

Data on older people is generally deficient. There is thus a need for data collection and research, especially that which looks specifically at older people's contributions to social structures and networks, and the key role they play in enabling families to cope in times of poverty and stress.

Income security, access to appropriate and affordable health care, transport and housing are key questions for policy makers across the globe. Collaborative policy making to deal with these questions together is essential for progress to be made. For example, income issues cannot be solved by pension schemes alone; in any case the security mechanisms utilized by most older people are outside the formal economy. Attention needs to be paid to the design of financial services that support sustainable incomes for the poorest in old age.

Livelihood strategies need to be supported by investment in older-people-friendly service delivery, especially in health, housing and transport. Without appropriate and affordable transport, centrally run services will not make an impact on health and well being. Policy decisions need to be informed by an understanding of the reciprocal arrangements within and between older and younger family members, as well as the understanding of the constraints facing older people to maintain livelihood strategies on which different generations rely.

Human Rights provision for older people requires greater international backing. The UN principles need to evolve into a charter which is legally binding; in

Why participatory research is vital for policy development

Social policy development on ageing is largely confined to and informed by the experiences of northern countries. In the South, where countries are still regarded as 'young', information and research bases to inform policy and practice on ageing questions are only recently developing. At the same time there is beginning to be global interest in the development of specific policies on ageing. Nevertheless, at national level there is a dearth of basic information, including statistical data, on older people. There is also a corresponding need to develop new perspectives on ageing from the viewpoint and experience of older people, using methods and approaches that measure older people's contributions and position in society, as well as their requirements as they age.

There is a growing body of experience in context-bound participatory research linked to policy development.[13] Participatory approaches are broadly aimed at eliciting the perspectives of poor people in order to deepen the understanding of poverty, and are increasingly included in research aimed at influencing policy and strengthening policy delivery frameworks. In relation to ageing there are opportunities both to draw upon and to contribute to this body of local expertise and knowledge. A small but growing number of governments have begun to employ such approaches to complement more quantitative research in the formulation of policy on ageing.[14]

Participatory studies are locally specific. Outcomes are relevant to specific social, physical, cultural and livelihood environments. This can increase rather than diminish their relevance for national policy. Insights drawn from a range of studies can contribute to national policy by revealing the areas of common experience and areas of diversity between them. Policy delivery frameworks can be informed by the identification of issues that are most appropriate for local level responses and those that are appropriate for national level policy responses. Issues can be related to sectors at all levels.

Participatory research attempts to bring together primary stakeholders and institutional stakeholders during the research process. The inclusion of older people as primary stakeholders enables their perceptions and priorities to be heard by those responsible for developing and implementing policy that affects them. Institutional stakeholders include members of government departments and civil society groups such as NGOs, church groups and academic institutions. The inclusion of institutional stakeholders across sectors facilitates the identification of issues relating to sectors and the transfer of lessons to national, regional and local level policy processes.

Training and capacity building with local research teams and those involved in translating outcomes to policy initiatives is essential. Training in research methods takes place prior to and during data collection and analysis. The role of stakeholders goes beyond the gathering and analysis of information, and includes developing research agendas beforehand, formulating strategies based on outcomes and disseminating results to achieve consensus on action. Links with participating communities need to be developed and maintained for future monitoring and learning about the impact of policy outcomes. Experience has shown that strategies for supporting these activities are the most crucial components of the policy research framework. However, some capacity already exists at local level, and this provides a valuable resource for research and policy initiatives focusing on older people.

the meantime the principles of independence, participation, care, self fulfilment and dignity need specifically to inform policies and programmes that affect the old directly. Additionally, the evidence of discrimination and lack of protection for the old demands international and national support for awareness raising and protection programmes, alongside accountable policies to deal with these problems.

More older-people-centred research and analysis which is multi-disciplinary and multi-method will enhance and improve the formulation of policy, programme and training frameworks that deal with issues facing older people. Anti-poverty strategies will have more chance of success if older people play a major part in identifying problems as well as solutions. Special efforts must be made to assess the impact and importance of older persons' contributions to the household and wider community so that adequate support can be given to older people to continue these

Local categories of well-being/poverty in Ghana

Site	Poor		Average		Rich	
	Local name	Description	Local name	Description	Local name	Description
Korle Wokun (Accra)	Ohiafo	• Can't afford a meal • Difficulty in maintaining house • Emaciated • Dresses poorly	Modenbofo	• Manages with few resources • Can afford daily meals • May have luxurious items	Sikatse	• Has a mansion • Has a car • Has a spouse • Has money • Has other assets
Tema Manhean	Ohiafo	• Does not educate children properly • No property • Borrows to eat • Mismanages	Modenbofo	• May have some property • Has well educated children	Niakye	• Solves financial problems • Well organized • Educates children • Fast with ideas
Amaasu	Ohiani	• Poorly housed • Cannot afford three meals a day • Small farm • May be sickly or handicapped	Modenbofo/ Totobidi	• Pays medical bills • Repays loan on time • Strength to farm • Sickness affects farming activities	Osikani/ Eye	• Can afford three meals • Has own work • Has money to finance own work • Has own house • Fulfils all responsibilities
Tronang	Ohiani	• Does not dress well • Looks sickly • Dependent • Does not maintain household well	Modenbofo	• Sustains oneself • Resources to fall on in times of need • Has difficulty with economic activities	Ebi Te Yie	• Has own cocoa farms • Has own house • Fulfils all financial obligations • Inherited property
Gwollu	Summu	• Borrows to eat • Not able to access social services • No money to buy fuel for lantern • Does not dress well	Boliniinaro/ Nikukwa/ Ukpikpa	• Manages with difficulty • No financial support • Inadequate support from children	Kuoro/ Kpatina	• Fulfils roles • Has many animals • Lives in good house – concrete and zinc roof • Solves problems independently • Helps others in cash and kind
Tumu	Nyabu	• Poorly dressed • Has difficulty in providing food	Ubi Kuoro	• Able to go about duties with little support	Kuoro	• Dresses well • Educates children • Has money and animals • Takes care of family

Source: Field site reports – Accra, Tema Manhean, Gwollu, Tumu, Tronang, Amaasu. HelpAge Ghana/HelpAge International research study, 1999

functions. Failure to do this will result in skewed and ineffective policies, which fail to utilize the important and often untapped resource of a key sector of the population.

The way forward requires the world community to make a conscious effort to seek out and include older people in the broad strategies to tackle poverty in the 21st century. All policies should be assessed with regard to their impact on older people. Strategies should include older people in the analysis of issues, and in the setting of standards to target both their own poverty and that of the wider community. Data collection, and research and training in relation to older people should be given priority.

Notes

1   Amanda Heslop is the Training and Research Manager for HelpAge International and is managing a research programme on the contributions of older people to development in Africa, based in Ghana and South Africa.
2   Neysmith, S & Edwardh, J, 'Economic Dependency in the 1980s: Its Impact on the Third World's Elderly' *Ageing and Society* 4:1, 1984. They argue that demographic and economic factors are more significant determinants of the status of older people than universal value systems.
3   Vincent, J, *Inequality and Old Age*, UCL Press, London, 1995.
4   Sen, K, *Ageing*, Zed Press, UK, 1993.
5   Chambers, R, 'Poverty and Livelihoods', IDS Discussion Paper, IDS Sussex, 1995, and *Whose Reality Counts?*, ITDG, London, 1997.

6   De Haan, A, 'Social Exclusion: An Alternative Concept for the Study of Deprivation?' and De Haan, A & Maxwell, S 'Poverty and Social Exclusion in North and South', *IDS Bulletin* 20:1, IDS, Sussex, 1998.
7   Chambers R (1995) *Poverty and Livelihoods: Whose Reality Counts?* IDS, Brighton. & (1997) *Whose Reality Counts?* Intermediate Technology, London.
8   Norton, Aryeety, Korboe & Dogbe, *Poverty and Social Planning*, Discussion Paper Series 83, The World Bank, Washington, DC, 1995.
9   De Haan, A, 1998, op cit.
10 The World Bank Policy Research Report, *Averting the Old Age Crisis: policies to protect the old and promote growth*, Oxford University Press, New York, 1994.
11 le Roux, P, *Poverty and Social Policies. Some Critical Policy Choices for South Africa*. Report of the Committee on Strategy and Policy Review of Retirement Pensions, Government of South Africa, 1995.
12 Heslop, A, *Participatory Needs Assessment in Clermont Township*, HelpAge International, London, 1996.
13 Much of the experience of participatory research with a policy dimension has been developed during this decade through the World Bank Participatory Poverty Assessments. For an overview of issues and experiences see Holland, J & Blackburn, J (eds), *Whose Voice? Participatory Research and Policy Change*, ITDG, London, 1998.
14 HelpAge International has supported participatory research with governments in Cambodia (1997), Tanzania (1998) and is supporting initiatives in Mozambique, Rwanda, Ghana and South Africa. Reports from Cambodia and Tanzania are available from HelpAge International office in London.

3 Gender and Ageing[1]

Edited by Deborah Ewing

Introduction

There is a double challenge in responding to the gender implications of global ageing. On one hand, there is an imperative to address the many disadvantages that the life expectancy 'advantage' holds for women. On the other, it is critical to recognize and support the successful efforts of older women to improve their quality of life and that of their families.

Too strong a focus on the extreme vulnerability of women in old age can obscure the indispensable contribution of women to the development process *despite* that vulnerability. Older women are one of the poorest population groups yet they are often the primary carers for the other poorest group – children. In several countries in Africa, the poorest older women – rural grandmothers – have taken on the responsibility of caring for the most vulnerable in their communities, that is children and grandchildren with HIV/AIDS, in the absence of any state

Sub-Saharan Africa's 15 million older women are projected to more than double in number to 33 million by 2025.
© Barry Lewis/ Network

support. This chapter looks at key factors in the experience of older women in the context of how they deal with that reality and how they can be enabled to cope better.

The actual situation of older women in developing countries is influenced by many (mis)perceptions about their capacity and activity. As with older people in general, older women have long been viewed – in their villages, in government departments and in the distant offices of development and aid agencies – as inactive recipients of support. Social custom and official policy have become concerned with the 'burden' of meeting the needs of older people. The responsibility to uphold the rights of people in their later years might be more readily embraced if there was greater awareness of the contribution they already make and of their potential to play a fuller role. This will only be possible if development policy stops regarding older people as a distinct but homogeneous mass, understands the different implications of ageing for women and men, and builds on their own, diverse strategies to live healthy, productive and fulfilling lives.

'Just as it is now accepted in development that women are not inherently 'unequal' but that gender inequality is built into society's economic, social and political systems, so it must be recognized that older women are not inherently vulnerable.'

The current status of older women in developing countries is the outcome of generations of systematic discrimination, through every stage of the life cycle. Given the neglect of basic nutritional and educational needs, the burdens of childbirth and childcare, and unpaid physical labour, the denial of property rights and the exclusion from decision-making that women face, it might be considered miraculous that so many survive to old age. Indeed, many women become 'old' in what should be their middle years.

Just as it is now accepted in development that women are not inherently 'unequal' but that gender inequality is built into society's economic, social and political systems, so it must be recognized that older women are not inherently vulnerable. Development policy needs to move towards investing in the vast human resource that older women command, in ways that they themselves judge will improve their quality of life. As Jon Hendricks[2] points out: 'Circumstances of older women do not come about by chance; they are socially constructed and reflect social priorities. To the extent that benefits are tied to productive roles in the public sphere, rather than reproductive roles in the private sphere, women must petition for benefits divided between the two, while males claim benefits based solely on activity in the public sphere.'

Demography – multiplying disadvantage?

In at least 75 developing countries, the number of women aged over 60 is projected to increase by more than 150 per cent between 1997 and 2025. In 1997, there were 15 million older women in sub-Saharan Africa and that number is expected to grow to 33 million by 2025. In Asia, there were estimated to be 144 million older women in 1997; by 2025, their number is expected to reach 355 million. In 1997, 9 per cent of older women in developing countries were over 80. By 2025, this percentage is expected to have tripled.[3]

Since older women are one of the poorest population groups, these statistics say to some economists, and development theorists, that in 25 years' time there will be three times as many very poor older women as there are now – three times the burden of care. The fact that older women's human rights and basic needs have been consistently neglected to make them so vulnerable to poverty in no way justifies such predictions about liability. Rather the statistics highlight the need to restructure social and economic systems and to rethink urgently – and in consultation with older women – how the many strategies they employ to cope can best be supported.

Longevity

Women outlive men in nearly all countries of the world. In developing countries, 7 per cent of females have a life expectancy at birth of more than 80 years (compared to 52 per cent in developed countries), while no males have a life expectancy over 80.[4] While this statistic reflects the trend in developed countries towards dramatically increased life expectancy, it hides tremendous disparities. For example, in Uganda, which like other African countries is suffering the impact of the HIV/AIDS epidemic, life expectancy for women has increased by less than two years since 1950 (in Japan it has increased by just over 20 years). In India, Bangladesh and Pakistan, women's life expectancy lags behind that of men.

Although the 'gender gap' is much smaller in developing countries (on average 3 years, compared to 7 years in developed countries, partly due to high levels of maternal mortality), it still impacts on the status of women. Older women are more likely than not to be widows and this likelihood increases with age. This means they are more likely to be dependent upon social support, to live in isolation, to be deprived of or unable to maintain any resources they may have enjoyed (such as farmland, marital home, livestock). They are likely to spend more of their older lives in a disabled state and are more susceptible to depression and psychological problems due to their isolation and reduced status.

Poverty

Female poverty is a universal phenomenon that becomes more pronounced with age. Only 18 per cent of countries in the developing world are committed to ensuring social security benefits in old age[5] and the amounts are rarely adequate. Even the small proportion of women who are eligible for pensions, having been employed in the formal sector, receive much lower benefits than men since they work in lower-paid jobs, with their periods of continuous employment interrupted by child-raising.

South Africa is one of the few countries of the South that has universal state pensions. However, where poor rural women are receiving these, they commonly use them not to provide for their own needs but to pay school fees for grandchildren and give loans to other family members.

Urban migration of younger, able-bodied people in search of work often leaves older people without their traditional support structures in rural areas. Older women then tend to bear the burden of responsibility of subsistence farming, household work and care of grandchildren with diminished resources.

Millions of people in developing and transitional countries are displaced or refugees as a result of conflict and natural disaster. Older people are likely to be separated from their families if they are unable or unwilling to join the forced migration. Older women are then most at risk, being more dependent on social support. If older people are displaced, they suffer particular hardships in refugee camps, physically – for example being unable to walk to food distribution points – and psychologically, for example due to separation from their ancestral home. The International Federation of Red Cross and Red Crescent Societies has responded to this by recognizing the value of older people's experience and employing them in refugee camps.[6]

Since women are rarely able to accumulate savings or assets, and often lose land and property on being widowed, they are more vulnerable to destitution. The very fact that women survive these conditions – and contribute to younger people's survival and well being – indicates their potential to participate in and benefit from the development process.

Economic contribution – invisible assets

Determination of old age in developing countries is linked to levels of activity and productivity. As these are perceived to decline, so the contribution of a person is

Despite multiple disadvantages, older women consistently work to improve their quality of life and that of their families – these efforts should be recognized and supported.
© John and Penny Hubley/ HelpAge International

perceived to decline. The implications of ageing tend then to be seen in terms of the 'burden' placed on more active and younger people.

As Dr Indira Jai Prakash[7] points out, this impacts particularly negatively on older women: 'Questions such as whether an ageing woman is an asset or a liability point to a basic anomaly in our way of thinking. It highlights the commercial streak in our social ideology which implies that a person has to be 'useful' to deserve to exist. It is also a loaded question that, if answered objectively, will show up women in poor light.'

All over the developing world, older people make an 'invisible' contribution to their families and society at large, performing domestic tasks and caring for children and sick or disabled adults so that other members of a household may engage in 'visible' economic activity. In addition, older people engage in a range of income-earning activities in the informal sector, which contribute to the household economy but are rarely acknowledged, or are seen only as 'reducing the burden' of their presence.

There is a strong gender dimension to the economic activity of older people, in terms of:

- the kind of tasks it is expected or accepted that they should do;
- the environment in which they perform these tasks;
- the recognition of their contribution;
- the remuneration they receive;
- the degree of control they have over any income from their activities.

For example, in Egypt older women in the villages control and contribute to a wide range of economic and social activities that provide essential services and attract status within a female hierarchy, but which are not acknowledged by those in public office. Because it is widely held to be shameful for women to participate in public life, they have established 'shadow' economic and social systems but their contribution is not officially counted and their specific needs are not addressed by public policy.

Just as it has been recognized that the economic contribution of women through household and informal sector activity must

> *'All over the developing world, older people make an 'invisible' contribution to their families and society at large, performing domestic tasks and caring for children and sick or disabled adults so that other members of a household may engage in 'visible' economic activity.'*

be taken into account in assessing national resources, so must the contribution of older women and men. The fact that older men, who once made a tangible contribution to national economies, are considered a burden on retirement hints at the low esteem in which women around the world are held when they cannot 'earn a living'.

Prakash suggests a more equitable way of considering this asset/liability issue. The disadvantages older women face must be recognized and the social system needs to be restructured to make ageing women partners in the developmental work. 'It is not ageing women who are a liability. Age becomes a liability for women.'

> 'The disadvantages older women face must be recognized and the social system needs to be restructured to make ageing women partners in the developmental work. "It is not ageing women who are a liability. Age becomes a liability for women."'

The economics of exclusion

Lack of access to credit, subsidies and labour for agriculture limit the productivity of older people in developing countries. Again there is a gender dimension to this exclusion. Both older men and women find it difficult to take loans, secure inputs for small businesses or farming, or help to work their land, due to their low incomes, lack of savings and collateral. However, women are further disadvantaged by the fact that they often have no independent income, no control over fixed assets and very limited exposure to business or the formal sector.

> 'International Labour Organisation studies of labour force participation by older people showed that, in 1993, in at least 20 African countries, between 74 per cent and 91 per cent of people over 65 continued to work. 'In fact, there is no retirement for an elderly woman until either death, dementia or disability claims her!'

Recent research in Ghana showed that credit markets there operated age and gender-neutral policies, which led to the exclusion of older people, especially women: 'These policies should be explicit and affirmative to serve the interests of different categories of older people.'[8]

Credit schemes supported by HelpAge International and other agencies in a range of developing countries indicate that the hurdle of collateral can be overcome through the collective responsibility of all savings and credit group members for meeting loan repayments if an individual defaults. Women in many countries have launched successful cooperative efforts to provide security in the absence of formal financing. For example, in South Africa, savings and credit groups called *stokvels* provide loans to members in times of need or for investment. The common interests and social bonds among members are their 'collateral'. Similarly, burial societies exist in almost every community, to help poorer people (again usually women) to set aside money for funerals.

Several researchers have found that as developing country economies have been steered towards investment in regions and sectors involved in international commerce, the economic situation of older women has deteriorated. Export dependency, debt and industrialization have drawn resources away from the areas where older women are most economically active – that is agricultural production and informal trade. In addition, reduction of social spending under structural adjustment has shifted the burden of care back onto the family, and particularly the older woman. Hendricks cites the pattern in Caribbean countries, where women work for cash outside the export sector; economic development subsequently marginalizes their role: 'Although Caribbean cultures are matriarchal, that matriarchy underwrites low-cost labour and provides sizeable pools of untallied resources.'

Despite the many restrictions on their activity, older women in developing countries continue to be active and productive even in the face of ill health and disability. The Ghana research suggests that older women actually employ a more diverse range of activities than men to sustain themselves and their families. International Labour Organisation studies of labour force participation by older people

Asset or liability? Older women contribute to a wide range of economic and social activities with little recognition. © Caroline Penn

showed that, in 1993, in at least 20 African countries, between 74 per cent and 91 per cent of people over 65 continued to work.[9] 'In fact, there is no retirement for an elderly woman until either death, dementia or disability claims her!'[10]

The politics of exclusion

As well as the economic contribution they make, older people often have leadership roles, such as conflict resolution and cultural, religious and health education. These may be highly visible but are not measured in terms of value to the community. Although older women are routinely expected to manage any crisis that arises in a household, and to be custodians of culture and tradition, they are far less likely than men to be consulted when community problems or dilemmas are anticipated.

The skills of leadership, diplomacy and financial management, and the vast experience as carer and counsellor that the older woman is likely to have acquired are rarely rewarded with a place in public or political life. Cultural taboos, lack of education and the sheer pressure of domestic and income-earning duties conspire to keep older women out of decision-making bodies. Yet where older women have led campaigns or organizations, served in parliaments and councils, their influence has been positively felt.

The transition from indigenous, communalist forms of governance, to colonial rule, to western-influenced parliamentary systems has affected the leadership role of older people and their participation in decision-making. Illiteracy and lack of formal education, experienced by many more older women than men, is a major disadvantage. Apart from excluding them from candidacy, it also leaves them very vulnerable to the pressures of patronage and coercion at election times.

Older women are more likely than older men to migrate to urban areas with their adult children. This may reflect their greater financial and physical dependency. However, migration often separates older women from the social and cultural networks in their villages, where they might have enjoyed some status and influence – perhaps as healers, oral historians or traditional birth attendants. This diminished social role and the fact that older women living in urban areas are likely to be financially dependent on their children[11]

A credit to perseverance

A pilot revolving credit scheme in Lima, Peru, shows how older women can increase their independence, self-sufficiency and dignity with access to small-scale credit and appropriate training.

Engaging in trade, commerce or service provision is often the only way an older person in a poor community can earn enough to remain independent, or to survive. Access to credit may be the key to success in such a venture.

However, the obstacles to older people in developing countries gaining credit are often insurmountable. Despite the skills and long experience they may have, banks (and even development agencies) consider older people high-risk. Ability to pay back long-term credit, a secure income and collateral are requirements that many older people, and older women in particular, are unlikely to meet.

For older women, the facts that they are less likely than men to have experience in paid work outside the home and more likely to be economically dependent also count against them.

The NGO Pro Vida Peru, with capital backing from CARE Peru, has established a revolving credit scheme to give older people loans to start up small businesses. The scheme was piloted with women members of a Third Age Club run by Pro Vida Peru in Lima. Its aim was to provide loans that would support the development of income-generating activities, help older people manage these activities and exercise their physical and mental abilities.

Women in the scheme chose three of their members to serve as a credit committee, with responsibility for approving loans, managing the accounts and reporting to members. This committee received training in management and administration from Pro Vida Peru and CARE Peru.

The criteria for approving loans are that the member is able to repay the loan punctually and that it will be used for production, commercial activities or service provision. Typical activities are making clothes and tools, running market stalls and shops, and providing services such as hairdressing.

Loans are paid back with interest of 5 per cent. In the formal banking system, interest is about 2 per cent but the scheme members wanted to build up capital to enable more women to take loans.

At first, the scheme ran into difficulties because some members used their loans to pay family expenses rather than invest in income-earning activities and their repayments fell behind. Loans were suspended for seven months until members became familiar with the idea of using the scheme to support sustainable ventures.

Many of the women have now established viable businesses – commercial ventures where they can save by buying in bulk have been most successful. These not only provide the women with an income but have also created work opportunities for family members in an environment of high unemployment. Only four of the original group of 14 dropped out – three due to family pressure. While some of the women reported that their husbands and children tried to trick them out of the money they borrowed, the majority received encouragement from their families.

Most of the income generated has been used to improve the family diet but some women have also bought items for their own use and expanded their businesses.

This credit scheme was the first targeted specifically to older women in Peru. In addition to the economic benefits, the women report that the ability to take and repay a loan has improved their levels of security, confidence and responsibility. The scheme has helped them to overcome barriers of inexperience, poor education, economic dependency and ill health. The women also report that their achievements have helped to change their image within their families and community.

undermines their self-esteem and contributes to loneliness.

Ways need to be found to integrate older people into social life where they have been displaced from their communities. HelpAge India has established practical schemes to develop the human resources of older people, for example involving them in development projects such as the rehabilitation of drug addicts and convicts.[12]

Belief in witchcraft threatens older women's rights

The bloodshot eyes, hunched posture, gnarled skin and solitary air of an old woman in a rural village may be easily attributed to her living conditions. Decades of cooking over smoky fires in confined spaces, of carrying children, wood and water, of labouring in the fields – only to be abandoned or neglected in your final years – takes a heavy toll on health and appearance.

However, these, and other characteristics, are often seen not as the harsher signs of ageing but as the marks of a witch. The belief in witchcraft is strong in many parts of Africa. Myths and superstitions about the identity and powers of witches have become entrenched over centuries. These are not easily dislodged by modernization and development if the ensuing change does not bring poor and isolated communities many benefits. If a child falls suddenly ill and there is no prospect of treatment, if the crops fail and there is no food to fall back on, if a family suffers recurrent misfortune and there is no explanation, sometimes a scapegoat must be found. Older women will often provide this scapegoat, being blamed as witches for all manner of death and disaster. Once such an allegation is made, say by a family where there has been an unexpected death, or by neighbours whose water supply has become contaminated, it may be repeated and accepted throughout the community. Traditional healers and diviners may propagate the belief in witchcraft in order to explain away phenomena that they cannot understand or control. They may initiate or reinforce the labelling of people as witches to maintain their power; for example, if a young person falls ill, as well as prescribing a cure, the healer might identify a 'witch' as the source of the illness.

The fate of someone accused of witchcraft may range from being ostracized, to being driven out of their home, or their community, to being brutally killed. Although the belief in witchcraft is ancient, witchcraft killings are regarded as a more recent response and the incidence of such killings seems to be increasing.

In Tanzania, an estimated 500 women are murdered every year after being accused of witchcraft. Many more are driven from their homes and communities, becoming destitute as a result. The power of the belief in witchcraft is so strong that the government and the courts find it hard to address the issue overtly.

A recent study in Tanzania by HelpAge International[14] found that widowhood exposed many older women to the charge of witchcraft. This was typically related to their solitude if they lived alone after being widowed: 'If she is not seen much around the village, an air of mystery may grow up around her, which contributes strongly to accusations of being a witch.'

The belief in witchcraft represents a double violation of the human rights of older women. They are already discriminated against as older people, in terms of their status and their access to support and resources. Their vulnerable situation is then exploited in order to deprive them of their limited assets or to punish them for unexplained hardships. While men may also be accused of witchcraft, women are much more likely to be targeted as they often do not have a family or community network to ward off the accusations; they are physically frailer and more vulnerable and therefore easier to attack. The Tanzania study also found that women are often seen as being 'cleverer' than men and therefore more capable of witchcraft.

In the Mwanza region of Tanzania, accusations of witchcraft were seen to link directly to the efforts of family and in-laws to prevent inheritance of property and possessions by widowed women. For example, grievances between a man and an older female relative might build up and become known in the community so that if a member of the man's family becomes ill and he consults a traditional healer or diviner, it is easy for that person to point at the female relative. The consequences can be tragic: it has been known for a defenceless older woman to be hacked to death under the guise of ridding the village of a witch; meanwhile, the man takes over the woman's home, fields and other belongings.

A study by the Tanzania Media Women's Association (TAMWA)[15] cites data from the Ministry of Home Affairs that in the region Shinyanga, in the 18 months from January 1996 to June 1997, 178 people were killed as a result of being accused of witchcraft. This represented nearly 40 per cent of all murders reported in the region in that period.

The vast majority of the 300 people surveyed said that they had witnessed at least one woman being killed for alleged witchcraft and that they had heard of other witchcraft killings. While nearly all those interviewed said they opposed witchcraft-related killings, 46 per cent of the respondents said it was up to the government to take action to prevent such attacks.

The research showed that nearly one third of those interviewed were afraid of getting old because they feared being targeted and attacked as a witch.

Older women and men have different needs and expectations, reflecting their different roles and priorities.
© Neil Cooper

Health

As women make up an increasingly greater proportion of the oldest old, their health and welfare needs have specifically to be recognized in social planning.

Health research has often excluded older people and where it has been conducted, it has tended to focus on men. There is very little comprehensive data on the health of older women in developing countries. This is due in part to the fact that lack of transport to clinics and money for medicines make them more likely to opt for self-treatment.

Women's health and access to health care are undermined by poverty and economic dependence, violence, gender inequalities in nutrition and food distribution, limited decision-making power and negative cultural attitudes. Poor education and lack of information are also factors – for example take-up of free health care is sometimes low because women are not aware of their entitlements. In any case, health care services directed at older people and outreach to women in rural communities are common casualties of structural adjustment.

Poor nutrition from birth, difficult and dangerous working conditions from girlhood, multiple pregnancies and domestic violence make the journey to old age one of declining health. Older women are affected by a range of preventable conditions that differ from those of older men – such as post-menopausal reproductive health problems – or which, because of their social and financial status, are less likely to be treated – for example, loss of vision due to glaucoma or cataract. Untreated infertility is a reproductive health issue which, for women in Africa particularly, has a negative impact in later life: childless older women are more likely to find themselves without essential family support.

One of the obstacles to improving the health status of older women, particularly the oldest old, is the widespread assumption that the ailments of older people are an inevitable result of the ageing process. In India, Alzheimer's disease has been called *sathaya gaya* (turned 60) and *satar-batar* (turned 70).[13] This is indeed a disease associated with ageing that is not reliably treatable. Its incidence increases so that up to 50 per cent of the oldest old might expect to be affected; this means

Addressing widowhood in India

A national seminar on the 'Need to focus attention on the plight of elderly females in India', in 1996, heard that:

'The condition of widows is considered one of India's most neglected social issues – in social science research, in the agenda of the women's movement, and in the media, which reacts only to the dramatic incidents of sati, or witch-hunting'.[16]

As in other countries, there is a high proportion of widows compared to widowers in India, because more men die before their wives, widowed men commonly remarry and women rarely do.

According to Dr Indira Jai Prakash,[17] widows make up 8 per cent of the female population of India and 64 per cent of them are aged over 80 years. Widowhood in India is regarded as 'social death', with constraints on dress, diet and public behaviour that isolate women.

The research that has been done shows that households headed by widows suffer dramatic decline in per capita income and that the mortality risk of widowhood was higher for women than men. Among basic causes of their vulnerability are restrictions on the residence, inheritance, remarriage and employment opportunities of widows. The situation of widows in North India is worsened by the system of patrilocal residence, whereby widows cannot return to their parents' home even though they are often rejected by their in-laws. An extreme but unique case is the woman of 64 from Udaipur, who was widowed within three months of her marriage to a man she had never seen.[18] Her in-laws took her jewellery and kept her dowry but both they and her parents refused to take her into their families. From childhood she worked as an agricultural labourer to support herself and knew nothing but the privations and stigma of widowhood. Widows who are rejected by their families are commonly sent off to temples under the guise of pilgrimage and rely on charity for their survival.

Patrilineal inheritance effectively denies widows' inheritance rights over their father's property, and their customary and legal rights over their husband's share of family property are often violated. Long after the abolition of sati, there continue to be reported cases of women being forced to kill themselves on the death of their husband, in order for relatives to seize their inheritance.

There are very limited opportunities for widows living in households without an adult male to engage in income-earning activities. Criticized for being dependent, widows are severely restricted by cultural norms in the kind of self-employment they can undertake to reduce that dependency. Prakash notes that while widow remarriage is not prohibited by most castes, it is rare (9 per cent of those in a 1994 survey) and does not accord great security to a woman.

A study of the psycho-social condition of women in rural and urban areas of Karnataka in 1996 showed that widows, compared to married women of the same age, suffered more health problems and received less support to deal with them. Rural widows were in the most precarious position, the majority having no access to social security benefits or pension from their husband. 'Very often, women are forced to give up independent living and move in with children or relatives, or even move from one child's house to another after the death of the spouse.'[19]

However, rural women have clear ideas of the kind of measures needed to ensure their well-being and protect them against discrimination and exploitation. Prakash cites some of these proposals for legal and structural measures to improve the status of widows. They are worth mentioning since they embody principles enshrined in most declarations of basic rights and illustrate how profound is the unequal treatment of widows:

- All land and property belonging to the husband should be in the joint name of the spouse.
- On the death of the husband, all these assets should be transferred automatically to the widow's name.
- All land records should be updated to facilitate easy transfers.
- Land allocated by the government to the husband for any purpose should also be in the spouse's joint name.
- Local laws should not contradict the fundamental rights of women.
- Forced re-marriage (arranged in rural northern India by in-laws to keep property within their family) should be abolished.

- Bigamy (which often results in the disinheritance of the first wife) should be punished under law.
- Government schemes for education and health of widows' children should be devised.
- Pensions should be a matter of legal right, for life, and defendable in court.
- Voluntary organizations should help widows access legal and financial support provided for in law.

The government of India has introduced several schemes specifically targeted at supporting poor widows but these have had poor coverage and do not address the deep psychological, social and cultural privation that widows endure in addition to economic problems.

Prakash argues for a systematic approach, involving the state, non-government organizations, communities and the media, to improve the conditions of widows. To make this effective, elderly women must be aware of their rights.

that most cases are found among older women. However, many diseases that are treatable or preventable are seen in the same light.

According to research in Rajasthan, many women in their 60s continue to enjoy good health, while no women over 75 rated their health status as good. As women tend to live longer than men, they might experience more disability-free years than men but as a proportion of their life-span, these years are lower than those enjoyed by men, and women form the majority of older people affected by chronic disease in old age.

Married older people are likely to retain better health than unmarried people. Since women are more likely than men to live alone in old age, having been widowed and not remarrying, they are again disproportionately vulnerable to ill-health. In addition to their isolation, changes in both the eating habits and lifestyles of widowed women contribute to poor nutrition and psychological problems such as depression.

In order to meet the challenge of ensuring maximum healthy life expectancy for older women, changes of approach and resource allocation are needed at every level. Considering nutrition as a key factor in good health, there is a need for older women to become aware of their nutritional needs and be enabled to meet them. Food security policies tend to allocate resources to households, wrongly assuming that all members will automatically receive adequate food for their individual needs. Other factors include:

- allocation of resources to preventive primary health care that is accessible to older men and women;
- training of health care professionals not to take for granted but to prioritize treatment of chronic conditions that enables older people to live more comfortable, active and independent lives;
- support and training to carers in communities to help them provide or access appropriate healthcare for older people;
- recognition and development of tradi-tional medicine, which is widely relied upon in developing countries as more effective, affordable and accessible than pharmaceutical medicines. Enhancing the role of older women as experts in this field has both economic and social benefits.

There are at least two compelling arguments to governments and funders to invest in the health of older women. Firstly, improved health of the older woman benefits the individual and her family and community – and minimizes the care and treatment cost to the state. Secondly, a healthy older woman is able to maintain for longer her contribution to family and community. Once that contribution starts to be counted in official measures of productivity, the value of older women's health might be recognized.

Gender dynamics of roles highlighted

The gender dynamics of older people's participation in development are clearly highlighted by a study of livelihood security in Ghana.

Research conducted by HelpAge International, as part of a six-country study of the contribution of older people to family and community life, found two key determinants. Firstly, older men and women have different (gender-based) roles, responsibilities and entitlements, which determine the livelihood strategies they adopt. Their sense of well-being relates directly to the fulfilment of these socially-assigned roles. Secondly, older people's participation is determined by the extent to which institutions are gender and age aware.

Other key findings were that:

* older women are predominantly the bedrock of support for the family;
* gender influences well-being and contribution of older people throughout the ageing process.

In relation to the second of these findings, the study revealed that the shift from dependency on economic sources of support (such as wages or trading) to dependency on social sources (such as provision by relatives) tends to be swifter for older men than older women. The reason for this is that while both men and women are circumscribed in their behaviour by social norms, women are better able to diversify their activities in times of need. For example, if very old people become homebound, the men are unlikely to remain economically active, while the women might still undertake petty trading activities.

In addition, while livelihood priorities were largely prescribed by gender roles, older women were able to adopt more flexible strategies to fulfil these roles. For example, older men have responsibility for providing for the household, while older women are central to the management of the household; they are regarded as more astute than men in the allocation of household income. Older men tend to assume responsibility for the purchase of assets such as land and livestock, which requires longer-term investment strategies. Women assume responsibility for daily expenditure and, therefore, adopt shorter-term income-earning strategies. As a result, women are more often in a position to economize in times of stress or to invest when they have small savings.

In the communities surveyed, it was found that older women, in addition to providing child care for the family, also offer physical care and financial assistance to older men. It was apparently a recurrent theme in the research that older men placed a high value on this support. However, according to the study, the contribution of older women was still less likely to be officially recognized.

Since the household and informal sectors account for much of the work of older people, their activities, especially those of women, are regarded as 'domestic', an extension of their normal responsibilities. One of the key messages presented in the research was that the contributions of older people needed to be accommodated in economic analysis and policy formulation.

The aim of the project was to help make policies and services more responsive to the needs and capabilities of poor and disadvantaged older people in African and other countries.

Notes

1   This chapter draws upon a wide range of sources, in particular the important contributions to the understanding of older women in Africa by Professor Nana Araba Apt.

2   *Older Women in Social and Economic Development*, Ageing International, June 1995.

3   *Gender and Aging*, International briefing of the US Bureau of the Census, December 1997.

4   *Ageing and Development Newsletter*, Issue 3, HelpAge International, London, February 1999.

5   ECOSOC, 1992, quoted in *Older Women in Development*, HelpAge International, 1995.

6   *World Disasters Report 1995*, quoted in *Older Women in Development*, HelpAge International, 1995.

7   *Aged Women – Coping with Life*, National Institute of Primary Health Care/Health Care Promotion Trust, New Delhi, 1998.

8 *The Contribution of Older People to Development* (Ghana study), HelpAge Ghana/HelpAge International, London, 1998.

9 *Ageing in Africa*, WHO Ageing and Health Programme, Geneva, 1997.

10 Prakash, I J, *Aged Women – Coping with Life*, National Institute of Primary Health Care/Health Care Promotion Trust, New Delhi, 1998.

11 *Older Women as Beneficiaries and Contributors to Development: International Perspectives*, quoted in *Older Women in Development*, HelpAge International, London, 1995.

12 Prakash, I J, 1998, op cit.

13 Chandra, V, *Alzheimer's Disease and Other Dementias, in Elderly Females in India*, Society for Gerontological Research and HelpAge India, New Delhi, 1997.

14 *The situation of older women in Tanzania*, Kate Forrester Kibuga, 1999.

15 *Killing of Old Women on Witchcraft Beliefs in Shinyanga Region*, TAMWA, 1997.

16 Nambiar, 1994, quoted in *The Status and Condition of Elderly Widows in India*, Elderly Females in India, Society for Gerontological Research and HelpAge India, New Delhi, 1997.

17 *The Status and Condition of Elderly Widows in India*, Elderly Females in India, Society for Gerontological Research and HelpAge India, New Delhi, 1997.

18 Ibid, p57.

19 Ibid.

4 Reinforcing Capability: Informal Community-based Support Services for Older People in the Developing World

Mark Gorman

For substantial numbers of people in the developing world, not only do poverty and ill health remain major risk factors in their old age, but services addressing their specific needs are undeveloped. Recession has highlighted the vulnerability of marginal groups such as older people to economic shocks and undermined the capacity of services to make effective responses.

There is an enormous diversity of need among older people and responses both of the formal and informal sectors have been equally wide-ranging. Rapid economic development in the past three decades has enabled some 'middle income' countries to develop or enhance the provision of public health and social services to their citizens, including older people. Growing affluence has also facilitated the emergence in some countries of groups of older people able to afford access to personal services. But in many countries there are virtually no public services to support older people.

The support offered by NGOs, families and communities (referred to here as the 'informal sector') needs to reflect the great diversity of national contexts. In Singapore, for example, there are well-developed public services, so NGOs can focus on covering the gaps in provision. This contrasts starkly with a country like Bangladesh, where there is neither comprehensive public service provision nor substantial NGO support to older people. In this situation NGOs need to engage in a range of activities crossing boundaries between health and social services. In the absence of a universal social security system, this may well include the promotion of income-generation activities and community-based welfare funds for older people.

Both in the more affluent and poorer societies of the developing world NGOs take on other roles apart from direct service provision. Advocacy on behalf of older people is an important feature of their work. Age-related NGOs work extensively with governments, inter-government and non-government organizations to develop policy, to improve practice and to raise awareness of issues affecting older people. Organizations of older people themselves are increasingly significant across the developing world. Spanning local, community-based mutual aid groups to associations of retired professionals, they combine a range of functions, in which service provision and advocacy play primary roles.

Family and community support is critical to the well being of older people but it too is affected by the socio-economic environment. A well-developed public service structure can provide additional resources to supplement (and in extreme cases replace) family and community support. If such a public service framework is lacking, informal support is rendered significantly more vulnerable to rapid change. More research is needed to understand the impact of change on family support for older people and on the contributions which older people make to the welfare of their families. If this is better understood it can inform policies designed to reinforce the capability of older people and their families to support one another.

This also holds true for community-based support, where a better understanding of the participation of older people in community life (and barriers to increased involvement) is indispensable to the development of effective assistance. In all cases the paramount principle should be that of consultation with older people. Their preferences and needs must be at the top of the agenda when solutions to their problems are being sought.

In this chapter we consider four key aspects of the lives of older people: income security, health services, family support and community participation. Drawing on models of good practice we illustrate ways in which service providers, families and communities can be enabled to enhance the lives of older people. The examples highlight a cross-section of countries, including societies where public services are well developed, as well as countries where services are offered largely by informal providers in the absence of substantial public provision.

Income security and support

In most developing countries most people have no prospect of a secure and sustainable income in their old age. Although nearly every country has some form of social security coverage for older people, in practice these benefits are often limited to a few occupational groups, typically retired government staff and employees of larger scale private or public enterprises. These workers make up only a small percentage of the overall labour force, and in most countries those in the informal sector – farm workers, day labourers, the self-employed and family workers – are excluded. Even in those countries with more developed systems, there tend to be large sections of the work force who are excluded from coverage.[1]

In these circumstances the first and most important task is to identify sustainable sources of livelihood in old age. In doing so it is also important to recognize the factors which may limit the capacity of older people to provide for themselves, and take steps where possible to accommodate these limitations.

Income poverty may be associated with poor health and/or frailty, inadequate or inaccessible health services, lack of family or community support, large numbers of dependants, landlessness, limited skill or capital to invest in productive activity, and low status.[2]

This is the situation in Cambodia, where the great majority of older people rely on their own labour or that of their children to provide them with a living. Few have access to capital or skills that would give them options besides rice farming or physical labour, a situation often worsened by the unwillingness of NGOs running credit schemes with younger age groups to extend credit to older people. Many older people have lost children during the war, or their children are themselves too poor to help. For most older people, and for nearly all those who are poor, making a living is the single biggest problem they face.[3]

In response to such situations, small-scale credit and income-generating projects for older people have been set up in a number of countries in Africa, Asia, the Caribbean and Latin America. In rural Mozambique, for example, a relief and resettlement programme for older returned refugees has developed a group-managed credit programme in 21 villages of Tete Province. Local committees assess loan requests for small-scale agricultural, trading and manufacturing enterprises, make loans and monitor repayment agreements.[4] An example of another variant from India is the co-ownership of community irrigation wells by an elders' group. Apart from the material outputs (increased cropping of rice paddy and greater protection from rain failures) is the active role which older people are able to take in the management of cultivation. This participation has a significant impact on family dynamics, since the older family members have a renewed role to play, which imparts respect. Income from an associated activity in the same programme has enabled older people to contribute (for example) to medical treatment, educational expenses and marriage costs for younger family members.[5]

These initiatives share common features, such as the low physical activity needed for them, and the small capital inputs necessary to start them. Evidence from many of these projects is that the creditworthiness of older people is high, with repayment rates typically exceeding 95 per cent. The overwhelming majority of group members tend to be older women, reflecting both their greater longevity, but also their greater poverty, due to lifelong inequities in access to resources. By setting entry criteria such as numbers of dependants in poverty, or a maximum landholding, credit groups can effectively target older women in their communities. In countries where it is culturally acceptable for women and men to belong to the same group, the inclusion of women on management committees is encouraged, enabling women to take on roles otherwise inaccessible to them.

In some places the main economic objective of establishing profit-making small enterprises has been succeeded by a progression into mutual solidarity groups, providing loans from accumulated savings. A further development is the creation of local welfare funds through the donation of a small portion of interest or savings to a fund, which supports the most vulnerable older community members who are unable to participate in income-earning activity. In Mozambique for example, these social

> *'In Mozambique for example, these social assistance funds have both provided material support for vulnerable community members and created peer pressure for the prompt repayment of loans to support the welfare funds. Such schemes may prove a viable community-based option in the absence of comprehensive national social insurance or pensions coverage.'*

Meeting at the 'Sala' – older people in Cambodia provide advice and support to vulnerable people in their community. © HelpAge International

assistance funds have both provided material support for vulnerable community members and created peer pressure for the prompt repayment of loans to support the welfare funds.[6] Such schemes may prove a viable community-based option in the absence of comprehensive national social insurance or pensions coverage.

This approach is not a universal panacea. Income generating and credit programmes are vulnerable to a variety of external factors, from market fluctuations to adverse weather conditions; lack of motivation or poverty may cause older people to remain outside group structures. Furthermore their long-term viability when the management support of the NGO is eventually withdrawn remains untested in many cases. Nevertheless these programmes provide the only viable community-level initiatives for meeting the income needs of older informal sector workers.

Health services

Health and well-being is of central importance to most older people everywhere. At an individual level the capacity to earn a living or to participate in family and community life, as well as a sense of personal well-being, are all governed by health status. At a population level health care provision is the most comprehensive of the public services offered by all developing countries.

Despite the critical importance of health care, both the extent and accessibility of health services for older people remains very limited in many countries. Health facilities and personnel tend to be concentrated in urban areas, while older people are still predominantly rural dwellers. Access to affordable health care is the major challenge for the health sector in developing countries during the next century.[7]

In the absence of comprehensive public health care older people adopt a number of self-help strategies such as buying western medicine without prescription, or seeking the assistance of local 'doctors' or others claiming health knowledge. In response to these strategies a number of initiatives have sought to establish community-based primary health care services.

Community gerontologists

An innovative project in the Philippines provides an alternative for older people unable to afford to access health facilities by setting up its own comprehensive local health service. The programme, launched in 1996 by the NGO Coalition of Services of the Elderly (COSE) in 21 communities of Metro Manila, has three components. These are: provision of out-patient and mobile clinics, training of older people as 'Community Gerontologists' and a health promotion programme. A core team (a doctor, dentist and nurse) is complemented by community-based primary health providers. Over the programme's first two years some 30 Community Gerontologists received initial training. This equips them to do basic medical checks, keep records and refer more complex cases on to the health professionals. They are unpaid, although they receive an allowance when assisting at the clinic, and are entitled to free medicines under the programme. An important feature of the programme is that the initiative to launch it came from older people themselves, through the consultation meetings, which are a feature of COSE's process. The programme is thus highly responsive to community need, and this is reinforced by the use of older people as primary health care workers at community level.[8]

Similar schemes are operated in many developing countries in a wide variety of community settings, though in most cases the core primary health care activity is carried out by teams of professional staff rather than volunteers. These teams work either from static or mobile clinics within the community. In the *barrios* of Lima, Peru, NGOs such as *Movimento Manuela Ramos* have identified key health needs in discussion with older residents. This has resulted in the establishment of health groups, whose regular meetings are both opportunities for discussion and to provide supplements to inadequate diets. Specialized attention at local health posts, the development of a health manual for older people and carers, and preventive campaigns (such as one to improve the eye health of older people) have also been developed.[9] In inner city Karachi a similar, but static service, is offered by Pakistan

Medico International. Consultation was made free of charge when it was discovered that even the minimal fees proposed by the NGO were beyond the means of many older patients.[10]

These examples illustrate the point that in many situations NGOs are providing services in the absence of accessible public health care. Where services are more developed the NGO role is very different.

Filling gaps in provision

In Singapore, the Tsao Foundation defines its community health role within the context of a well-developed public health framework as:

> '[identifying] key services which are lacking and seeking to be the primary facilitator and an active provider'.[11]

Tsao Foundation's community health programme offers services to homebound older people and to those who are more active, through a combination of mobile and static clinic services and a day health programme. Their target is older people from low-income backgrounds or lacking family support. In both the mobile service and the seniors' clinic the approach is a multidisciplinary one, recognizing that health problems may be only one among a number of issues faced by older people. Psycho-social and financial problems may also be pressing, and may impact on health status. Team members are therefore multidisciplinary, including not only a doctor and nurse but also a social worker.

This case management approach also seeks to coordinate and harness available community resources through informal support mechanisms such as neighbour visiting, which can provide significant additional support for older people.

This holistic approach is also reflected in the Tsao Foundation's involvement in a locally-based Community Care Network. This groups non-governmental and public service organizations together so as to integrate services for older people in

Mohammed Taher, aged 69, in his carpentry workshop in Kassala, Sudan. With a series of loans, Mr Taher has expanded his business – he can now support his family and employ others.
© Andrew Webb/ HelpAge International

Singapore's Western Region. The network aims to provide a 'seamless' service framework, and to add value to the individual services offered by different agencies. Such inter-agency collaboration can work both at a community level and more broadly across national boundaries. Training courses are one example of the way in which knowledge can be shared between professionals. A number of successful collaborative training programmes developing the skills of community-level health workers have been held in recent years, providing a model with much potential for further expansion.[12]

Family support and living arrangements

'Growing old in one's own home among kith and kin and in one's own community is the overwhelming preference for most people'.[13]

Throughout the developing world there is a strong consensus on the importance of the family as a basic component of the social structure, and a key role assigned to families is that of providers of care at every stage of life.

Care in old age is still perceived as a special responsibility, particularly in the absence of alternatives in the form of public support structures. However the rapid demographic transition of recent decades, accompanied by other changes such as migration, urbanization and the increasing numbers of women entering formal workforces, have called into question the continuing capacity of the family to provide effective old age care.

Despite these concerns the available evidence is that family support systems for older people throughout much of the developing world remain robust and effective. Indeed in Cambodia family care has been described as 'the most widely used survival strategy for older people'.[14] In other parts of the developing world also, there is evidence of the durability of family support. For the overwhelming majority of elders in developing countries ready family support, whether in the context of extended families, co-residence or otherwise, remains available.[15]

Other features of these living arrangements should also be noted. Firstly, family support is perhaps a necessary but not sufficient guarantee of old age security. Poverty remains a significant intergenerational risk factor: if a family is trapped in endemic poverty the capacity of younger adults to assist older relatives may be severely impaired. Secondly, descriptions of living arrangements need to acknowledge the reciprocal nature of intergenerational support. Older people are by no means simply passive recipients of care but may also be active contributors to household economies through cash transfers or in-kind contributions such as child-minding or domestic chores. Finally, while acknowledging the pervasive nature of family support systems, this begs the question of what quality of support is available to those older people without family resources on which they can rely.

This discussion indicates that best practice in the provision of family support services should focus on sustaining existing arrangements, and compensating for their absence in the cases of older people who lack family assistance. A number of programmes address these issues, using a combination of strategies. In the Republic of Korea, where co-residence of older people with their children has undergone a dramatic decline in recent years,[16] an initiative which began life as a local project in parts of metropolitan Seoul in 1986 has become a nation-wide, government-supported programme of home care. The programme, developed by HelpAge Korea, is founded on a structure of voluntary home visitors. The volunteers visit older people to help with household tasks, shopping and cleaning. They also offer friendship and support, through shared social activities or simply through conversation with their older clients. In many cases this contact is the only extended social interaction enjoyed by the older person.

The programme emphasizes a strong supportive framework for the carers through training and regular support group meetings, which has resulted in a very low attrition rate of volunteers over the life of the programme. The formula is now being replicated nationally, with partial government funding and managed by a national body, the Korea Association of Community Care for Older People. In addition to the home help service, a day centre network and short-stay respite care facilities are also being developed as part of the national programme.

Support for family caregiving can provide vital stability in situations of great stress. In the townships of Durban, South Africa, the Muthande Society for the Aged provides a range of supports to family caregiving for (and sometimes by) older people. These include not only home nursing but counselling and not infrequently conflict resolution. The emotional dimensions of care, including difficult issues such as caregiver stress, and coping with death and bereavement are also addressed. There is a growing recognition in many countries that psychological and emotional problems have a significant impact on the well-being of older people and their carers. Services to respond to needs in this area include the establishment of counselling facilities, and in Singapore SAGE operates a free telephone service advising on caregiving issues as well as providing information on other services available. Individual counselling is also offered by those seeking help with personal problems.

Community participation

Throughout the world a consensus exists as to the desirability of enabling older people to participate to the fullest possible extent in the life of their own communities and wider societies.

Representatives to the Asian and Pacific Ministerial Conference on Social Development (Manila, November 1997) emphasized the need to create an environment supportive of 'active ageing' and one delegate believed that 'social integration of the elderly is a pressing moral imperative'.[17] However, the barriers to the effective community participation of older people are many. These include limitations on access to income-earning opportunities, lack of 'user-friendly' social environments adapted to older people's requirements such as public buildings without adequate access, inadequate transportation and physical insecurity. Above all, there is the invisible barrier of age prejudice, which thwarts the attempts of older people to participate.

Despite these barriers, it is clear that older people, in common with other age groups, want and seek out opportunities for community participation. Best practice in support of this clearly needs to focus on creating such opportunities, and this may be done by fairly simple means. In Bangladesh, for example, the traditional 'adda' or informal social gathering of close neighbours is by far the most favoured form of interaction.[18] Where elders clubs modelled on this traditional pattern have been established however, they have provided a number of different opportunities for members. For example, the clubs are not only centres for collection and disbursement of loans under community credit programmes, but simultaneously have become centres where people can enjoy recreational pursuits, and are forums for the discussion and mediation of local disputes. Thus the provision of physical space for one purpose may be adapted to other ends by the older users.[19]

The success or otherwise of such facilities is very dependent on their appropriateness to social norms and customs. In many parts of the developing world religious observance plays a central part in the lives of older people. In rural Cambodia the wat (temple) is the centre of social life for older villagers.[20] In communities where there is no *wat* the establishment of a Bhuddist community centre (*sala chortein*) is a priority, and NGO support for the development of these centres is therefore a particularly appropriate activity. As in Bangladesh, such community centres for older people acquire multiple uses. They provide meeting places and facilitate social contact among older people in a culturally appropriate way. Centres provide venues through which the development of Older People's Associations (OPAs) can be encouraged.

These OPAs have an important community-level welfare function, assisting those who are sick, or lacking family support, and helping with funeral arrangements. The centres thus provide a measure of physical security, since through the OPAs

'Above all, there is the invisible barrier of age prejudice, which thwarts the attempts of older people to participate.'

a sustainable internal village support system is established for the most vulnerable. This is a revival of a more comprehensive, traditional form of village-based social security which has otherwise virtually disappeared.

Psychological security is also increased, as isolated and potentially vulnerable older people have a place to meet others, where they know they will be looked after. This increases their self-confidence and morale. The *sala chortein* is also used for other community activities such as training and immunization campaigns. This, and the recognition which comes from seeing similar groups being set up in neighbouring communities (as has happened in Cambodia), increases the self-confidence and solidarity of older community members.[21]

The provision of day centres for older people is a common feature of NGO programmes throughout the developing world. As in the Cambodian example, these centres often acquire a range of activities, which enhance both the physical and psychological well-being of older people. The provision of meals, for example, has an important social meaning. So too does practical 'income generating' activity, even if the economic return is low. Facilitating the social contact of older people also has a value even for those who are suffering from severe impairment. In Cochin, India, the establishment of a day centre for older people with dementia has the dual function of enabling the centre's clients to benefit from a stimulating environment, and giving their family caregivers a break from their responsibilities.[22]

The involvement of older people can be facilitated by using a range of interconnected strategies. In the Bolivian Altiplano region, a project initiated by an NGO to substitute for the lack of free public health services for older people has become an integrated community development programme.

The NGO CIPE identified a number of components that contributed to the health status of local older people in 19 rural and small town communities of the northern Potosi region. Thus actions to promote the revival of traditional medicine and primary health care were supplemented by the development of small-scale economic activities. The latter included the re-establishment of traditional farming practices on land depleted by indiscriminate use of chemical fertilizers, and the introduction of new varieties of vegetables, some grown under locally-constructed greenhouses of plastic sheeting. Small community centres have provided a focus for this activity, as well as workshops where craft goods are made for local sale. The centres combat social exclusion by enabling older people from isolated communities to meet together. Increased incomes and improved diet, the enhanced ability of older people to contribute to family economies and increased demand for traditional medicines for minor ailments have been outcomes of the programme.[23]

> *'Increased incomes and improved diet, the enhanced ability of older people to contribute to family economies and increased demand for traditional medicines for minor ailments have been outcomes of the programme.'*

Lessons learned

An examination of best practice in support of older people needs to start from first principles. A common theme running through much of the activity described in this chapter is that the preferences and needs expressed by older people themselves were central to the development process. The experiences of older people are complex and diverse, and arguably grow more so with increasing age. The knowledge and expertise accumulated by people over their lifetime are the primary resources on which they rely in old age, and are also assets of enormous value in planning and delivering services involving older people. Identifying and utilizing effective consultative processes both in the planning and delivery of services are therefore of critical importance to the development of appropriate models.

Best practice should be sensitive to the social and cultural perspectives of older

From mutual assistance to advocacy

Older people's groups may also move on from practical mutual assistance to a broader advocacy role. *Defensa Del Anciano* is a Bolivian network of more than 20 older people's organizations and of NGOs working with them. The member organizations, many of them service providers, came together in 1996 following a campaign that resulted in the ratification by Presidential decree of basic rights for older citizens.

Through the decree the then government approved the payment of the *Bonosol*, an annual payment to all Bolivians over 65. The authorization of the first payment in 1997 brought to light the problem of 'undocumented' older people, a particular issue in Bolivia, which has one of the highest rates of unregistered citizens in the world.

Registration for documentation with the National Identification Department normally requires the applicant to be accompanied by two (documented) witnesses who are at least ten years older than the applicant. This was clearly a problem for many over 65. In negotiation with the government *Defensa Del Anciano*, working in collaboration with the Church and the University, established an alternative system of registration, enabling 5,000 older people in La Paz to register. The majority of these were older women. This exercise enabled these older people to receive the *Bonosol*, and to be eligible to vote for the first time.

In the aftermath of the registration exercise, hurriedly carried out following the introduction of the *Bonosol, Defensa Del Anciano* has subsequently established two legal aid centres. They act as 'clearing houses' for older people, helping them to access the services to which they are entitled, including health care, housing and legal assistance. They also act as meeting places for older people, and one of the core founding groups of *Defensa Del Anciano*, the La Paz-based Council of Venerable Older People, meets at one centre regularly. One result of this has been that a group of older beggars who approached the centre for assistance, was inspired by the group meeting they encountered to create their own group, *Nuevo Amanecer*, and to apply for membership of the Council.[24]

people. Factors such as religion, family, home and community grow in importance as people get older. There is a belief in many countries that priorities change significantly in old age; there are certain roles which are particularly appropriate for older people to assume. In Cambodia for example, the importance of religious observance for older people is expressed by the view that 'younger people make rice, older people make merit'.[25]

It is also important to be sensitive to the special requirements of older people in other ways. The ageing process involves increasing restrictions on physical activity for many individuals, and means frailty or disability for some. It is therefore a key aspect of best practice that older people are not treated as though they were exactly like younger adults, but that programmes of support recognize changing capacity. This is not to imply that older people should become the passive recipients of care, but that the principle of their full involvement in activity to address their needs is always followed to the greatest possible extent, notwithstanding physical or mental impairment. In a number of the cases quoted above, the involvement of older people in the initiation and development of programmes is a core element of the process.

A further primary principle of best practice is that of maximizing the local-level impact of support services involving older people. This implies a number of the strategies discussed above. The involvement of family and community members, whether formally as volunteers within a programme structure, or through the support offered to informal caregiving and other assistance, can compensate for the lack of other resources. The principle of involvement remains crucial,

> 'The knowledge and expertise accumulated by people over their lifetime are the primary resources on which they rely in old age, are also assets of enormous value in planning and delivering services involving older people.'

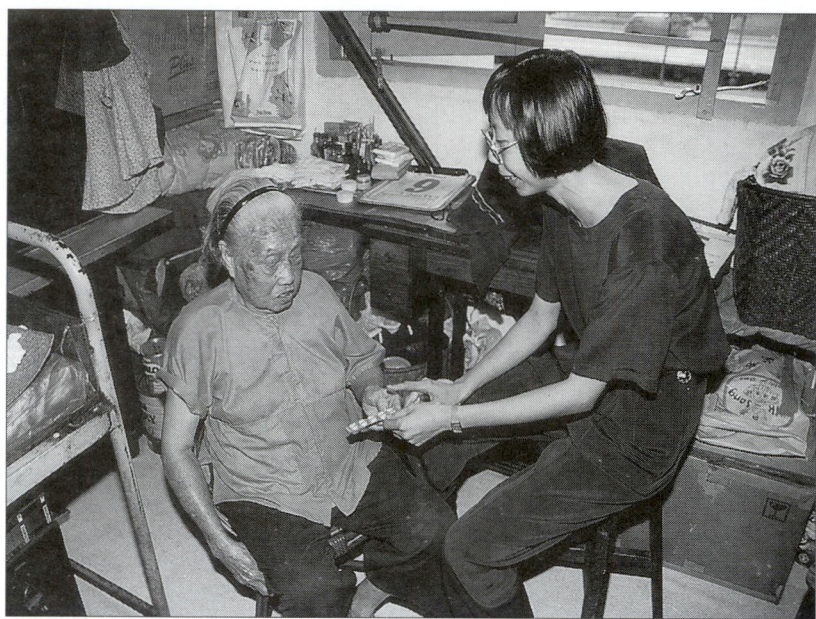

Madam Lee Kwai lives with a friend in her home in Singapore. Now both in their eighties, the two women receive regular visits from the Tsao Foundation mobile clinic.
© Tsao Foundation

and volunteer training and ongoing support are ways of encouraging this.

Apart from these examples of linkage of individual organizations and community structures we have also noted models of networking between organizations, which may work for a variety of purposes. Training and information exchange are clear benefits of inter-agency collaboration, but so too are joint initiatives in developing and maintaining direct services. There is also great potential to develop further cross-regional links to exchange learning and skills.

Making best practice count

Best practice needs to serve two purposes. One is to support high quality, innovative activities which have an immediate impact on the lives of older people, even if the number of people affected is relatively small. The other is to scale-up such local experience in order to have an impact on policy and practice at a much broader level. It is vital that good practice at community level is communicated to policymakers in government and inter-government organiza-tions, and to seek mechanisms to enable

this to happen. Two key requirements thus need to be met.

First, experience needs to be recorded. Grass-roots work properly emphasizes practical responses to perceived needs or problems. However this is often to the detriment of recording the experience, and knowledge which is left unrecorded is all too easily lost. A balance needs to be found between activity and reflection so that experience and knowledge can be shared.

Second, channels for passing on and sharing experience need to be identified. Reference has already been made to some of the ways in which this can be done. Seminars and workshops at local, national and inter-regional level play a vital role in collating and sharing what can otherwise be fragmentary information, and making resources available for such forums is an important priority for the consideration of institutional donors. Other forms of infor-mation exchange, through newsletters and increasingly by electronic means, also need to be fostered. In all such exchanges there remains the basic principle of enabling the voice of older people themselves to be heard by creating forums which are recep-tive to them.

Effective policy to support older people

What are the issues which emerge as the critical ones for older people at the end of this century and into the next?

Clearly the overwhelming question is the extent to which people of this and future generations will be able to ensure a reasonably comfortable material existence in old age. There has been much discussion in recent years about variants on pensions systems, with the World Bank advocating far-reaching reforms which would introduce fully funded, mandatory, preferably private pensions, replacing existing pay-as-you-go systems.[26] However, as the World Bank itself concedes, in most parts of the developing world, 'the informal system for income security – with no governmental and little market involvement – is still the mainstay' for the great majority of older people.[27] Informal systems therefore need to be a key focus of attention for policy development.

Given the importance of informal systems, and the extent to which many people will need to continue providing for themselves in their old age, a priority issue is ensuring a basic level of functional capacity for as many older people as possible.

This has a number of dimensions. We have noted the critical problem of access to affordable health facilities, and examined initiatives to bring services closer to older people. The development of these isolated initiatives into far-reaching service provision is a task which can only be taken on by governments, although there is also clear potential for development of effective partnerships between public and NGO provision in this area. As with curative service provision, so with the development of preventative health. To ensure that the rhetoric of 'lifelong healthy ageing' becomes a reality will require an investment in public health education for all ages (including older people themselves) which can only be made by governments. NGOs and civil society play an important role in advocacy, developing best practice and ensuring that older people can pursue their basic rights.

A key variable for both the material circumstances and the health of older people is the role of the family. The overwhelming majority of older people in the developing world have some form of family connection. The family in Korea has been called 'the most central avenue of social integration and the basic ground of support',[28] a description which applies practically throughout the developing world. Policy makers need to find appropriate ways to offer support to family caregiving.

The clear focus of policy relating to the family needs to be on provision of support structures which ease the caregiving burden, and wherever possible on fostering opportunities for contributions by older people to family life. Direct interventions in support of families, such as caregiver training or respite care, need to be supplemented by government policy. For example, fiscal measures can be used to encourage co-residence of older people with their children.

Family structures are affected by the same stresses as other social institutions. Being part of a family is not a necessary guarantee of material and psychological security for an older person. A growing number of older people may not have immediate access to family support, and the potential for the growing isolation of this group needs to be addressed. Finally, the role of caregiving very frequently falls on female family members, and their needs will require the close attention of policymakers in future. In other words, it will be important for policy development not to view the family as a given, but as an evolving structure whose various elements will require a variety of supportive strategies.

Responses to these emerging issues will be varied. However, one consistent approach should be the continued effort to link governments, inter-government agencies and the non-government sector together, through activities which range from direct service provision through to inter-regional networking to share information, learning and experience. In these ways it would be possible to foresee a strong and effective response to the emerging needs of the growing older populations of the developing world.

Notes

1 Social Security Administration, *Social Security Programs throughout the World – 1997* Research Report 65, August, Washington, DC, 1997.
2 HelpAge International, 'Credit and Livelihood. HelpAge International Cambodia Programme', unpublished report, 1998.
3 Ministry of Social Affairs, Labour and Veterans Affairs/HelpAge International, (MSALVA/HAI) *The Situation of Older People in Cambodia*, HAI, Phnom Penh, 1998, p22.
4 HelpAge International, unpublished report, October 1998.
5 'Community Action for Rural Development', unpublished report to HelpAge International. Tamil Nadu, India, January 1998.
6 HelpAge International, unpublished report, October 1998.
7 World Health Organization, *World Health Report 1998*, WHO, Geneva, 1998, p189.
8 Masulit, S P, 'Assessment of a Community-Based Health Program for the Elderly: Implications for Future Initiatives', unpublished MSc thesis, De La Salle University, Philippines, 1998.
9 HelpAge International, unpublished report, 1995.
10 Ibid.
11 Tsao Foundation, information materials, Singapore, no date.
12 See, for example, the training course programmes of the Asia Centre on Ageing, Chiang Mai, Thailand, for 1997 and 1998.
13 Tsao Foundation, *Age Concerns* 4:10, June 1998, p1. Singapore has adopted ageing in the home with the family as a national directive.
14 MSALVA/HAI, 1998, op cit, p25.
15 See the comprehensive discussion of these issues in UN ESCAP, *Asia-Pacific Population Journal* 12:7, December 1997.
16 From 78 per cent in 1984 to 49 per cent in 1994. See also discussion of the situation in Korea in Kinsella, K & Taeuber, M, *An Aging World II*, US Bureau of the Census, Washington, DC, 1993.
17 UN Economic and Social Commission for Asia and the Pacific, *News Bulletin on the International Year of Older Persons* 1, 1998.
18 Khan, A H, 'An Evaluative Study on Elders' Community Based Service Projects in Bangladesh', unpublished report, Resource Integration Centre, July 1998, p25.
19 Khan, A H, 1998, op cit, p15.
20 MSALVA/HAI, 1998, op cit, p30.
21 HelpAge International, *Cambodia Programme*, unpublished report, 1998.
22 *Urban Community Dementia Services and Day Care Centre* of Tropical Health Foundation of India. HelpAge India, unpublished report, 1998.
23 HelpAge International, unpublished report, 1998.
24 Packman, N, unpublished report, HelpAge International, April 1999.
25 MSALVA/HAI, op cit, 1998.
26 World Bank, *Averting the Old Age Crisis*, Washington, DC, 1994.
27 Ibid, p49.
28 Jong-Jo Yoon, 'Population Aging and Changes in Family Factors' in Sung-Jae Choi et al (eds) *Aging in Korea*, Chung-Ang, Seoul, 1995.

5

Ageing and Health

Alex Kalache and Kasturi Sen[1]

'The one who has health has everything'

Introduction

Population ageing represents a triumph of social development and public health. Throughout this century, improvements in hygiene, water supply, control of environmental hazards, and prevention of infectious diseases through immunization have greatly reduced the risk of premature death for hundreds of millions of people throughout the world. In addition, antibiotics and new medical technologies are providing the means to avoid early death caused by diseases of all age groups, resulting in the survival of much larger populations to even older ages.

Ageing of the population is a desirable and natural aim of any society, and it is an irreversible process once it starts. But if ageing is to be a positive experience it must be accompanied by improvements in the quality of life of those who have reached or are reaching old age.

The challenge for society at large is maintenance of autonomy and independence for the majority of its elderly citizens. Health policies must respond to the need to improve access to social and health resources enabling improvement in the quality of life of both present and future cohorts of elderly populations.

From a demographic perspective the view of ageing as a crisis must be rejected: ageing has a lead-time of decades rather than years and provides societies with the opportunity to prepare themselves through appropriate policies and programmes for an ageing population. The real crisis of ageing is the personal crisis of day-to-day existence – a present reality faced by many older individuals and their carers. This is reflected in the primary concern among older people across nations and cultural divisions: the issue of old age income security particularly in relation to the rising cost of health care.[2]

'The real crisis of ageing is the personal crisis of day-to-day existence – a present reality faced by many older individuals and their carers. This is reflected in the primary concern among older people across nations and cultural divisions: the issue of old age income security particularly in relation to the rising cost of health care.'

The state of older people's health

In the past, the main threat to life in a less developed country occurred in the early years of life. Now, in addition, populations face the prospect of long periods of morbidity and disability and chronic degenerative disease. Life expectancies of middle aged and older persons in developing countries are not significantly lower than for those people in the same age groups in the developed world. A middle class woman aged 60 in San Paulo, for instance, still expects to live for 23 years. However numerous local and national level health surveys are beginning to indicate that despite low levels of awareness, older people in developing countries have a high prevalence of disability. This is due in part to the long-term effects of diseases that occurred in childhood and early adult life such as poliomyelitis, leprosy, tuberculosis, rheumatic fever, schistosomiasis, Chagas' disease and infections not properly treated

in their early stages. In addition, common problems that can be successfully dealt with through secondary prevention, often lead to complications and permanent incapacities in poorer countries. Examples are hypertension and stroke, diabetes and peripheral vascular disease, trachoma and blindness.

A major survey on social economic health profiles of elderly people in India,[3] covering 5000 households over 8000 villages and 4500 urban blocks, showed that 45 per cent of both men and women and rural and urban dwellers reported chronic illnesses. In two smaller Indian studies on older people in rural areas, virtually everyone included in the study had multiple symptoms. Close to 90 per cent had visual deficits, 40 per cent had muscular-skeletal problems, 20 per cent had cardiovascular symptoms, 20 per cent problems with the central nervous system and 16 per cent respiratory problems. In addition 43 per cent suffered from some form of depressive illness.[4]

Both in the developed and the developing world, ischaemic heart and cerebrovascular diseases are the main causes of death in old age, followed by various forms of cancer and then respiratory diseases, largely pneumonias. Rates increase steeply with age, although cancer-related diseases are less frequent in the very old age group. There are however some differences in degree; in developing countries, infectious and parasitic diseases still kill at the older ages, cerebrovascular diseases are more important than ischaemic heart disease and the group of other heart diseases are also prominent, as are injuries, compared to developed countries.

Although most older people live in developing countries, little research has been carried out into the prevalence and incidence of dementia – one of the most disabling later-life mental disorders. In developed countries the prevalence doubles with each five-year increase in age from 3 per cent at 70 to 20–30 per cent at 85.

Health is essential to survival – for many older people the ability to work and fulfil one's role in society depends on their physical well-being.
© Carol Lee/Network

While reliable figures for developing countries are not available, if the age specific prevalence is the same, 24 million people in developing countries would be suffering from Alzheimer's Disease and similar conditions in 2025.[5]

Gender and health

In most countries women live longer than men. Currently in the developed world, differences in mortality favour women at all ages and especially so at the oldest ages. Female death rates are lower than male ones at all ages and in most countries of the world. In developing countries these trends are apparent, although there are considerable variations in the years of the gender gap. For example, in Uruguay, the Republic of Korea and Hong Kong, the gender gap is similar to that in the developed world – typically 3–6 years. In parts of south Asia, for instance India, north and sub-Saharan Africa, the inverse may apply owing to the excess in female mortality during the reproductive period and in early childhood. Whilst the gap between male and female life expectancy is likely to be reduced in the coming decades, the majority of the world's elderly population continues to consist of women.

Most important to policy are the issues of family based care. Marital status and living arrangements are affected by longevity – fewer men than women are widowed, owing to the age and mortality differentials. Higher life expectancy coupled with lower age at marriage for women, means that widows outnumber married women in most developing countries by the age of 65 years.[6]

Women's health and access to health care are often disproportionately affected by high levels of poverty and economic dependence, experiences of war and violence as well as gender inequities in nutrition and food distribution. These are often compounded by negative cultural attitudes in both developed and developing countries. As a result older women are often excluded from research programmes and routine data collection. Such information in the form of both cross-sectional and longitudinal studies is essential to plan preventive strategies and reduce the impact of diseases that affect older women – coronary heart disease, dementia, osteoporosis and other disabling osteo-muscular diseases. A handful of western studies also indicate a high prevalence of depression among older women as the cumulative effect of a life time of double-roles of production and reproduction. These studies are only exploratory, but need to be examined for similarities and differences with developing countries in order to inform policy.[7]

The health transition

As developing countries change socio-economically and demographically there are far reaching consequences for health services. Brazil provides an interesting example: In 1940 more than 40 per cent of deaths were caused by infectious and parasitic diseases, 50 years later they were responsible for only 7 per cent. In the meantime, cardiovascular diseases and neoplasms (cancers) increased from 14 per cent and 4 per cent of total mortality in 1940 to 32 per cent and 12 per cent respectively in 1980.[8]

This shift, the 'epidemiological transition', reveals only part of the picture. Already, in the mid-1980s the main causes of death in Brazil as a whole were non-communicable diseases. The second most common set of causes was closely associated with poverty – illnesses originating in the peri-natal period and respiratory and intestinal infectious diseases. The third group embraced external causes of death related to the hazardous environment and to social violence. A similar picture is now emerging throughout developing countries: diseases associated with ageing coexist with the 'traditional' problems of underdevelopment together with problems arising from environmental hazards.

There is a very important difference between the demographic transition in developing and developed countries. Substantial increases in life expectancy and significant reductions in birth rates occurred in Europe before the advent of the recent dramatic development of medical technology. Control over death and birth was mainly achieved through a gradual improvement in living conditions. People in Europe and North America no longer died of tuberculosis, gastro-enteritis and similar causes of premature death. This was not because they were being actively prevented, for example by immunization, or successfully treated by antibiotic or other drug therapies. It was because of substantial improvement in the overall quality of life. Such improvements were reflected in better nutrition, improved housing, sanitary conditions and healthier working environments. By comparison in developing countries, hundreds of millions of people continue to live in absolute poverty, yet medical technology has in recent years provided the means to prevent or cure many once fatal diseases, regardless of the conditions in which people are living. The reality is that developed countries became rich before they aged; developing countries are now ageing at unprecedented speed while most of their populations are living in poverty.

Health policies in developing countries

Desirable as it is, the ageing of populations is fast progressing against a background of unsolved infrastructural problems. Ageing

Ceremony to 'swear in' new volunteer health workers. These older people in the Philippiness have been trained to support the most vulnerable older people in their neighbourhood.
© Ed Gerlock/COSE

is progressing while basic developmental problems affecting the population as a whole – adequate education, sanitation, control of the environment – still await solutions.

Many developing country governments are operating in conditions of extreme budgetary pressures on already strained health and social services systems. Even those countries which first witnessed significant ageing of their populations are having to review their past policy responses in the face of rapid social, economic and political change. They are experiencing an increased need for care of frail old people as well as a need to increase health promotion for those now growing old.

The 1997 World Health Report[9] clearly indicated that by 2020, over two-thirds of deaths in the developing world would be caused by ageing-related non-communicable diseases. The very nature of these diseases – long-term, potentially costly, incurable and often disabling – will further strain the health and social care systems of countries already burdened with the challenges of communicable diseases that no longer kill as often, but continue to be major public health threats. This 'double burden' is unprecedented. By the time their popula-

tions had aged, most developed countries had already overcome the problems related to infectious diseases. Furthermore, current trends towards nuclear families, urbanization, participation of women in the workforce and the development process – all contribute to the erosion of traditional forms of care.

Nonetheless, it should not be forgotten that although more older people will mean greater demands for services, this sector of the population also represents a precious resource for society. In many societies for example, older persons are expected to and do continue to provide support for the family in terms of raising income through small trading among other factors, also looking after grandchildren. This should not be overlooked. The cost of care, in particular health care, is currently a much-debated issue, but relates in our view not only to ageing but also to the kind of therapeutic measures undertaken in the treatment of older people.

Support for elderly people as part of comprehensive provision for all vulnerable groups in the realms of health care thus has huge potential pay-offs. By ensuring that older persons continue to contribute positively to society instead of being just receivers, their role as providers of care will be considerably extended: instead of being a problem, they will be part of the solution. This will increasingly become an imperative following changes in the dependency ratio of countries without the capability to provide social security schemes to large segments of their populations. Healthy older persons are a resource for their families, their communities and the economy.[10]

Health, old age, inequality and poverty

Health, old age and poverty are intimately linked. In most societies, a disproportionate number of the 'poorest poor' are very old. This has profound implications for countries where social inequalities are severe and/or increasing. In Brazil for example, considerable differences in standards of living have developed. Life expectancy at birth is nearly 16 years higher in children of professional parents than in those at the bottom on the social scale, for whom infant mortality rates are at least three times higher.[11] Regional differences are also sharp. Life expectancy at birth in San Paulo is 70 years, while in the State of Penambuco it is around 57. Paradoxically, the highest proportions of elderly people will not necessarily be found in the wealthiest regions. Migration is a phenomenon mostly of the young who leave behind older relatives who often have neither physical help nor financial support as they lack the necessary skills to compete successfully in skilled job markets. Such inequalities influence the quality of life of millions of elderly people trapped under the poverty line.

Appropriate responses to health and ageing

Health in old age as a result of the life course

A life-course perspective on ageing is indispensable in order to understand the process of ageing in all its dimensions: physical,

social, psychological, spiritual.

Health in old age is greatly determined by the patterns of living, exposures and opportunities for health protection over the life course. The patterns of living that enhance health are formed in early life and are not easily changed. Furthermore, the most frequently occurring ageing-related diseases – such as cardiovascular diseases and cancer – are long-term disease processes. Promoting health and well-being throughout the lifespan is part of the process of achieving greater quality of life (and longevity) for older people.

Pathogenic, disease-led approaches cannot meet the challenges of global ageing. Statistical correlations relating age and disease/disability, as adopted by the Burden of Diseases approach and originating in the World Bank, tend to result in a focus on ageing as problematic and the aged as ill, leading many to believe that the changing age distributions will only cause problems. Such pessimism is unwarranted and inhibits the development of effective health policy and services. Longitudinal studies have shown that physical and mental status can improve in successive generations of older people. The challenge is to understand and promote the factors that keep people healthy, with a focus on both personal and external resources.

Functional ageing

Assumptions that there is a chronological threshold – 60 or 65 years – which clearly demarcates old age are deeply unsatisfactory in the context of global inequalities. Individual ageing reflects, most of all, prior living conditions. If a women aged 50 has spent the whole of her life working beyond her physical capacities, has experienced ten, perhaps more, full-term pregnancies and lactated between each and since childhood has been undernourished and deprived, she will not reach 50 with the same degree of fitness as a woman who has enjoyed a comfortable life from birth. Similarly, a poor peasant man with a history of tuberculosis or chronic malaria, who has worked an 11 hour day since childhood,

Learning is life long.
© Rural Yotala/Pro
Vida Peru

will be old by the time other, more fortunate men are celebrating life 'starting at 40'. The proportion of old people in developing countries is therefore an underestimate since only those 60 years and older are included.

There is an urgent need to measure functional status reliably in a variety of contexts, in order to provide information for service priorities, planning and evaluation and particularly to explore the potential for healthy ageing and independence despite reduced functional status.

Health services for older people

In most developing countries public investment in health care provision is facing a crisis. A policy focus on efficiency and cost saving advocated by donor agencies such as the World Bank (in the main) has drastically reduced investment in public health and welfare provision. In India for example, there has been a progressive decline in central government grants to state governments for health services from 41 per cent in 1984–1985 to 29 per cent in 1988–89 and falling sharply to 18.5 per cent in 1992–93.[12] This has not kept pace with population growth nor with demographic and epidemiological changes increasing the need for access to public health care. Instead the main policy focus has been on 'efficiency' and cost effectiveness and a narrow economic interest in patterns of health care utilization alone and how this may impact upon the future demand for different types of health care provision.

Lack of support for public provision coupled with a decline in investment means that a large proportion of the population has to depend upon the private sector for health care in India. In 1990 for example 75 per cent of health care expenditure consisted of out-of-pocket private expenditures borne by households.[13]

The widening gap between public and private sector provision is compounded by pre-existing inequalities in the distribution of health care resources (public) between urban and rural areas and the total absence of a functioning health infrastructure in rural areas. Thus health care resources, availability and access are often substantially different in urban and rural areas and between different states. Urban areas as in other parts of the developing world are in receipt of sophisticated and high technology-oriented medical care for treating chronic conditions such as heart disease and cancers. This type of care is costly and often inaccessible to the majority of the population, which continues to lack the basic essentials of health care. Primary care and prevention is an essential strategy for improving health status in later life.

The growing discrepancy in India between public and private sector provision is also reflected in recent five year plans which show the government spending on the health sector amounting to less than 2 per cent of GDP (against a 5 per cent minimum recommended by the WHO). Annual per capita household expenditure on curative health care is several times higher than the investment made by the public sector.

While the surviving elderly face the double burden of communicable and non-communicable disease, mortality among the poor continues to be high for communicable diseases, with high rates of infant mortality and child deaths from infectious disease. Those among the poor who are also affected by non-communicable diseases, are unable to purchase the high cost care needed to treat them.

The extent to which older people are dependent upon private sector provision relies on a handful of local area studies from which the cost of treatment of chronic conditions for older people has to be derived. This is likely to underestimate the real/actual cost to individual families. Estimating costs and patterns of utilization is further exacerbated by the lack of data on morbidity and disability at older ages.

A number of studies have shown that poor people have a much greater need for access to public health services owing to higher levels of poverty and sickness throughout the world related to greater exposure to environmental and social hazards. However, studies in places such as India, Vietnam and parts of Africa, show that utilization is much higher among those better off and able to pay for costed services, despite the fact that levels of morbidity are lower.[14] The growing cost of health care, in parallel with the demise in public sector provision, places enormous burdens upon households (especially those caring for elderly relatives) for the treatment of chronic and non chronic ailments. This is a serious issue faced by many elderly people and their families and is largely neglected by policy makers world-wide.

The current increase in the privatization of health care in parallel with the process of demographic and health transition in a country such as India, does not augur well for the future of older people. The social consequences of ageing with inadequate infrastructural support are serious. Family based care is under threat, with insufficient consideration from policy makers at the national as well as international levels. This would be especially ironic at a time when the issue of family support is critical to debates on ageing and social policy.

International policy responses on healthy ageing

The practical implications of the demographic and epidemiological transition for many developing countries are far reaching: the numbers are increasing, the resources are limited and the perceived social priorities lie elsewhere. Yet the reality is that as more people reach old age, they will make increasing demands on the communities in which they live. The response to such demands has to be well-orchestrated, multisectoral and based on systematic planning.

The first step is advocacy. It is increasingly important to raise the awareness of policy makers to the multiple issues related to population ageing. This is particularly urgent in countries that are already experiencing a rapid change in their age structure. As well as the relevant professionals, politicians, leaders of old people's organizations and officials from pertinent international agencies should be targeted. Failing to gain their understanding and positive support will only result in perpetuation of piecemeal approaches which are invariably ineffective and potentially disastrous.

The second step is proper training. Care of older people is a complex process. Local values, cultural patterns, prevailing attitudes and expectations all have to be considered. Models of care unquestioningly transplanted from elsewhere will no doubt fail. They may serve as useful examples of how particular problems were tackled in other countries but local circumstances should ultimately dictate the most appropriate way forward.

Good training goes hand in hand with an adequate basis for knowledge. This can only be achieved through research; otherwise myths and fallacies are perpetuated indefinitely. Good research pays off even in the short term and should serve as the basis for meaningful longer-term policies. Inevitably neither training nor research of the necessary high standard required is possible if funds do not become available. A systematic and scientific approach to research and training is essential. A suitable body of methods and instruments has now been developed by what may be termed the epidemiology of ageing. Epidemiology in its broadest sense offers the perspective of defining and examining concepts and practical policies for promoting the well-being of the population under study. For older persons, the multidisciplinary nature of epidemiology ensures that it is particularly relevant.

A database of good examples of research and training in age-associated problems is urgently required. A process of cross-fertilization between local, regional and national groups greatly helps the development of practical and successful models of care. NGOs can also play an active role, and the example of HelpAge International deserves particular mention. Within only a few years the work of this organization has permeated across all continents. Its non-patronizing approach, respect for the realities of the local situation and its effective use of limited resources should act as a model for anyone interested in the well-being of elderly people in developing countries.

Of particular importance is the catalytic contribution that international agencies are making to the process of calling attention to the importance of ageing for global development. In this context the WHO restructured its previous programme on Health of the Elderly, now called Ageing and Health. It is driven by perspectives which emphasize the importance of the life course, health promotion, cultural settings, gender, inter-generational and ethical issues such as undue hastening or delaying of death, human rights, long-term care, abuse. The purpose of the programme is to promote health and well-being through the lifespan, but ensuring the attainment of the highest possible level of quality of life for as long as possible for the largest possible number of older people.

One of the programme's main activity components is information base strengthening – ensuring that quality information is disseminated to older people themselves, to NGOs, health and social care workers, policy makers, informal caregivers and all who can contribute to maintaining optimal quality of life as individuals age.

The programme pays particular attention to policies aimed at generating community based programmes – support and health care of informal carers is an example. Such priority activity areas require in the background a well-organized programme integrated with advocacy and involving NGOs, to raise awareness of ageing as a major but neglected public health issue. Training is essential and involves defining the gerontological component in the curricula of health and social care professionals and developing training material for primary health care workers. Research is needed to define priorities and establish a worldwide healthy ageing research programme.

Health and social planners will be increasingly asked to conceive, develop and implement imaginative and innovative strategies of care for the elderly in developing countries. It is imperative to assist them in the task of initiating practical policies for the promotion of well-being of older persons within the considerable constraints dictated by the realities of local situations. It is time that health professionals were

NGO *perspectives on health provision for poorer older people in rural Ghana*

The meaning of good health

Common elements in older people's perception of good health relate to the absence of disease, physical strength, mental soundness and social responsibility. While recognizing that there are certain ailments that are associated with ageing, older people are of the opinion that physical well-being is the ability to work and to fulfil one's role in society.

An older person is in good health when she or he is mentally sound, that is, has no worries. More than this, people should have the ability or support necessary to access health services. An interesting distinction arises between older men and older women in defining good health. While men emphasize the ability to work, women seem to be more concerned with the mental well-being of the person.

Common ailments

Through focus group discussions with older men, older women and medical staff the common ailments of older people were identified. They included immobility, instability, incontinence and 'unusual' behaviour. Older people also mentioned specific diseases such fever, asthma, colds, piles and hernia while medical personnel added kidney and liver problems, adult malnutrition and urinary retention.

Health status, livelihood and seasonality

The health status of older people changes with the seasons. Better health usually coincides with periods of food availability, good income and good weather. In the rainy season and dry 'harmattan' season disease prevalence increases. The harmattan season is characterized by cold and older people usually complain of colds, bodily pains and hernias. For farmers, the rainy season is the period of increased labour demand, increased farm expenses and food insecurity. Older people have to work to survive and this exacerbates health problems. However, the ill health caused by seasonal work demands is not always visible in medical records. Older people have no choice but to put up with ill health while they get farm work done.

For both farmers and fisherpeople, harvest periods mark the beginning of good nutrition, better income and good health. At these times more people can afford to make reasonable payments for health care for themselves and dependants and hospital attendance may increase.

Older people as health care providers

Older people are acknowledged health care providers. Older people usually administer home remedies and since skill with herbal treatment usually comes with experience, most herbalists tend to be older people. Older women have an important role as traditional birth attendants. Bonesetting is a task usually performed by older men. Older people are responsible for the health care needs of dependants: older men are expected to provide money while older women take physical care, such as accompanying patients to the clinic.

Access to healthcare and sequencing of treatment

There are common trends in health care strategies of resource-poor older people that suggest that choice of health care provider follows a rational pattern. Some older men pointed out that:

'when somebody is sick you start with home medication, if you are not successful you go to the herbalist, then the pedlar, clinic and finally to the hospital – a last resort.'

Where clinics are available most people will use them before going to the hospital. The nearness of health care provider to the community is very important for two reasons: it reduces transportation costs and time spent. The clinics usually make referrals to the district or regional hospitals. While acknowledging the usefulness of orthodox medicine, especially the quality of care it offers, older people identified the hospital as the most expensive place, followed by the clinic. Older people associated the quality of health care with the general attention that they were given and the depth of inquiry during diagnosis. This contrasts with their perception of the quality of care they receive from the herbalist where, apart from the initial diagnosis, the medicine is given with very little or no subsequent attention from the herbalist. In almost every hospital, older people are very sensitive about the way they are treated and this shapes their perception of service delivery. The time consuming procedures at the hospital are known to have in-built systems for illicit payments at every stage of the process.

Some reflections on cost exemption

Very poor and aged people in Ghana are exempt from payment of user fees for health services. User fees are part of Ghana's cost recovery programme and have the stated aims of: raising revenue, improving the supply of drugs, and improving services, specifically primary health care. In most communities, user fees are complemented by sharing the cost of health financing through in-kind contributions for the construction and maintenance of health facilities.

Exemption from fees offers great relief to older people. If exemption is to be applied more widely then progress needs to be made to improve information delivery, the sustainable supply of drugs and the integrity of staff.

Exemption guidelines appeal to medical staff to use their discretion to identify the very poor and the old. While the use of discretion may work in very small communities, it presents problems for larger ones. Medical staff do not find it easy to implement, given the large number of people who use the health facilities. That few older people seemed to be meaningfully aware of the existence of the fee exemptions implies that health management teams need to improve the coverage in their information, education and communication campaigns. It appears that urban dwellers were better informed than rural dwellers.

Medical personnel stress that free treatment for older people is contingent upon the availability of drugs. Where prescribed drugs are not available older people have to purchase them and no reimbursement is available. This confuses people who are aware of the fee-free provision. Those best placed to administer cost exemption are in hospitals which have a regular supply of drugs. A typical example is the Tumu district hospital, where Danish health care assistance includes the provision of drugs. Some hospitals have flexible payment regimes but these are reported to be fraught with problems as people abuse the offer and do not settle their debts.

While older people are supposed to get waivers on the formal fees, illicit fees paid along the consultation chain add to the cost and in addition most older people incur transport costs. Where information is kept from older people, and where discretion is a basic administrative principle, the system may be abused, especially in the absence of proper supervision. Drugs are prescribed for patients after consultation, but there is no guarantee that the patient will receive them or that explanations will be offered to clarify the situation. This partially explains why older people complain about staff attitudes towards them. The need to stand in queues for long hours is also a problem for them. It should also be noted that some hospital staff complain of the attitude of some older people.

To promote participation in financing health care delivery, especially to sustain the provision of drugs, several suggestions were made including involving communities in managing and financing health care since everybody pays something towards it. Where wealth is held in the form of animals these can be sold in times of crisis. Some of these animals, it was argued, could be sold and the money kept in the bank or used to purchase government treasury bills. Older people also talked about schemes where those in the informal sector such as farmers make their contributions immediately after the harvest. Some workers also mentioned the need to hasten the establishment of the health insurance scheme.

Source: The Ghana Study, HelpAge International/HelpAge Ghana, 1999

prepared for this new and stimulating challenge which is now well established as part of the already long list of priorities for the developing world. A healthy older person is more likely to be an active contributor to society – an asset for the process of socio-economic development.

Notes

1   Dr Kasturi Sen is Senior Research Associate at the Department of Community Medicine, University of Cambridge. She works on comparative perspectives of public health and policy in the era of reforms with an emphasis on vulnerable groups in Europe, the Middle East and countries of south Asia. Dr Alex Kalache is Chief, Ageing and Health Programme of the World Health Organization.

2   Chawla, S, *Generations* 17:4, 1993, pp20–23.

3   Kumar, V, 'Disability, morbidity and mortality in old age: an epidemiological transition' and Shah, B, 'Ageing in India', both in C Ramachandran and B Shah (eds) *Public Health Implications of Ageing in India*, ICMR New Delhi, India, 1994.

4   Rao-Venkoba, A, *Health Care of the Rural Aged*, Indian Council of Medical Research, New Delhi, India, 1996.

5   Prince, M, 'The need for research on dementia in developing countries', *Tropical Medicine and International Health* 2:10, October 1997, pp993–1000.

6   Kinsella, K, 'Demographic Aspects' in Ebrahim, S, and A Kalache (eds) *Epidemiology in Old Age*, BMJ Publishing Group, London, 1996.

7   Sen, K, 'Health sector reforms and the implications for later life from a comparative perspective', in *Health Care in Later Life*, 1:2, Edward Arnold, UK 1996, pp73–83.

8   Ministerio da Saude, DNDCG. Coencas Cronico-degenerativas: Evolucao e Tendecias Atuasis – 1, 1988, p56; Centro de Comunicacoes, Brasilia.

9   World Health Organization, *World Health Report 1997*, WHO, Geneva, 1997.

10 World Health Organization, WHO Brasilia *Declaration on Ageing*, Who Brasilia, 1996.

11 Ramos, LR, Veras, RP and Kalache, A, 'Envelhecimeto populacional: uma Realidade Brasileira', *Rev Saude Publ* 21, São Paulo, 1987, pp211–24.

12 Tulsidhar, VP, 'Expenditure Compression and Health Sector Outlays', *Economic and Political Weekly* XX V111:16&17 and nos 45–6.

13 Ibid.

14 Sen, K and Koivusalo, M, 'Health sector reforms and developing countries: a critical overview', *International Journal of Health Planning and Management*, John Wiley and Sons, Chichester, 1998, pp199–215; Duggal, R, *The Cost of Health Care*, Foundation for Research into Community Health, Bombay India, 1989; Sauerborn R, Notara A, Latimer E, 'The elasticity of demand for health care in Burkina Faso: differences across age and income groups', *Health Policy and Planning* 9 (2), 1994, pp185–192.

6 Older People's Strategies in Times of Social and Economic Transformation

Peter Lloyd-Sherlock

To date, most research about the welfare of older people has focused on issues such as the reform of formal social security programmes. These are important, but do not include a range of concerns which are much more relevant for the great majority of poor older people living in developing countries. This chapter shows that patterns of social and economic change in poorer countries are complex, and that we should not assume that they are simply repeating the experiences of the north. As yet, our understanding of these processes of change and their impact on older people is very patchy. Many generalizations are made, but these do not provide a secure foundation for appropriate policies. The sheer speed of change in many developing countries has created great challenges for all age groups, and it may be that older people are less well equipped to deal with some of these. However, the examples presented in this chapter show that older people are more than capable of meeting these challenges, if the correct policies are in place.

Retirement is not an option for most older people.
© Alison Tarrant/ HelpAge International

Don Maximo, aged 94, at his loom in Bolivia. This weaving project raises older people's standing in the community and enables them to remain financially independent.
© Nicky Packman/ HelpAge International

Migration and Older People

Over the past 20 or 30 years, the social and economic life of many developing countries has changed beyond all recognition. Rapid population growth and the emergence of new employment opportunities in cities have fuelled unprecedented levels of rural to urban migration and led to sudden changes in family structures. In most cases, migrants have mainly been young adults, and older people have remained in the villages. As such, an issue of pressing concern is how older people have responded to being left behind. Have they maintained contact and do they receive remittance payments from migrant children? Have they been able to take over the roles which younger groups once performed in the villages? What happens when older people are no longer able to work the land or support themselves? For example, in Thailand, where the proportion of total population living in urban areas rose from 13.3 to 22.6 per cent between 1970 and 1990, a recent government report observed that:

'With more job opportunities in the big city, many young people moved from rural areas to urban areas to take jobs as unskilled labourers. Many elderly are left behind to care for small children or live alone, especially in the rural areas. Many elderly do feel neglected, because of the out-migration of younger people.'[1]

When old people living in rural areas are no longer able to cope alone, they may have no option but to migrate to cities and live with relatives there. The process of migration is challenging for all age groups, but is particularly traumatic for older people who may be ill or very frail. The box opposite describes some of the problems faced by elderly Aymaras who migrate to La Paz, Bolivia.

Of course, even young rural–urban migrants will themselves reach old age one day. In some cities this process has already begun. While the lucky few may be able to retire from work and return to their regions of origin, most remain in the city, either to retain contact with their family or simply because they cannot afford to go home. The slums and shanty towns of poorer countries are still characterized as being over-run with children and adolescents. However, a combination of falling fertility

Poor, old, Aymara: *and living in the city*

In Aymara communities in Bolivia older people are held in respect for their wisdom. People ask them for advice and listen to their opinions. Traditionally the community accepts responsibility for the care of older people who are left alone for whatever reason.

Currently this traditional behaviour is being transformed as many Aymara people are migrating to the cities in search of work. Aymara migrants often end up living in marginalized areas of the city in conditions of extreme poverty. Many of them decide to move their older relatives to the city, in particular widowed mothers, because they don't want them to be left alone in the rural areas. For older Aymara people the cities are alien places. The cultural structure of their ancestors is practically non-existent there, and they feel unprotected.

There is much discrimination in Bolivia. Being Aymara is a disadvantage. Being Aymara and poor is worse, and being a poor Aymara living in the city is an even greater disadvantage. But the worst human condition is to be Aymara, poor, in the city and old.

A group and a home

About 11 years ago, in a part of La Paz called Pampajasi, four older Aymara women founded a group to help themselves and avoid being a burden to their children. The group – called 'Awicha', or 'grandmother' – enables them to meet and find solutions to their problems together. It has gained the respect of local people in the neighbourhood.

Originally, the main activity was spinning alpaca wool. Contacts were made with a group of older people in Linköping in Sweden, who helped sell the wool there. With this income and other fundraising efforts the older women began to construct a home for themselves, room by room. Now they have a small house which gives a home to nine older women who don't have anywhere to live or who don't want to be a burden to their children. Three years ago a dining room was added and some 20 local older people come there for lunch every weekday.

Other 'Awichas' meet there once a week. They have a spinning and weaving workshop and a loom. There is a small pharmacy of traditional medicines and a *yatiri*, or traditional healer, comes to the house once a week. There are also recreational activities like music and theatre and each year they prepare a dance for their local fiesta.

The most notable aspect of this group is their sense of self-management. They decide what they are going to do, how they will do it, establishing their own rules and evaluating how well their projects work. All this in spite of being old, illiterate and unable to speak Spanish. One of the women, Doña Francisca, says:

> 'We have to know how to manage our dining room. I was responsible for the money and as I don't know how to write, I invented my own way of working out the money and the accounts with twigs.'

Another 'Awicha' explains that their method of working for themselves is:

> 'much more cost effective than an organization coming in from outside. We can do things at half the price ourselves, because we know where to buy'.

The group is strengthening the self esteem of the people in it simply by the fact that they are their own bosses and are not just receiving a service. Although they need support from the group in Sweden and from younger members of their community, they have been able to create a thriving organization from their needs, and their initiative has enabled them to survive in a difficult environment in a dignified way.

Source: From an article by M Mercedes Zerda, a psychologist who works with the group, which was originally published in the HelpAge international bulletin, AGEWAYS

Few older people are eligible for pensions – most continue to work in old age, often despite chronic and disabling illness.
© Jan Hammond

and localized ageing will soon lead to a significant change in their age structures. Developing countries need to make preparations for the emergence of a substantial poor, urban elderly population. The box opposite focuses on the problems of older people living in *favelas* in São Paulo, Brazil.

Older people living in slums frequently suffer from extreme social isolation, are only able to obtain down-graded forms of employment, and their needs are often ignored by urban planners, NGOs and government welfare agencies. Many had not expected to grow old: they did not see their own parents reach old age and so it comes as a surprise for which they and their families were often unprepared.[2]

> '*Older people living in slums frequently suffer from extreme social isolation, are only able to obtain down-graded forms of employment, and their needs are often ignored by urban planners, NGOs and government welfare agencies. Many had not expected to grow old: they did not see their own parents reach old age and so it comes as a surprise for which they and their families were often unprepared.*'

Coping with rapid social and economic change

Historical research has largely scotched the myth of a 'golden age', when older people were the objects of veneration and enjoyed considerable power and prestige, both within the household and in society at large.[3] Even so, there is general agreement that the rapid changes of recent decades have had an unfavourable effect on the social relations of the aged. Studies from developed countries conclude that increased access to education for younger age groups, and the growing technological sophistication of labour processes have rendered many of the more traditional skills of older people obsolete. The social isolation of older people has also been worsened by the increased separation of workplaces from the home. Some studies from developed countries argue that the growing size of elderly populations has intensified competition for resources between them and other age groups.[4] For developed countries, these negative social effects have partly been compensated for by a general improvement in the economic welfare of the majority of elderly people, thanks to the up-grading of social security programmes.

To date, most research into these issues has been carried out in the developed world. It is generally assumed that the

Old age, migration and poverty in the slums of São Paulo

All older people living in Brazilian *favelas* suffer from serious social and economic difficulties. A study of two *favelas* in São Paulo found that the timing of migration to the city had a very large effect on the welfare of older people. People who moved when they were already old ('late comers') were relatively disadvantaged *vis-à-vis* those older people who had originally migrated at an earlier stage in their lifecycle ('early arrivers'). Early arrivers had mainly come to obtain employment in the city. Late comers usually migrated because they were unable to cope with living alone or because of poor rural health facilities.

Early arrivers were much more likely to be home owners. Although they did not usually obtain any direct income from this, home ownership increased their social standing within the household and led to better levels of overall care. Access to affordable drugs and medical facilities was a major problem, and older people had to develop complex procurement strategies. According to one early arriver:

'I use medicine when they have it in the chemists in Vila Prudente, I get it there...But it's more often the case that they don't have any. So then I go to the catholic mutual association, to see if they have it or maybe they don't. I try to sort it out there, because for me going to Glicerío [the main hospital] is too difficult, as I have to take a bus there, but I'm too ill and 'nervous', now that I just get 100 cruzieros [basic pension]...and sometimes I have to go without medicine, so I just drink some herb tea and have a rest.'

For late comers, who had few social networks, and who were unfamiliar with and afraid of their surroundings, these barriers to access were usually insurmountable. Late comers were much more likely to remain hidden inside the São Paulo welfare programmes.

Source: Peter Lloyd-Sherlock, 'Old age, migration and poverty in the slums of São Paulo, Brazil' *Journal of Developing Areas*, 1999 (in press)

experiences of developing countries are fairly similar. For example, as long ago as the early 1960s one anthropological study in rural Mexico observed:

'It appears to be the consensus that less and less respect for old people is being shown...there are more sources of conflict between the older and younger generations because of recent social and economic changes'.[5]

Social and economic change has been particularly abrupt in many developing countries, and so it is only to be expected that the position of older people will have been adversely affected. At the same time, the lack of formal social security in many such countries will have meant that these social trends have been paralleled by (and may also have contributed towards) growing economic hardship for the aged. This means that, while the social problems of older people in developed countries have in some ways been compensated for by economic factors, both effects are much more likely to be negative in the developing world.

Even so, the social and economic impacts of modernization should not be considered a foregone conclusion. Very little substantial research has been undertaken into these issues, the notable exceptions being Nana Araba Apt's study of ageing in Ghana and Peter Lloyd-Sherlock's work in shanty towns in Brazil and Argentina. These largely support the view that modernization is detrimental to the social and economic status of the aged.[6] Araba Apt observes that rapid change had, among other things, reduced the central role of elderly Ghanaians in cultural and religious rituals and their influence over property inheritance.[7] The box on page 77 summarizes some ways in which older women in Ghana have attempted to deal with these challenges.

Three generations of
wood cutters, Kabul,
Afghanistan.
© Jenny Mathews

Social isolation and mutual support

The dangers of generalizing about social change in developing countries are made apparent by a recent survey of living arrangements of older people in Mexico.[8] This found that older people in urban areas were less likely to be living alone and more likely to be in extended families than were their rural counterparts. It suggested that higher housing costs in cities obliged people to live in larger household units. The study also found that there had been no important variations in the living arrangements of older people between 1976 and 1994. It may be, then, that some developing countries are not emulating the patterns of social change found in the developed world, and that extended families will remain the dominant social form.

Another widespread assumption is that older people living with other relatives, particularly children, are more likely to receive social and economic support from them. Consequently, when household size falls, the welfare of older people is adversely affected. However, several

> 'How then can policy help to support intergenerational links so that older people are not marginalized and their economic and social welfare put at risk by urbanization and other processes of change?'

studies have questioned this belief.[9] Older people in Buenos Aires for instance were found to have received more financial support from children who moved away than from those who remained with them.[10] This was because the decision of children to set up their own households reflected a degree of economic success, whereas those who remained were more likely to be unemployed or incapacitated in some way.

It has been argued that societies in poorer and less 'modern' countries place more emphasis on mutual support and family responsibilities than in richer countries. An extension of this argument is that most responsibility for caring for older people can be left to the family, so excusing governments from taking any action at all. The World Bank takes this argument a step further, claiming that the extension of formal pension programmes in regions such as sub-Saharan Africa runs the risk of undermining these informal sources of support.[11] However, the real threat to effective family support of elders (if it ever existed in the first place) comes from the speed and extent of

The value of intergenerational support

A well-balanced exchange of services among the generations has been a feature of traditional Ghanaian life. However urban living means that old and young are less frequently found inhabiting the same household. Older people thus live apart from the most economically active generations.

Traditional domestic arrangements had intergenerational support built into them but such arrangements are increasingly difficult to sustain. A case in point is doorstep trading.

Women predominate in the trading sector in much of West Africa. Sophisticated practices exist for transferring businesses as going concerns from mother to daughter or other female relatives in exchange for subsequent support to the mother. The customary arrangement has been that when a mother transferred her market trading business to her daughter, she would then take up a minor trading role on the doorstep of the common home.

In the past, as mothers and daughters exercised their rights to residence in the family house, the transfer of business took place within the same household unit. Now, as mothers and daughters tend to live in separate households, this practice has become less efficient as an insurance mechanism for older women traders. Similarly, the provision of child care services by older female relatives is more complicated and support of her mother becomes less advantageous to a daughter.

Widowed women face a particularly difficult set of circumstances. The funeral expenses of burying a husband can result in prudent businesswomen losing their life earnings and with reduced capital for trading. The ability of widows to re-accumulate sufficient capital is weak, as older women have very poor access to credit.

Access to credit could enable daughters both to assist older relatives in prolonging economic activity and older women would be less likely to suffer from social exclusion.

How then can policy help to support intergenerational links so that older people are not marginalized and their economic and social welfare put at risk by urbanization and other processes of change?

Many social policy efforts are founded on the identification of particular target groups such as children, people with disabilities or women. Little attention is given to how a change in the fortune of one target group will affect those with whom the target group interacts. For instance, provision of institutional care for young children may result in the removal of an important social and economic role for older people. The loss of this role may damage self-esteem and result in new social welfare problems of how to integrate older people back into the social and economic activities of the community.

Policies designed to assist and maintain the incorporation of older women in commercial, domestic and educational structures need to be accompanied by policies that ensure their financial incorporation. In much of Africa women have poor access to formal financial services and informal savings and credit groups have been established. A current policy issue is how best to link the very substantial level of African women's informal economic activity into the formal sector. This discussion needs to be harnessed to understanding and meeting the needs of Africa's older women.

Source: Adapted from Grieco, M and Araba Apt, N, 'Interdependence and Independence: Averting the Poverty of Older Persons in an Ageing World', *The Bulletin on Ageing* 2 & 3, 1996, pp10–18, United Nations, New York

social and economic changes. Yet, the governments of many developing countries continue to view the family as a panacea for ensuring the quality of life of older people. This complacency must be replaced with policies which enable the aged to take an active role in the promotion of their own welfare.

Not all the effects of social and economic change on older people are negative. With economic development

come new drugs and technologies, some of which may be affordable and have a significant impact on their quality of life. The box on page 78 gives details about advances made in the field of cataract surgery. Increased female labour force participation may conflict with women's traditional role as carers for older people, but this may offer elders a more central position in the household as carers for grandchildren and providing general domestic support. Also in

Access to cataract surgery for older people

During the past 20 years, there have been tremendous developments in the field of eye surgery. This has resulted in improved quality of vision following cataract surgery, due to new technologies such as microsurgery and intra-ocular lenses (IOLs). IOLs were initially expensive, costing several hundred pounds each – well beyond the means of most older people living in developing countries. However, today good quality IOLs are available for around five pounds each, and a cataract operation can be performed very successfully at a low cost, with the patient returning home the same day.

Even so, there are still serious problems of access to cataract surgery for many older people. A study from Tamil Nadu in India found that fear of surgery and financial worries (both the cost of the operation and the loss of working time) were important barriers for many cataract sufferers. Often the decision whether or not to use the service is taken by other household members who may not prioritize the needs of older relatives. Many of those in greatest need are elderly widows –a group often overlooked by communities.

Source: Interviews with Allen Foster of Sightsavers International and Martine Donoghue of the London School of Hygiene and Tropical Medicine

rural areas, remittance payments sent by migrant children may mean that older people have a higher standard of material wealth than ever before.[12] However, over-dependence on remittances may become a problem when it encourages older people to sell land, which would have provided economic security at times of crisis.

Coping strategies

Older people can respond to the challenges and problems resulting from rapid change in a variety of ways. One possibility is to form local-level associations. These can perform a range of functions including leisure activities, income generation (providing informal credit, establishing workshops etc), the provision of basic health care and education, and, in countries where social welfare programmes for older people exist, providing advice and support for obtaining benefits and assistance. Perhaps more importantly, they can reduce the sense of isolation experienced by many of the aged and enable them to exchange experiences, articulate concerns and develop confidence, whilst raising the profile of older people in the community at large.

Experience has shown that effective associations for more vulnerable social groups do not develop spontaneously and often need support from outside agencies, particularly in the early stages of development. To date, most developing country governments have not taken a large interest in supporting such initiatives. This is surprising, given the huge sums spent on old age pensions in some countries, particularly in Latin America. At little extra cost, a more holistic approach to social welfare could be taken, complementing high-cost pension programmes with a range of wider measures designed to help older people to help themselves. One clear exception to this trend is Argentina, where a para-statal agency had established a network of over a thousand day centres for older people by the early 1990s.[13] These provided a wide range of services and proved to be highly popular. Unfortunately, these day centres did not target the poorest and most vulnerable aged, and the responsible agency has accumulated enormous debts due to a combination of maladministration and corruption.

Older people can gain greater control over their own lives if policies and development programmes support their own strategies for coping. Income security in old age could be greatly enhanced by improved access to credit and by the ability of older people to exercise their rights to the

Including older people in credit programmes

Support structures that existed in the past are no longer there according to older Cambodians. Families have suffered great losses, many older people have no children of their own and their lives have been profoundly disrupted by war.

HelpAge International reviewed the cases of 783 poor and vulnerable older people – about half of whom had taken part in a loan scheme. One hundred and fifty-five borrowers were interviewed to improve understanding of the ways in which older people have used loans and the conditions for success.

The target group for these loans was very poor and vulnerable people over 55 and widows over 45 with children without any form of support. Loans of between US$20 and US$50 could be taken out for six months, repaid monthly and each person was able to borrow up to three times.

The majority of money loans were taken out by women (72 per cent) with an average age of 62. Half the borrowers only had land for a house, a quarter had a garden and a quarter had rice land. People who took loans of fertilizer, pigs or cows had a similar profile, except that fewer were women (55 per cent).

Borrowers were asked to assess their situation. Had it improved, remained the same or deteriorated over the period?

Perceptions of interviewees on changes since access to credit as percentages of total number interviewed

Factor	Improved (%)	Same (%)	Deteriorated (%)
Food	46	30	24
Clothing	30	46	24
Household goods	37	43	20
Health	46	43	11
Making merit (Wat)	48	39	13
Debt	17	67	15
Confidence	17	83	0

The loan provided the opportunity for many older people to engage in business for the first time and helped to make the transition from a situation of 'no occupation' with no reliable income to one where they can generate additional income.

For many clients taking a loan is learning process. The first loan provides the opportunity for a person to try out a business. The second gives them the chance to try a different business or the confidence to continue in the same activities. The third loan enables people to start to earn sufficient income.

Those who chose not to take a loan gave reasons of frailty, illness, lack of ideas and fear of debt.

Those for whom circumstances have improved reported that they had been able to buy mats, dishes, pots, and watering cans or to pay schools fees for their children. A third had been able to buy clothes and nearly a half said that their health was better. Forty-eight per cent said that the loan enabled them to participate in funeral ceremonies and give rice to monks on their daily alms round. The reasons older people gave for these improvements were:

- Reduced worry
- Increased ability to buy medicine
- Increased food security resulting in better diet and increased strength

Those whose circumstances remained the same or had deteriorated, were most often in a situation where there were many dependants, family problems or illness. It was found overwhelmingly to be the circumstances of the borrower, rather than the activity or business, which affected the success of the loan. A quarter of borrowers said that their food situation was worse than before because livestock had died, crops had failed or the older person simply did not have the strength to do the work involved in improving their circumstances.

Older people engage in a large number of different small-scale activities. A person might labour to carry water or clear a field or cut grass; they might scavenge in the fields or cut wood or bamboo in the forest, they might sell cakes or buy and sell fruit and vegetables. As they do not have the skills to earn more than what they need from day to day, they have no reserves and are vulnerable to any change or emergency. They rely on their strength to survive and if they fall ill their situation is likely to become desperate. In these circumstances older people can easily become caught in a spiral of debt, paying exorbitant interest rates – usually 20–30 per cent a month. This in turn leads to increased vulnerability. If rice is borrowed the interest rate is usually 100–200 per cent a season.

Loan schemes need to recognize these diverse sources of income and the vulnerable situation of many older people. Loans help with immediate needs – obtaining food from day to day. But on their own, loans are unlikely to impact on the multiple and interrelated problems experienced by poor, older people. Alongside other forms or assistance, access to credit can make a significant impact both long and short term.

Source: HelpAge International Cambodia, 'Evaluation of Loan Scheme Component of the Relief and Rehabilitation Program', September 1995

---

benefits to which they are entitled. The boxes on pages 79 and 80 illustrate the ways in which access to loans and the provision of legal advice and social support can enable older people to improve the quality of their lives and their ability to support themselves.

The task of supporting local-level associations for older people has been left largely to NGOs and voluntary organizations. Ideally, the role of the outside actors is reduced over time, so that older people themselves become responsible for the entire administration of their activities.

Improving access and entitlement to pensions

The 'Youngsters of 1990' Centre in Villa Jardín, Buenos Aires was set up in 1990 to provide legal advice and a social forum for local elderly people in this shanty town, as well as serving as a pressure group. The original initiative was taken by a locally based NGO, which had already developed successful centres in other poor parts of the city. The NGO began by arranging a series of social events and discussion groups for the aged, out of which arose the idea of setting up a permanent centre. By late 1992 the 'Youngsters' had 265 members, including 187 women.

The main aim of the Centre was to help members obtain means-tested pensions. The majority of older people living in the area were eligible for these, but many had difficult in handling the paperwork and general bureaucracy of making applications. Many were illiterate, had lost their papers or were physically unable to do the rounds of the various state welfare offices. By the end of 1992, the Centre had helped 81 members to obtain some kind of pension.

Members were requested to pay a small monthly contribution, although this was waived for the very poor. This money, along with the proceeds of a range of fundraising events, went towards social activities, including barbecues, monthly dances and theatre productions staged at local schools. The Centre ran daily classes, which helped several members develop basic literacy skills, and organized day trips, which were offered at reduced prices thanks to support from local government agencies.

During the first three years of operation the Centre had succeeded in improving the economic position of many members, had raised the profile of elderly people in the community and had done much to break down the social isolation associated with later life. It also increased the organization skills of local older people, so that the local NGO had been able to gradually reduce its direct involvement. Sadly, no efforts have been made to repeat this experience in other poor parts of the city.

Source: Lloyd-Sherlock, P, *Old age and urban poverty in the developing world: the shanty towns of Buenos Aires*, Macmillan, London, 1997

Notes

1   Government of Thailand, National Statistics Office, *Population ageing in Thailand. 1990 Population and Housing Census*, Bangkok, 1992, p47.

2   Lloyd-Sherlock, P, *Old Age and Urban Poverty in the Developing World: the Shanty Towns of Buenos Aires*, Macmillan, London, 1997; Lloyd-Sherlock, P 'Old age, migration and poverty in the slums of São Paulo, Brazil' *Journal of Developing Areas*, 1999 (in press).

3   Kertzer, D and Laslett, P (eds), *Aging in the Past. Demography, Society and Old Age*, University of California Press, Berkeley, 1995.

4   Cowgill, D, 'Aging and modernization: a revision of the theory', in J Gubrium (ed), *Late Life: Communities and Environmental Policy*, Thomas, Springfield, 1974.

5   Lewis, O, 'Life in a Mexican village: Tepoztlan revisited', *Urbana*, 1963, pp411–12.

6   Araba Apt, N, *Coping with Old Age in a Changing Africa. Social Change and the Elderly Ghanaian*, Aldershot, 1996, pp 34–46. Similar concerns are expressed in studies of other developing countries.

For example, Vatuk, S *Old age in India*, in P Stearns (ed), *Old Age in Preindustrial Society*, Avebury, London, 1982, pp70–103.

7   Araba Apt, 1996, op cit.

8   Solís, P, 'Living arrangements of the elderly in Mexico', paper presented at the 1999 annual meeting of the Population Association of America, 1999.

9   Ramos, L, 'Family support for the elderly in São Paulo, Brazil', in H Kendig, H Hashimoto and L Coppard (eds), *Family Support for the Elderly*, Oxford University Press, Oxford, 1992.

10   Lloyd-Sherlock, P, 1997, op cit.

11   World Bank, *Averting the Old Age Crisis. Strategies to Protect the Old and Promote Growth*, Oxford University Press, New York, 1994.

12   Very little research has been carried out into this issue. Tout, K, *Ageing in developing countries*, Oxford, 1989, pp88–90, found that remittances in India most frequently occurred between parents and their children, rather than directly to the elderly.

13   Lloyd-Sherlock, P, 'Healthcare provision for elderly people in Argentina. The crisis of PAMI', *Social Policy and Administration* 31:4, 1997.

7 Economic Security in Old Age: A Family–Government Partnership

The key to the income security of older people is, first and foremost, dependent on what individuals and families do. That is true for people in all nations – developed and developing. Governments can and should assist but the economics of old age should always be viewed as a joint process, involving individuals, the family, employers and government.

In this chapter we review approaches to maintaining income in older age in developing countries and explore the potential for feasible, sustainable and effective policies. Too often discussion of pensions is informed by misconceptions about the economics of old age: a failure to recognize that most older people work and are part of family and community economies. Older people's livelihoods, family lives and rural/urban issues are explored before an examination of social protection policies in developing countries. The challenges for reforming provision for old age in developing countries are set out along with the case for a partnerships based approach.

Paradoxically, while there has been little interest in 'the aged', there has been a great deal of interest in pensions in the developing countries.
© Alain Le Garomeur
Panos Pictures

For most of their adult life, people assume responsibility for their own economic welfare (many until they die); but some cannot. The problem of providing for elderly individuals unable to provide for themselves has faced all societies throughout history. In the absence of special provisions for distributing income and wealth, people everywhere in the world are threatened when they are unable to work and earn – either temporarily or permanently because of sickness, disability, or age.

As the World Bank observes, 'More than half the world's old people are estimated to rely exclusively on informal and traditional arrangements for income security.'[2] Children and grandchildren are often the main sources of support for people when they are no longer able to work.[3] The economic situation of older people in the world is intimately tied to the more general situation of the extended family as a whole.

Worldwide poverty and older people

Nearly a quarter of the world's population lives in 'absolute poverty'.[4] Aged poverty mirrors the general poverty of nations as a whole, with its rural character and its feminine preponderance. In many parts of the world, *poverty in old age is the last phase in a lifetime of deprivation.*

Clearly, one of the best ways to combat poverty in old age is to pursue a successful development programme of pro-poor, equitable growth with explicit gender policies that expand women's opportunities. But causes of poverty which need to be taken into account for older people are their declining ability to work, the death of family members, or geographic separation from relatives.

Poverty and declining work opportunities

When people grow older access to work, and hence remuneration, becomes less secure and societal expectations regarding work decrease. Today, more than ever, countries are embracing the incentive-control mechanisms of markets. But the market incentives that promote efficiency, innovation, and growth also cause labour dislocation, unemployment, social disruption, and inequality.

In China, for example, a dramatic shift is occurring, away from a system where almost all non-agricultural workers were assigned jobs by an administrative allocation process and protected by the 'iron rice bowl', to a more open system of labour market mobility and job choice. Guaranteed lifetime employment has declined dramatically.

Rural areas experience drastic changes as product markets shift, as new agricultural practices compete against the old ways, and as the fertility and ownership of land changes. Increased migration, growing dependence on wage income, and fluctuating crop prices affect the welfare of many families and especially impact older people:

> *'Village life has changed drastically over the past few decades, sweeping away many conditions that gave security and stability to the lives of older people. Many villagers today no longer have free use of a plot of land, or their plot is too small or arid to support them.'[5]*

Older people's work roles: urban/rural differences

Many people think that older people do not work. They are stereotyped as frail, inactive, and retired. In developing countries this is certainly not the case. Labour force participation rates for older workers are relatively high.

Moreover, unless we expand the scope of analysis to include the informal sector, many of the important economic activities carried out by older people (especially women) are overlooked. Work associated with the home (cooking, water collection, cleaning, childcare, and repairs) is a major responsibility that does not stop when

Labour force participation rates for men and women over 65, selected countries

Country (year)	Male Participation (%)	Female Participation (%)
Malawi (1987)	85	72
Indonesia (1988)	56	25
Pakistan (1989)	56	2
Philippines (1989)	59	29
Guatemala (1987)	63	14

Source: Kinsella, K and Taeuber, CM, 1993, 'An Aging World', International Population Reports P95/92–3, US Bureau of the Census

people get old. Also, since shared living arrangements still predominate in developing countries, the older members of the family often take major or primary responsibility for the home while the younger adults of the family work outside the home.

National labour statistics hide important differences among various sectors of the population. Agriculture remains an important part of the economy in most countries, and formal economic support systems in these rural areas are relatively undeveloped. The result is much higher labour force participation. In China, for example, about a quarter of men (60 and over) and women (55 and over) were in the labour force in 1982. Of these, 86 per cent worked in agriculture, forestry, animal husbandry, or fishery jobs.[6] In the Republic of Korea, about 40 per cent of men (age 60 and over) living in cities were in the labour force. In contrast, the rate for men in rural areas was 63 per cent.

Family composition

Almost all individuals throughout their lives are integrated into households, families, clans, tribes, and communities. This 'family solidarity' promotes the security and social viability of both individuals and the larger society.[7] When people reach old age, they are likely to have spouses and children who are able to assist them in times of need.[8]

But the extent of potential support for some may be meagre or even non-existent because of the death of a spouse, divorce or separation, childlessness or migration of family members.

Aged without spouses

A large proportion of older people are 'not married' – that is, single, widowed, separated, or divorced. Data for six Asian countries in the early 1980s shows that the proportion ranges from 37 per cent in Bangladesh to 50 per cent in Singapore.[9] On average, nearly half of the aged in both industrialized and developing countries do not currently live with a spouse.

A very high proportion of older women are widowed. Typically in Asia around two thirds of older women are widows.[10] Loss of a spouse weakens the support network that operates in time of need, and is often a direct cause of immediate problems for the surviving marriage partner. Often the deceased spouse was still working, and thus a major source of income shared by the couple ends. When pension income is available, it often stops (or is reduced drastically) when the eligible retired worker dies. Divorce often has serious economic consequences for women and, like widowhood, can lead to social isolation and a deterioration in status.[11]

The little data available indicate that older people without children are a minority but numerous in both developed and developing countries. Their vulnerability represents an important policy issue for every country. Information from the WHO surveys of people over 60 in South East Asia[12] found that 3–6 per cent of the older population had no living children.

Even if older people have children, there is no certainty that these children will be *available* to provide assistance. The global population living in cities more than doubled between 1950 and 1975, in large part accounted for by younger people leaving rural areas.[13] For example, in the early 1970s there were only 80,000 people living outside of their 'home province' of Sichuan, China; today there are about 6 million![14]

HelpAge Korea's volunteer home visiting scheme enables many older people to remain independent.
© HelpAge Korea

While many younger migrants send remittances back to their parents, some choose not to – or are unable to do so.[15] Older people are also vulnerable to migration arising from natural disasters and political upheavals. 'The first problem to confront the elder in a disaster situation is that he or she may be left behind by the mass migration. When refugees came into Sudan from central Tigray, Oxfam estimated that up to 40,000 elderly people had been left behind without adequate support.'

When the family cannot provide

While most children acknowledge an obligation to care for their parents in old age (if needed), responsibility becomes less clear when there are no children or they do not (cannot) provide the necessary support. Many countries have laws that legally obligate children to provide support to their parents. Often other relatives provide help, and sometimes neighbours, charities, or community groups assist the person in need.

With urbanization, modernization, and international migration on the rise – and fertility in many countries on the decline – it is not sufficient for policy makers to assume that the family will take care of older people. As ESCAP notes, in a context of limited resources and programmes, highest priority at the national and community levels should be accorded to older people who are alone and vulnerable.[16]

'Social solidarity'

The most common means of social protection in developing countries is reliance on personal saving and family support. The major problem with the family for sharing risk, however, is that the number of people involved is relatively small. The danger is that there will not be enough producers to support the unproductive. Illness, crop failure or some other disaster can bring the proportion of earners to non-earners to a level at which the group cannot function. This leads to the need for insurance.[17]

The need for better collective arrangements to deal with the economic problems of old age has always been with us and nations have developed a rich array of cultural traditions, interpersonal mechanisms, and collective programmes to

Social service for the familyless elderly in Korea

The average lifespan in Korea is 71 years and expected to increase to 74 by early in the Millennium. It is clear that Korea is rapidly becoming a society where the numbers of elderly people will be very substantial.

Nursing care and other help given by families to older members has decreased in recent years. Over two thirds of families are now nuclear families, and nearly a quarter of the population over 65 are living alone.

Official Korean policy is 'family protection first, social protection second', which assumes that traditional methods for addressing the problems of older people will be used within the family unit. A HelpAge Korea survey identified the social networks used by older people. While support systems do exist within the community, they are mainly on a one-off basis and not a foundation for continuous long-term care.

HelpAge Korea has established a wide network of volunteer Home Helpers, recruited through the media. These helpers are assigned to the familyless elderly on a one-to-one basis. In the late nineties the programme was expanded to include paid helpers. There are now around 800 paid helpers and 4000 volunteers.

This initiative for community based care has had a major impact on the approach taken by the government. The Ministry of Health and Social Affairs incorporated the home help programme into the Act for the Elderly in December 1989 in an attempt to provide legislative backing. In 1993 the Korean national policy on supporting older people was amended to put more emphasis on community based service, and a new programme comprising a home help service, a day care centre programme, and short stay or respite care was included. The target is to extend government funded community care so that there are 520 teams of home carers across the country.

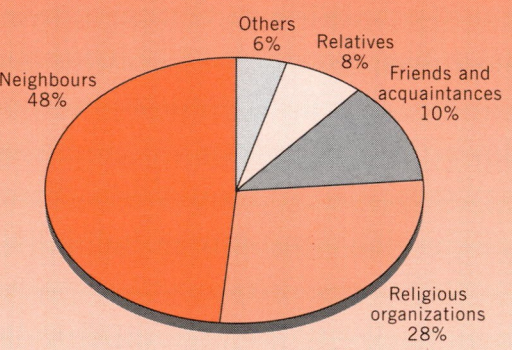

Social support networks used by older people in Korea

Neighbours 48%
Others 6%
Relatives 8%
Friends and acquaintances 10%
Religious organizations 28%

HelpAge Korea has recommended that the home help service be formalized, not only for the familyless elderly but also for those where children are working or where families lack the resources to help their older relatives. It is thought that only through such an expanded programme will elderly Koreans will be able to enjoy a better quality of life and security while they are still living with their families or alone within the community.

Source: HelpAge Korea

deal with the problems. The variety of these programmes can be classified into the following major categories:

- *Social assistance* provides cash benefits to individuals who can demonstrate that they meet specified eligibility criteria typically including 'means tests' of income and/or assets.
- *Mutual-benefit societies* are occupational or industrial groupings of members organized under the principles of solidarity and mutual aid

in times of need. Benefits are provided through member contributions and decisions made by members collectively. They often operate under the supervision of government ministries or regulatory agencies. There are large numbers of mutual benefit societies, insurance companies operating on mutual benefit principles, and a growing number of agricultural mutual benefit organizations.

- *Social services* are in-kind or non-cash benefits such as homemaker or home-meal services or adult day-care centres. Benefits are sometimes means-tested or paid for by user-fees.

- *Employer Liability Programmes*, such as employer work injury insurance programmes, legally require employers to provide designated benefits to their employees and/or dependents, either directly or under an approved insurance policy.
- *Occupational pension programmes* are payments – periodic or lump sum – by employers or unions who take principal responsibility for administering a plan. Payments are conditional on a specified employment record and encouraged by governments through tax incentives.
- *Mandated Defined Contribution Programmes* require workers and/or employers to contribute into individual accounts for retirement or other needs, with the moneys invested by a selected private financial institution on behalf of each individual (the so-called Chilean approach).
- *Savings incentive programmes* encourage personal savings. Governments sometimes provide tax subsidies on monies invested in 'retirement accounts' that cannot usually be withdrawn before a specified age.
- *Provident funds* are compulsory savings organizations for workers. Employers (and often workers) make contributions into a publicly administered fund with a separate account for each employee. A lump sum is payable on specified payout criteria – or most commonly old age.
- *Social allowances or universal (demogrant) programmes* provide benefits to all elderly residents or citizens without respect to income, employment, or other means.
- *Social Insurance national programmes* are legislated and administered by or under the supervision of the government. They provide periodic cash payments for unemployment, old age, death, survivor's needs, disability, sickness or maternity, work injury, and/or the birth of a child.

Programmes in the developing world

Ageing issues have not been a major concern of leaders in developing nations of the world for at least four major reasons.

First, pre-industrial societies are predominantly *rural* societies. In these societies, the economic and political position of older persons relative to younger persons is generally strong. Families, by both structure and necessity, are supportive of needs in old age. Older people are able to remain economically productive for a greater portion of their lifetime. And much of the population is outside of wage-dependent markets.

Second, older people have been a relatively small proportion of the total populations of such nations.

Third, governmental development priorities favour expenditures that invest in the long-term productive potential of the young.

And fourth, older people are viewed as impeding development because they are considered to be resistant to change and are less adaptive human capital.

Paradoxically, while there has been little interest in older people, there has been a great deal of interest in pensions in the developing countries. Most developing countries have legislated for social insurance pension schemes. But coverage in most countries is still quite minimal, with critics arguing that many programmes redistribute income to elite segments of the population who are less in need.

There is a growing awareness of the important relationship between social programmes and demographic changes resulting from development policies. Development in both the urban and rural sectors brings with it changes in both family size and the support roles of family members.

In countries where population ageing is most advanced, there has usually been government-led population planning to reduce fertility. Economic support in old age has been provided traditionally through large families that insure the survival of at least one child, preferably a male child,

Pensioners as a percentage of people over 60 years old, selected countries	
Countries	Pensioners as a percentage of people over 60
Cote D'Ivoire	5.7
Madagascar	4.1
China	22.5
Indonesia	9.8
Philippines	7.0
Bolivia	17.8
Colombia	10.0
Costa Rica	36.4
Guatemala	13.0
Jamaica	27.0
Nicaragua	19.9
Peru	17.6
OECD	84.1

Source: World Bank, 1994

who provides support to the parents in their old age. To be fully successful population planning policies must be complemented by income security mechanisms that reduce the reliance families have been forced to place on their children in the past.

Reforming provision for older age: the reality and the challenge

In recent years social insurance programmes in developing countries have come under sharp attack. For example, in an influential publication, 'Social security in Latin America,' economist William McGreevey comments:

> 'In addressing [various social risks] … through social insurance, governments everywhere confront moral hazard – the fact that public benefits once proffered will be taken up by those who may not need them – greatly inflating the costs of protecting against the risks themselves. In a broader political setting, benefits once proffered come to be regarded as entitlements and hence no longer subject to review even if they fail to serve the objective for which they were created. With the passage of decades … the needs of the populations have evolved and the problems of the poor, especially in rural areas, have become more pointed and explicit. The services offered to urban employees through social security seem luxurious by comparison to what governments are able to do for the poorest segments of society.'[20]

There is a clear need for nations around the world to reassess their approaches to income maintenance in old age. But in developing countries the need is driven by the changing realities of rapid demographic ageing and the new international economic environment combined with growing dissatisfaction with current provision and major financial problems.

What benefits? For whom?

While there are serious resource constraints, there are also political obstacles to introducing and reforming social security in developing countries.[21] Serious political issues arise from the fact that in many developing countries social insurance coverage is not available to most of the people, is

Taking account of the one-child policy in China[18]

Projections of the number of people over 65 in China demonstrate the importance of taking ageing into account in population policy. Based on a two-child or voluntary projection between now and the middle of the next century, 17–20 per cent of the population would be over 65 in 2050. Based on the one-child projection, 41 per cent of the population of China would be over 65. The significant issues raised for social security and the country as a whole are clear.

Rebuilding with credit – in Tete, Mozambique, HelpAge International has provided credit to enable returning refugees to rebuild their lives.
© Stacey Walker/ HelpAge International

'too generous' for some who get it, and is often inadequate for many of the other recipients.

In the early stages, social insurance coverage is almost always limited to urban workers, and *different* programmes are often created to respond to the needs of *different* groups. Even for urban workers coverage is often restricted to workers in certain occupations/industries. Those in

A brief history of pensions in developing countries

As in the industrialized West, social insurance pensions were preceded by pensions for military and civilian officials employed by governments. Pensions in many developing countries, however, have also been influenced in a major way by pension schemes designed to cater largely to the needs of expatriate workers in the urban areas of various colonies before independence. With the needs of expatriates in mind, provident funds were established in many British colonies, impeding the development of social insurance programmes in most of these countries. Comparing these provident funds to social insurance, Dixon concludes:

'[The capacity of provident funds] ... to provide adequate social security protection is generally constrained: (a) by the relatively low level of their individual members' deposits, (b) by their inability to ensure that lump-sum payments are used to provide long-term social security protection, and (c) by their inability to provide their members with a hedge against inflation ... None, however, has found the solution to the fundamental dilemma that makes them ineffective social security institutions – namely, how to provide adequate social security protection on the basis of compulsory savings.'[19]

A second development in the colonies was the creation of formal mutual benefit societies. These societies now exist in countries as diverse as Algeria, India, the Ivory Coast, Malaysia, Nigeria, the Philippines, Senegal, Tanzania, and Zaire. Mutual benefit societies are modelled after the European 'friendly societies' of France, Belgium, and Great Britain. Over the years, some of these mutual benefit societies (especially in Latin America) have evolved into or have been replaced by pensions.

smaller firms, or in certain regions, towns, or cities are often not covered. The result is a patchwork of different programmes – programmes that cover *some* groups (but never *all* groups) in the population.

When countries stop and reassess the results of their political histories regarding social insurance development, they often do not like what they see and think about change. But as Giovanni Tamburi warns in reaction to the various proposals of foreign advisers for pension reform in Eastern Europe, in making changes today one cannot assume away the 'benefit culture,' obligations, and citizen expectations created in the past.[22] Each country has a history of providing certain benefits to certain groups, and it is politically difficult *in any country* to 'turn back the clock' and start again. Hence, reform is almost never easy (to the great irritation of some economists who are used to assuming away political considerations in their models). Not surprisingly, therefore, a large part of the history of social insurance is a continuous debate over 'what benefits and for whom?'

It is clear that pensions should be *available*, *adequate*, *fair*, and *understood*. Unfortunately, social insurance programmes in most developing countries today can be criticized with regard to their success in achieving all four goals.[23]

Availability: the coverage problem

Social insurance coverage is a major issue.[24] Most people would agree that individuals in similar circumstances should not be arbitrarily excluded from coverage under a plan or excluded because of issues such as age, sex or race. But the matter of who is actually included in a pension plan is often complicated by administrative, technical, political, and economic considerations. In almost all developing countries large numbers of workers in rural areas and in the informal sector are not covered. There are very real logistical, technical, and administrative problems in extending cover-

> 'It is clear that pensions should be available, adequate, fair, and understood. Unfortunately, social insurance programmes in most developing countries today can be criticized with regard to their success in achieving all four goals.'

age to both these groups: registration, communicating with plan participants, compliance, record-keeping, estimating wages or income in agricultural settings, delivering benefits.[25]

Rural populations, most with very low incomes and very little *money* income, find it difficult to contribute financially to collective schemes.[26] Moreover, politically it has been difficult to develop redistributive financing schemes that finance rural benefits from urban revenues. The 'extension of the current system to cover the total population is infeasible in most countries because of the costliness of the current package of benefits.'[27] The result in Latin America, for example, is that 'a minority of the population is covered against all risks, while the majority of the population has no protection at all.'[28]

Many developing countries are frustrated by the obstacles to providing social protection to a greater proportion of their populations.[29] The slow progress indicates the difficulty of the problem; there are no ready answers to the dilemmas.[30] Current proposals for reform that may help deal with the lack of collective social protection for large portions of the population include:

1 Shifting greater responsibility onto other mechanisms:[31]
    • Increasing government efforts to support and strengthen family support, especially in rural areas; or
    • Expanding social assistance programmes that target the poor in general.
2 Rethinking and changing the financing approach:
    • Financing more universal benefits (or better 'targeted' programmes) by saving money (for example, through actions described below) and/or by developing new financing mech-anisms to replace or supplement the traditional 'payroll tax';

No chance of a pension – Eda Preston, aged 77, like many older people worked all her life in the informal sector. She used to do 'days work' as a maid and sell coal near Vineyard Town, Jamaica to supplement her savings.
© Tanya Ward/ HelpAge International

- Reducing the costs of current programmes by consolidation of programmes and/or by cutting back on benefits to those currently covered; or
- Creating a first tier of 'basic benefits' to be extended to all and a second (and perhaps third tier) of supplemental benefits provided through a combination of public/private programmes.

3 Rethinking the benefits provided:
- 'Unbundling' the many different benefits and services offered by social security institutions into those that could be extended to the poor and those that are 'affordable' only by middle- and upper income groups;

- Protecting the rural, and poor population generally, through specialized programmes more appropriate to their situation (eg, crop insurance programmes and 'guaranteed income' programmes);[32] or
- 'Prioritizing' benefit needs, which are likely to be different in urban and rural areas; giving priority attention in rural areas, for example, to primary and preventive health care, disability protection, and assistance to widows and old persons without access to family support.

Adequacy

The existence and coverage of a pension programme should not be confused with the *level and amounts of benefits actually paid*. A particular pension plan is often only one of a number of collective programmes operating to provide economic security and cannot be viewed in isolation. Eligibility or benefit determination under one programme is sometimes related to benefits received from another programme (ie, benefits are sometimes 'integrated').[33]

In developing countries, there are two major adequacy concerns: one, that the benefits will be too small; the other, that the benefits will be too generous. Adequacy will also be affected by high inflation, which erodes the real value of benefits where pension payments are not indexed. This has caused a capricious redistribution of benefits from workers with long service and high incomes to those with short service and low incomes.[34]

Unrealistic promises – for instance 70 per cent or more replacement wages during retirement or disability – mean that social security institutions will never be able to serve the needs of the poor. If the benefits offered by these institutions were reduced to, perhaps, 40 per cent of the basic urban wage, then it is possible that poorer groups could benefit as well as contributing workers.[35]

Pro-poor benefit structures could include:

- Eliminating excessive 'early retirement' options, raising the normal retirement age, and/or making the retirement age for men and women the same.
- Providing better, but not necessarily unlimited, protection from inflation.
- Incorporating redistributional provisions into programmes (eg, 'a weighted benefit formula' that replaces relatively more pre-retirement income for lower income individuals than for higher income persons).
- Elimination of seniority pensions that are based on years of service, regardless of age, and therefore allow retirement at very early ages (eg, as early as age 40 in Brazil and Uruguay).

Equity

Analyses of equity questions tend to focus on financing – how much do the benefits received cost the individual in contrast to other benefit recipients and, possibly, non-recipients?

An important consideration is the extent to which a pension scheme is designed to redistribute income within the relevant population. In plans that redistribute major amounts of income, there is generally a very weak link between, on the one hand, a worker's personal contributions, total payroll taxes, and reduced wages (to pay for pensions) and, on the other hand, the benefits the worker ultimately receives. Yet the link between pay-in and benefits received is often one major criterion for judging pension equity.

Another issue is the amount of 'unintentional redistribution' that occurs in a plan. 'Unintentional redistribution may result from the effects of inflation on the distribution of benefits within and across generations, but it may also be caused by changes over time in the provisions or performance of different schemes.'[36]

Also, redistribution may occur as a result of particular financing arrangements. Concern has been raised by some economists with regard to the redistributional impact of payroll taxes in developing countries. If the uncovered population, many of whom are poor, partially pays for the benefits of the covered population through higher prices of consumer goods, then a serious inequity would seem to exist.

In addition to action related to the coverage and adequacy issues, social insurance could be made more equitable by:

- Introducing financing methods that offset the 'regressiveness' of the payroll tax: exemption of wages up to a specified level; a progressive contribution rate structure; or tax credits for certain categories of earners.
- Raising or eliminating the payroll tax contribution ceiling that limits the payments of high earners.

- Utilizing special taxes to subsidize benefits to low income individuals (eg, luxury taxes of the Brazilian type, or tax on the payroll of urban enterprises and agricultural production).
- Stricter penalties and prosecution of businesses that avoid or delay payroll tax payments.

Being understood: informed participation

People should, as a minimum, know whether they are covered by a pension plan, what the conditions of entitlement are, what benefits they (or their family) are likely to receive, and what the risks of losing benefits are. In practice there is serious lack of knowledge and misinformation about expected pensions, both public and private. As pension programmes grow many of them become more complicated. Their complexity weakens informed participation. However, all too rarely are assessments made about employees' ability to understand pension programmes and integrate them into their personal finances.

Informed participation could be improved by:

- Education by governments (and pension organizations) to explain the strengths and limits of existing programmes.
- 'Consolidation' to minimize the number and complexity of programmes to reduce inequity and confusion that can result from many programmes covering different groups.

Administration and implementation

The administration of pension schemes can be a major expense, influencing the amount of benefits ultimately paid out. In Latin America, the percentage of administrative expenditure over total expenditure in the system is very high, fluctuating from 7 per cent in Costa Rica, Chile, and Uruguay to 10 per cent in Peru and 18 per cent in Mexico, percentages far above those in the developed countries.[37]

Good administration also requires a high-level of trained personnel. But such people are in short supply for all of government, and personnel for pension provision are usually given a low priority.[38]

A major administrative problem is payment noncompliance by both governments and private employers and the need for an adequate enforcement structure to deal with this situation.[39] In some countries, noncompliance is generally ignored; in others the penalties are not significant enough to encourage speedy compliance.

While some countries operate their public pension programmes on a pay-as-you-go basis, there are other countries where the social insurance programmes (or provident funds) accumulate sizeable reserves. However, in some cases, the rates of return on the investment portfolios are quite low. Reporting on eight Latin American countries, for example, Mesa-Lago finds that only three of the eight countries had a positive average annual real yield on investments from public pension reserves.[40]

The volume of pension funds makes them vulnerable to fraud and corruption in developed and developing countries alike. Programmes in developing countries are especially vulnerable: monitoring and regulation are often less rigorous and legal processes often underdeveloped and of low priority.

Competition and privatization

The most common proposal for promoting competition in the provision of pensions is through 'privatization' of government-run activities: the aim is to boost organizational efficiency and raise the quality of the products/services provided.[41]

Given that effective competition is significantly weakened in many sectors by the growth and dominance of large firms, it is not surprising that privatization in many countries has been, in fact, the turning of public monopolies into private monopolies.[42] In private ownership, managers are often driven to strategies and practices that make essential products/services unaffordable or unavailable to large segments of the population.

Whether public or private, people want pensions schemes to deliver value for money, but also to be without corruption, carried out using appropriate performance standards, and accessible to participants.[43] The experience of industrialized countries that rely in a major way on employer-sponsored pensions is illuminating. The vast majority of plans have been free of major problems, but there has always been a significant minority where there was misrepresentation, fraud, and mismanagement – necessitating public supervision and the creation of large regulatory agencies. Regulation does not come cheaply and is only as good as its regulators. Privatization and competition does not guarantee against dishonesty and empirical evidence indicates that neither private nor public pension schemes are immune from this problem.

> '*Whether public or private, people want pensions schemes to deliver value for money, but also to be without corruption, carried out using appropriate performance standards, and accessible to participants.*'

Trust: the foundation of public and private pensions

Basic to the success of social insurance is the trust that people place in the institution itself. Social insurance 'solidarity,' 'actuarial soundness,' the 'intergenerational compact,' benefit equity, administrative efficiency, informational 'transparency,' solvency and integrity risks are concerned with the trust people place in the future promises of the social insurance approach.

Lack of trust in a social insurance system undermines its viability:

> '*it is vitally important that any social insurance programme have an effective set of mechanisms for reviewing the general operations of the programme and especially for assessing the financial integrity of the fiscal operations.*'

- Individuals who do not believe they will get promised benefits, or are not covered by the programme, are unlikely to support it politically.
- If governments continue to fall behind in the payments they are required under law to pay on behalf of their employees, they set an extremely poor example for other employers.
- Administrative corruption and graft not only reduces political support but is likely to increase payroll tax avoidance and recipient fraud.
- Lack of explicit actions to protect social insurance pensions from the ravages of inflation seriously undermines support and compliance.

There are positive steps that countries can take to promote trust. The experience in the industrialized countries indicates that it is vitally important that any social insurance programme have an effective set of mechanisms for reviewing the general operations of the programme and especially for assessing the financial integrity of the fiscal operations.

Each developing country needs to pay serious attention to the mechanisms for public review that currently exist and consider ways of improving them. All too often, the financial conditions of the social insurance programme have been allowed to deteriorate to the point that remedial action is not only difficult but sometimes impossible without major changes to the system of economic support.[44]

Conclusion: providing adequate income in old age

The need for social protection is growing, not diminishing, around the world – in both developed and developing countries. In fact, the rising tide of market solutions to economic development issues promises an accelerating need for mechanisms that assist individuals in dealing with the risks and social disruptions arising out of social, demographic, political, and economic change.

In the years to come, increasing numbers of individuals will reach old age.

A retired Tanzanian officer's perspective on pensions

A retired officer from Mukalize, Tanzania contended that the national government does not consider retired people:

> *'I worked for this country for more than 30 years, but now that I am retired and in need of money for an operation, they do not want to know about me'.*

Retired officers also complain about the pension system, which pays out the same money now as it did 30 years ago. There are lengthy procedures and pensioners had experienced long delays in receiving their terminal benefits from the government. A retired teacher for instance said, 'I had to go to Dar es Salaam twice before receiving my terminal benefit – by the end more than half of that sum had already been spent on those trips alone.'

Ex-employees of the government also insist that the salaries are so meagre that, once retired, people have no chance of carving out a new life for themselves – instead they have a life of destitution to look forward to. This has encouraged corruption amongst government officials, who are tempted to channel cash off into their own style of 'pension fund'.

Many will be unable to work. Others will expect the growing leisure increasingly associated with this time of life. When work stops, for any reason, where will the income support in old age come from?

'The need for social protection is growing, not diminishing, around the world – in both developed and developing countries.'

Nations learn over time from their historical experiences in providing for old age. Each is confronted with an evolving demographic structure, fluctuations in economic growth, and pressures arising out of other macroeconomic developments, all of which influence the ultimate choices of policies and programmes that are made and the nature of reforms. This is why national income policies for older people can never be static.

What governments do also strongly influences the options of individuals. Governments create opportunities, moderate risk, provide information, compel compliance, and so forth. Or they can do the opposite.

The key to the security of older people is, first and foremost, dependent on what individuals and families do. That is true for people in all nations – both developed and developing. Of course, governments can (and should) assist in greater or less degree – depending on the particular income security approach a nation takes. Thus, the 'economics of old age' should always be viewed as a joint process among partners – the individual, the family, employers, and the government.

Notes

1   Dr James H Schulz is Professor of Economics and Kirstein Professor of Aging Policy at Heller Graduate School, Brandeis University, Waltham, MA 02254, USA

2   James, E, 1994, *Averting the Old Age Crisis: policies to protect the old and promote growth*, World Bank Policy Research Report, Oxford University Press, New York, p5.

3   The ASEAN surveys found that in Malaysia, for example, children and grandchildren were the main source of support for 38 per cent of aged men and 67 per cent of aged women.

4   United Nations Development Programme, 1997, *Human Development Report 1997*, Oxford University Press, New York.

5   Paul, Susanne and James, 1994, *Humanity Comes of Age*, WCC Publications, Geneva.

6   China National Committee on Ageing, 1989, 'Population Ageing in China', *Asian Population Study Series* No 95, UN Economic and Social Commission for Asia and Pacific, Bangkok.

7   See, for example, Lopata, H Z, 1979, *Women as Widows: Support Systems*, Elsevier, New York and Nangen, D G, Bengtson, V L and Landry, P H, 1988, *Measurement of Intergenerational Relations*, Sage, Beverly Hills, CA, 1988.

8   To a lesser extent, they also receive assistance from other relatives and members of their 'community'.

9   International Labour Office, 1997, *Ageing in Asia: The Growing Need for Social Protection*, ILO Regional Office for Asia and the Pacific, Bangkok.

10 Ibid, Table 7.

11 A discussion of what can happen is provided in Ellickson, J, 1988, 'Never the Twain Shall Meet: Ageing Men and Women in Bangladesh', *Journal of Cross-Cultural Gerontology* 3, pp53–70.

12 Martin, L G, 1989, 'Living Arrangements of the Elderly in Fiji, Korea, Malaysia and the Philippines', *Demography* 26, pp627–43.

13 Kinsella, K and Taeuber, C, 1992, *An Ageing World II*. US Bureau of the Census International Population Reports P25, 92–3. US Government Printing Office, Washington, DC.

14 'China on the Move', *The Economist*, 6 July, 1996, pp33–34.

15 See, for example, the discussion of this point in Oberai, a S and Manmohan Singh, H K, 1983, *Causes and Consequences of Internal Migration: A Study in the Indian Punjab*, Oxford University Press, New Delhi, for the International Labour Organisation.

16 Economic and Social Commission for Asia and the Pacific (ESCAP), 1987, 'Population Ageing: Review of Emerging Issues', *Asian Population Studies Series* No 80, ESCAP, Bangkok, p9.

17 Kenneth Boulding, K, 1958, *Principles of Economic Policy*, Prentice Hall, Englewood Cliffs, NJ.

18 See Fennell, S and Zhu, L, 1996, 'Ageing and Pension Policy in China' in P Lloyd-Sherlock and P Johnson (eds), *Ageing and Social Policy*, Global Comparisons, LSE, London.

19 Dixon, J, 1987, 'Provident Funds: An Assessment of their Social Security, Social, and Economic Performances and Prospects' in J H Schulz and D Davis-Friedmann (eds), *Ageing China: Family, Economics, and Government Policies in Transition*, Gerontological Society of America, Washington, DC, pp173–193.

20 McGreevey, W P, 1990, 'Social Security in Latin America: Issues and Options for the World Bank', World Bank Discussion Paper 110, World Bank, Washington, DC.

21 As McGreevey and Mesa-Lago (among others) have correctly observed (Notes 20 and 28), 'political obstacles are perhaps as important as economic ones in both initially *introducing* and then *reforming* social security programmes throughout the world. Similarly, Esping-Andersen's recent book examining the evolution of the welfare state in the West makes that point abundantly clear.

22 Tamburi, G, 1992, 'Misunderstanding Pension Privatisation – the Case Against Do-It-Yourself Pension Kits', Benefits & Compensation International, March, pp2–8.

23 This paper focuses on social insurance in developing countries. The statement in the text should not be interpreted to mean that the author does not think there are problems in industrialized countries with regard to these attributes. Certainly problems and debates over these same issues are also frequent in the West.

24 It is also a major problem with regard to employer-sponsored plans.

25 See, for example, International Social Security Association, 1980, *Social Security Protection of the Rural Population in Developing Countries*, ISSA Regional Office for Asia and Oceania, New Delhi. In this connection, it is interesting to note that in the highly industrialized country of the US in the 1940s, policymakers still found it difficult to extend coverage to farmers, the self-employed, and other groups because of problems associated with collecting the equivalent of payroll contributions. See Berkowitz, E D (ed), 1987, *Social Security After Fifty*, Greenwood Press, New York, p20. See also International Labour Office, 1985, *Informal Sector in Africa: Jobs and Skills Programmes for Africa*, ILO, Geneva.

26 Tracy, 1991, op cit, points out, for example, that extension of social security coverage to Mexican farmers in the 1970s had to be rescinded because the farmers had insufficient funds to make the required contributions.

27 McGreevey, 1990, op cit.

28 Mesa-Lago, 1989, 'Portfolio Performance of Selected Social Security Institutes in Latin America', World Bank Discussion Paper 139, International Bank for Reconstruction and Development/World Bank, Washington, DC, p8.

29 See, for example, Mallet, A, 1980, 'Social Protection of the Rural Population,' *International Social Security Review* 33, pp359–393.

30 Ibid. Conclusions were reported over a decade ago(!) at the General Assembly of ISSA in Manila

(1980) by Christine Cockburn.

31 But the reader should take note of our earlier discussions on the limits and problems of alternative mechanisms.

32 Examples of programmes that might be studied include the IMSS-Solidaridad in Mexico, Peasant Insurance in Ecuador, the 'indigent' programme of social insurance in Costa Rica, the Agriculture Workers' Pension Scheme in Kerala, the Social Assistance Programme in Maharashtra (India), and the Social Guarantee Programme in Gabon.

33 Leavitt, T D and Schulz, J H, 1983, *Pension Integration: Concepts, Issues and Proposals*, Employee Benefit Research Institute, Washington, DC.

34 Vittas and Skully, 1991, *Overview of Contractual Savings Institutions*, World Bank, Washington, DC, p17.

35 McGreevey, 1990, op cit, p19.

36 Vittas and Skully, 1991, op cit, p5.

37 Mesa-Lago, 1989 op cit.

38 Of course, this is a problem that plagues *all* organizations (public and private) during the initial stages of development.

39 The ILO reports, for example, that there have been 'record high levels of non-payment [in the Americas]: in Barbados, 44 per cent of payments are late; in Brazil, delays and evasion are of the order of 60 per cent; in Jamaica, delays are at 44 per cent; in Peru, evasion is at 33 per cent.' See International Labour Office. *Social Security and the Process of Economic Restructuring*. Report II, 13th Conference of American States, Members of the ILO.

40 Mesa-Lago, C, 1989, op cit.

41 See, for example, Vernon, R, 1988, *The Promise of Privatisation*, Council on Foreign Relations, New York. Vernon provides extensive information on privatization activities in developing countries.

42 Vickers, J and Yarrow, G, 1991, 'Economic Perspectives on Privatisation', *Journal of Economic Perspectives* 5(2), Spring, pp111–132.

43 Ibid, p36.

44 This is the explanation for the abolition of the Chilean social insurance programme in the early 1980s. See, for example, the discussion in Myers, R J, 1985, 'Privatisation of Chile's Social Security Program', *Benefits Quarterly* 1(3), pp26–35.

8 Change, Family Life, Coping Strategies and Seniors

Denise Eldemire-Shearer[1]

The family is defined by the UN as 'those members of the household who are related, to a specific degree, through blood, adoption or marriage'. The family is considered by many as the fundamental unit of society and as such supports and nurtures its members, recognizing and facilitating satisfaction of age related needs throughout the life course.

In discussing the family and seniors it may be helpful to begin by identifying the relationships which exist and why. At the outset it is important to recognize the role of the family in helping all its members meet their needs. Development is constantly occurring during the life-course and the family plays a role in helping seniors through life-course transitions. The care and support of senior members is but one of the demands made on the family. There are competing needs from different age groups and family members.

Two recognized forms of the family are nuclear and extended. The nuclear family is one in which only two generations live and is found in

Today's seniors are the survivors – research is needed to identify their coping strategies and examine how they can be supported and replicated.
© Neil Cooper

more developed countries whereas the extended family – several generations living in one unit – is more likely to be found in the developing world.

The family in its numerous forms reflects the multiplicity of forms of social organization and cultural and religious values, but has traditionally accepted responsibility for all its members including older persons.

Like everything else the family is experiencing changes. The changes are many and varied including demographic, socio-economic and cultural. The changes are causing the need for adaptation and innovation by families and communities in how they meet their traditional roles and functions.

> '*In recent times it has been said that the extended family is breaking down. Not all research supports such assertions but suggests instead that the extended family format is changing and under pressure but still recognizes its responsibility to its members even if it is not able to fulfil it. Such findings suggest that it is the* ability *to care and support needy older members that needs to be addressed rather than the* willingness.'

In recent times it has been said that the extended family is breaking down. Not all research supports such assertions but suggests instead that the extended family format is changing and under pressure but still recognizes its responsibility to its members even if it is not able to fulfil it. Such findings suggest that it is the *ability* to care and support needy older members that needs to be addressed rather than the *willingness*.

Changes in society and family

Decades ago the family was physically close. This facilitated cohesiveness. Modernization, urbanization and industrialization have led families to live great distances apart, communicating through modern technology and therefore unable to help each other meet certain physical needs. In addition the age structure and size of the family is changing as population policies reduce the number of children per family so reducing the number of potential caregivers for each elderly person while increasing the number and longevity of older persons. Economic circumstances are also impacting on gender roles and more women are enter-

ing the work force so reducing further the number of potential caregivers.

This economic activity also reduces family-orientated time, threatening family cohesion because of absence and reduced time for supervision. In addition marriage is losing its status, as cohabitation becomes more acceptable. People are marrying later and having children at older ages. Divorce is also increasing, leaving more single women with children. Increased life expectancy means longer widowhood.

Such changes all influence inter-family distribution of power and affect family composition and function. At the same time, families are subject to external influences as society's value system is influenced by change and higher levels of education and exposure to a wider range of experiences through television and other forms of communication.

The issue is complicated by the great diversity among seniors and the need to avoid narrow stereotyping. This century has experienced great social change especially among developing countries and each cohort of seniors has its own peculiarities, which make generalizations difficult. Each senior is a product of the opportunity and experience of their earlier years and therefore has different values and expectations from present generations. This can be interpreted by younger family members as stubbornness, rigidity and difficultness among seniors, and can have a negative effect on relationships.

Life is a series of transitions. How personal transitions are experienced, successfully or with difficulty, impacts on how the family deals with family issues. An unhappy discontented family member is not likely to be able to contribute positively but rather to need help themselves.

For successful ageing one must first negotiate mid-life. But, mid-life as a transition period has received very little attention and its impact on both caregivers and those receiving care can be quite significant. It is not always recognized that menopause is not only a women's issue but also a family issue.

Mid-life is an important transitional phase, a prelude to active ageing and a period of adjustment in family life, work and personal identity. Families have a role in helping the future senior through this adjustment period. This is the period when many of the gender differences and new issues impacting on senior years emerge, including health and income. Families are often uninformed and unprepared to deal with the social conflicts of this period. Breakdowns in relationships can happen both between spouses and between parents and children. Often these are not resolved causing additional conflict and resentment in senior years. The result being a senior who appears difficult to please leading to additional stress among family members who then feel unappreciated.

Families are therefore microcosms of many interacting forces and systems. Policy makers considering care of older persons have to make decisions in this context of changes in traditional family roles. Health, productivity, social participation and relationships between generations are key issues. Policy has to consider what positive contribution it can make in the best interest of the family unit and all members, including seniors.

Seniors' contribution

Much of the current discussion focuses on how family support of seniors can be maintained. Such a discussion could be seen as one-sided – 'supporting' seniors. But inter-family relationships are rarely one-sided as in reality grandparents often make an unmeasured and unrecognized contribution to maintaining family life – socially and emotionally. Recognition of this contribution might give the present discussion on providing care new insights and directions. Grandparents are 'at home' due

to retirement – they are 'on the spot' and in many cases the day to day management of the household is their responsibility – a very important consideration given the other changes previously noted.

In reality seniors (grandparents) are the educating and motivating forces for many children. Seniors are repositories of accumulated skills, knowledge and experience – a living database of life, which they share through story telling. It is the interaction between children and adults which develops knowledge and should be encouraged.

It must be recognized that there is another view, which thinks that the role of the grandparent in the family is also changing at least in the public perception. The view of seniors as the seat of authority, wisdom and experience is being challenged in some developing countries, especially those experiencing technological change. Modernization has led to the less educated grandparent being seen as outdated. The value previously placed on heritage and culture is lessening. In addition, because of teenage pregnancies, many grandparents are themselves very young, thirties and early forties, and not seen as 'older persons' with wisdom and experience.

This perception is often not shared by the senior who still sees him or herself as head of the household. Such differences in perception often lead to inter-family conflict as young persons ignore directives from seniors. The changing view of seniors by younger generations, society's sometimes negative view of old age and the family and seniors' unpreparedness for ageing suggest the need for education on all aspects of the subject. Family Life Education programmes need to be evaluated to ensure that they not only take a life-course perspective but address all ages in the life cycle.

Many emphasize the teenager, the young adolescent and reproductive issues with little

> '*The changing view of seniors by younger generations, society's sometimes negative view of old age and the family and seniors' unpreparedness for ageing suggest the need for education on all aspects of the subject. Family Life Education programmes need to be evaluated to ensure that they not only take a life-course perspective but address all ages in the life cycle.*'

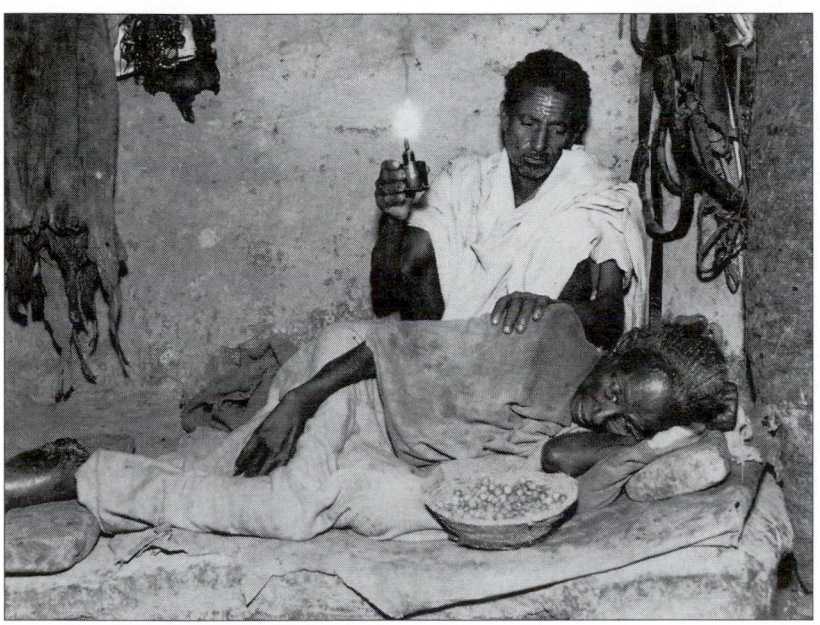

It is the family's ability to care and support needy older relatives that needs to be addressed, rather than their willingness.
© REST

on family relationships, the mid-life years, menopause and senior years. Better preparation of all family members for each stage should improve life for all through increased understanding and tolerance.

Changing perceptions

An approach to ageing needs which recognized the contribution of seniors to life alongside their need for support would be more positive and reduce the emphasis on the 'burden of old age'. For this to happen the measurement of dependency ratios needs to be rethought along with a re-examination of the present emphasis on economic productivity to the exclusion of social productivity. Another area for re-examination is the definition of 'work' and how to calculate the value of traditionally called, 'unpaid work'. For the family to remain a viable option for many seniors, ways will need to be found to ensure that the socio-economic environment in which they live provides ways for them to remain active. This is a real challenge for developing countries given the large young populations and high unemployment but vital to avoid age based wars over resources.

In many countries religious institutions have found ways to accommodate all ages. Seniors are very active in committees and groups and no doubt there are lessons to be learnt on how services can be re-oriented to enable seniors to stay involved.

The media has played a role in helping to perpetuate negative perceptions of older persons as the majority of news stories about seniors are about problems. Successful ageing is rarely seen as news. The media helps to form attitudes and as such is an area for consideration in policy development. The media is seen as very youth oriented so aggravating the problem of 'old age' prejudice which is detrimental to society and the youth themselves as they grow old. Efforts are necessary to change the approach to an equally positive one.

Support

Support to many means financial support and families often feel they have failed if they are unable to meet all the financial needs of their seniors. Poverty is a crisis faced by many in the developing world and the reality is that many families cannot afford to financially support their senior members. This will need to be addressed especially as it is mainly women who are seen as being responsible for the provision of care. Women often have less money to contribute than men.

But support is broader than just finance. For many seniors the social and emotional support they require from family is more important in their minds. Yet many younger people, feeling guilty about financial inadequacy, stay away from the senior not realizing that love and social interaction are more important to them at this time of their life than money.

Family networks have unique resources: proximity, affection, lifelong commitment and knowledge of each other and this is appreciated by the senior. Too often society and families do not realize that the senior has human needs like anyone else, but, unlike younger generations, has fewer ways of meeting their needs for love, self esteem and worth. Policies which help seniors meet these needs – beginning with education, reduction of social marginalization, support for the family through domiciliary services, home help care, respite care, activity centres, support groups and caregivers programmes – will relieve pressure on families and encourage them to keep their senior at home. In offering support to families, the church and other religious institutions have been mentioned as models to be encouraged and replicated by community groups.

Communities are extensions of families and are also resources. A chief resource is the younger 'able' retired senior, as well as youth groups and other volunteer groups. They can be encouraged to develop community supports especially using the inter-generational model which could include a good neighbour scheme, visits and practical emergency services such as changing lightbulbs and paying bills. The benefit is two-fold, meeting the need of the senior, but also exposing the younger person to a

senior and hopefully removing their fears of old age.

Such programmes could be the beginning of lifelong opportunities and service that educate about the ageing process, provide opportunities to plan for retirement and decrease dependency while increasing autonomy and supporting families. They also address a double need: that of families adapting to increasing numbers of seniors while seniors adapt to a changing family.

The latter is very important as seniors sometimes have unrealistic expectations of their families based on their childhood experience or refusal to accept changing social patterns. Survey findings also emphasize that economic ability without social structures available for help does not meet the caregiving needs.

Gender considerations

The traditional care system has been the responsibility of the females in families. The majority of younger women have no choice but to enter the work force. They are simply not available to look after grandparents or children. They will offer money to finance the care but many developing countries do not have in place community care systems even for those able to pay.

In examining the issue of family support for older persons, gender considerations are important as there are significant male/female differences for caregivers and caregiving. The last decade has seen an emphasis on the needs of older women due to the increased poverty, ill health and economic marginalization which puts older women at increased risk, especially economic risk. However, studies are indicating the need to also focus on the older male who, unlike the older female will not have his need met by economic solutions. The older man is at risk of being abandoned by his family in

> '*In examining the issue of family support for older persons, gender considerations are important as there are significant male/female differences for caregivers and caregiving. The last decade has seen an emphasis on the needs of older women due to the increased poverty, ill health and economic marginalization which puts older women at increased risk, especially economic risk. However, studies are indicating the need to also focus on the older male who, unlike the older female will not have his need met by economic solutions.*'

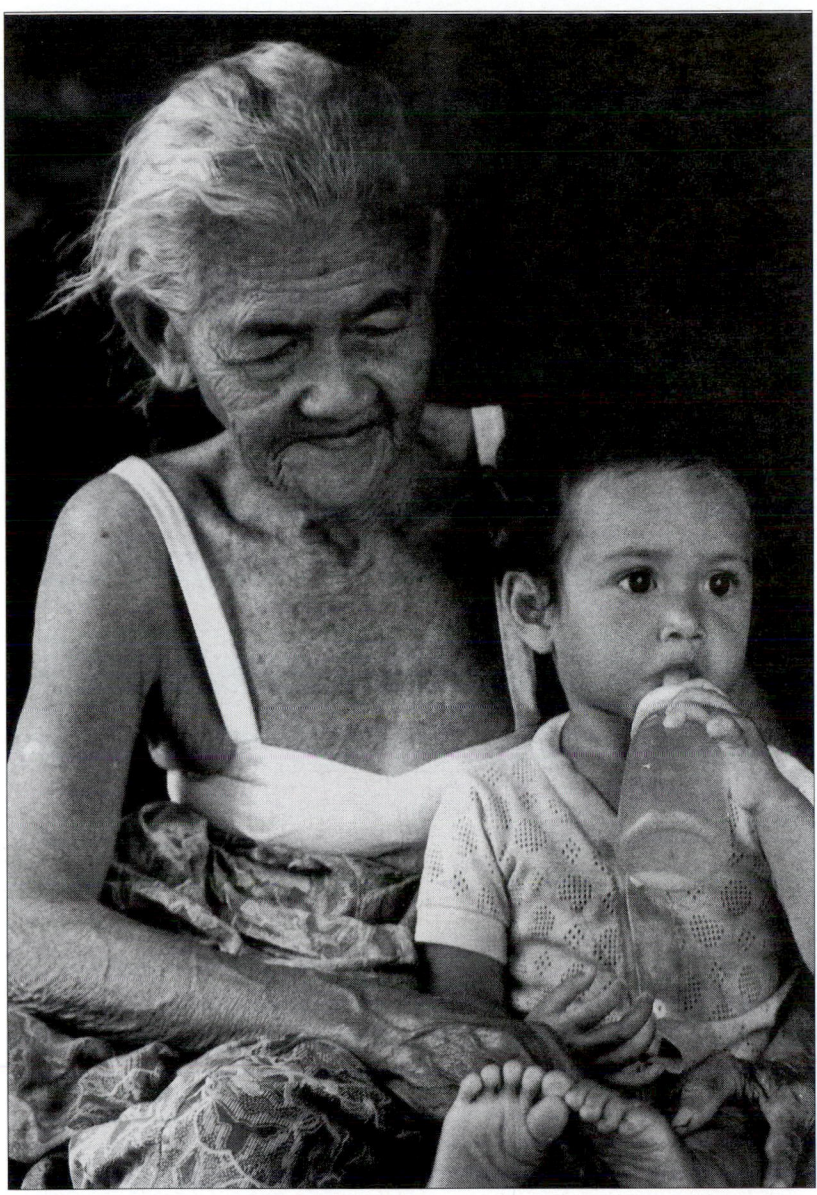

Grandparents are 'on the spot' and in many cases the day-to-day management of the household is their responsibility.
© HelpAge International

times of need, sometimes due to his previous abandonment of them in his young adulthood.

Therefore even if finance is available there is no one who will take on the responsibility. Efforts to change this will need to include educational programmes for young men stressing the need to fulfil social responsibilities from an early age as the only investment for 'old age'.

The way forward

It is not enough for countries, particularly developing countries that do not have the social service infrastructure, to point out that even some developed countries are having problems addressing ageing populations. Creative and innovative ways need to be found to offer families and seniors support.

Older people as active contributors to the household

The focus on the capacity of family support networks to care for older people often ignores the reciprocal nature of this intergenerational support. Older people are by no means simply passive receivers of care, but more often are active contributors to household economies. In subsistence economies older people contribute their labour, providing for their own survival until they are no longer physically capable. The following example from rural Mozambique illustrates how these contributions are maintained even in situations of vulnerability, in this case, severe drought:

'Portina is 70 years old and lives in her own hut in a family compound. She stated that a good harvest on her mashamba would yield five bags of maize, and she would give three of these to the family. The rest would be stored and used for her other needs... During the last two years of drought she has given all that she is able to produce to the family. She now lacks the resources to complete the walls of her hut; she receives no assistance from the family and views this as her own responsibility.'[2]

Other activities such as child minding and domestic work, often unacknowledged, provide a significant part in family survival.

Another example from Ghana[3] illustrates intergenerational interdependency among female traders in an urban environment. The practice of 'gifting' businesses to younger female family members provides an 'informal insurance system' for older women. Ill health is taken as a signal to reduce trading activities but not to stop. While the business, located in markets and involving long hours and physical work, is taken over by younger women, older women take up 'doorstep trading' at the family home. In addition to generating income for their upkeep, they provide child care services and security for the home, freeing other members for outside work.

Drawing policy lessons from Asia on ageing and family life

Albert I Hermalin[4]

Understanding the choices open to older people about where and with whom they live

It is important in formulating policy to distinguish form from function in terms of family structure and relationships. With increasing incomes and supply of housing, elderly parents and children may choose to live apart to gain more space and privacy, but this may not imply any diminution in levels of material or emotional support. Programmes that are generated on the basis of these trends on the assumption that they indicate growing isolation or vulnerability of the elderly may be wasteful and overlook more pressing needs on the dimensions of well-being. To be properly informed, policy makers need to utilize and encourage research that ascertains the preferences of the elderly with regard to living arrangements, measures the allocation of duties within households and the two-way flows that take place between elderly parents and children, and be attentive to the location of kin not in the household, since in many places it is customary for children to live nearby even when not coresiding with parents.

This is not to suggest that policy makers should not develop programmes that influence choices in living arrangements and other behaviours which enhance the well-being of the elderly. Singapore, for instance, provides tax incentives or housing priorities for children coresiding with or caring for elderly parents. In addition, the retirement programme in Singapore, the Central Provident Fund, contains provisions for use of accumulations for the educational expenses of children, developing expectations for later repayment and support from children. Some health plans in the region allow parents to be included as dependants under a worker's coverage, thus providing the mechanism for financing health care of the elderly in advance of the development of broader health programmes. In these and other ways, policy makers in the region have demonstrated the ability to innovate programmes that take into account emerging needs and trends but sustain desirable elements of traditional family arrangements. Continued development of programmes with these dual features can pay big dividends within the region and provide leadership to other countries facing similar issues.

Possible shifts in levels and patterns of coresidence are one manifestation of the accommodations within existing institutions that are likely to occur with on-going demographic and socio-economic changes. To develop sound policies and programmes, it is important to track the adjustments in behaviour and social relationships that families and individuals make in the face of rapid social changes. Often these give rise to special needs and/or produce groups with special vulnerabilities. Research, both qualitative and quantitative, that traces changing norms and attitudes and emerging needs can be valuable in this respect.

A second perspective important for the development of sound policy is taking account of changes over the life course as well as of changing cohorts. As the figure suggests, the well-being of the elderly is partially a function of their characteristics, and earlier behaviours, as well as their familial and social networks. This means that programmes can seek to affect later well-being through interventions at various stages of the life cycle. For example, a programme that discourages smoking at younger ages can produce better health and reduce health costs at older ages. A job retraining programme for workers as they age can keep older workers productively involved in the labour force for longer periods.

The time dimension also arises in recognizing that future cohorts of the elderly are likely to be very different in their characteristics compared with the current cohorts because of the demographic and socio-economic changes that have taken place throughout the region. On average, they will be better educated, more urban, with smaller families, and probably with better overall health than current cohorts of elderly persons. These differences must be accounted for in fashioning programmes that will extend into the future. Future needs and demands from the elderly for recreation, medical facilities, transportation and housing may look quite different than they do currently.

Policy makers need to encourage research that provides detailed insights for sound decision-making. It is obvious that the income of older people can affect their health, and that labour force activity will have an impact on income. But the system is complex and there are subtle problems of cause and effect. Income can affect health; but to what extent does poor health affect income and asset accumulation? Coresidence with children may promote physical and emotional health, but poor health may be a cause of coresidence. To develop sound policy, it is important to understand these and other subtle interrelationships.

These considerations point to two important criteria for effective research on ageing. One is the need for surveys and related data-collection efforts that contain all the factors of interest – that is, studies of sufficient breadth so that key interrelationships across different domains can be examined. The second critical element is the need for longitudinal data. It is doubtful that we can sort out all the key cause-and-effect relationships without longitudinal information, and given the subtlety of the information needed, this usually points to a panel design with reinterviews rather than reliance on retrospective reporting, although some histories can and should be obtained.

Source: Asia Pacific Population Journal, 1997.[5]

A key area for attention is support of caregivers and caregiving. Families are the main source of care of physically dependent seniors and, as has been repeatedly stated, sometimes are simply not able to meet even basic needs. Innovative solutions and answers will have to be found. Today's seniors are 'the survivors' and have developed coping strategies. Given the economic barriers to developing the social support systems seniors require, research is needed to identify existing coping strategies and examine how they can be enhanced, even replicated by the changing social order and structures.

In conclusion, it should be recognized that the family is one institution that has survived the challenges presented over many centuries and will have to survive the 'senior challenge'. The mission needs to be to find ways to support and help the family through present uncertainty to the benefit

Too often, society and families do not realize that the senior has human needs like anyone else but, unlike younger generations, has fewer ways of meeting their needs for love and self-esteem.
© HelpAge International

of the senior, the family and society itself, recognizing that it has to meet competing demands from its members.

A major attitudinal change is required by all – not just policy makers. A new culture or vision of ageing is needed in which older persons are seen as both agents and beneficiaries of change and development. Such a vision must have a balance between supporting those who are dependent and investing in the continuing development of seniors through retraining and alternative income earning opportunities. It must recognize the family as crucial. Development of opportunities for seniors will need to be included in national plans as the potential of the mid-life and senior years can only be maximized in the absence of social upheaval and poverty. The present emphasis on educational investment in earlier years needs to be broadened to include approaches for the family as a whole and mid-life including senior years. Educational investment for the latter three aspects will release the potential of these groups for development, reduce the risk of poor health, reduce social isolation and eventually reduce the high economic and human cost of decline and isolation of families and seniors.

Well-being in families and for seniors depends on fostering age-inclusive family networks and community enterprises. Family acceptance and care of seniors will be supported by mutual benefits experienced by both parties. Efforts to improve the well-being of seniors by improved health and other measures including skills development and greater incentives for pensions and savings will increase the capacity of the family to cope. This demands coordinated and integrated approaches rather than individual, ad hoc efforts.

Integrated approaches across the generations will reduce age competition, encourage inter-generational solidarity and increase the opportunities for participation by all. If a society invests in improving the health and well-being of its members and includes support of the family on the national agenda, tomorrow's seniors, all of whom are born already, will have a better life.

As families age – family care needs to be encouraged and supported as well as educated and informed. A mixture of informal (family) care and formal care needs to emerge, with adequate systems to identify and support those in need – both financially and socially, including emotional support. Policies that address the issue should always be sensitive to the need to preserve maximum independence and dignity, foster self help and enabling environments wherever possible and be based on equity, reciprocity and interdependence between generations in the family.

Notes

1   Dr Denise Eldemire-Shearer is Professor of Community Health and Psychiatry at the University of the West Indies, Jamaica. She is Executive Secretary of Action Ageing Jamaica and Chair of the National Council on Ageing, Jamaica.

2   Heslop, A, 1995, 'Needs Assessment in Changara for the Development of Resettlement Programme in Tete Province', HelpAge International, unpublished.

3   Apt N, Koomson, Williams, N & Grieco, M 1995 'Family Finance and Doorstep Trading: Social and Economic Wellbeing of Elderly Ghanaian Female Traders', *Southern African Journal of Gerontology* 4(2), pp17–24.

4   Albert Hermalin is Professor Emeritus of Sociology and Research Scientist, Population Studies Center, Institute for Social Research, University of Michigan, 426 Thompson St, PO Box 1248, Ann Arbor, MI 48106–1248, USA.

5   The research was supported in part by a grant from the United States National Institute on Aging for research on 'Rapid Demographic Change and the Welfare of the Elderly'. A number of ideas were first presented at the conference Emerging Policy Issues on Aging in Asia and the Research Response, held at Taipei in January 1997.

9 Conflict, Humanitarian Assistance and Older People

Anthony Zwi[1]

This chapter seeks to highlight current challenges for those working with older people affected by the changing nature of conflict and of the humanitarian response. Given that conflicts are increasingly internal and specifically seek to undermine social structures, civilians of all ages are affected. The chapter raises questions about how older people are specifically affected and argues that they need to be centrally involved in determining the humanitarian response to their needs. Particular vulnerabilities are described while also drawing attention to the important potential role that older people can play in re-constituting their communities in an attempt to put behind them the distress and burdens of violent conflict. There is limited documentation on how best to identify and respond to the needs of older people, or on how best to recognize their role within affected communities. There is a great need to develop a strong evidence-base upon which more effective future policy and practice can rest.

Introduction

The Kosovo crisis of 1999 has once again highlighted for Western observers the nature, form, and impact of present-day conflicts on populations. As with the crises in (for example) Rwanda and Cambodia in recent years, there has been on the one hand a brutal internal conflict which led to heavy loss of life and the fracturing of social structures. On the other hand, a large-scale international response accompanied by a vigorous debate regarding methods and strategies. On the ground in Kosovo and surrounding territories the impact was dramatic: 850,000 refugees and close to a million internally displaced people in Kosovo itself, the latter precariously seeking to meet their basic needs and to determine what has happened to missing family members.

Older people are present among the refugees, among the internally displaced, among those left behind when the rest of their family has fled, among those killed and ill, but little, if any, attention has been devoted to their particular needs. Even less attention has been given to their potentially crucial role in re-establishing their communities and rebuilding the social fabric in the years to come.

This chapter seeks to highlight current trends in complex political emergencies, and to consider their impact on populations with a particular focus on older adults. Older people are at the same time both a vulnerable group and a resource; consideration of this ambiguity lies at the core of this chapter.

Current conflicts

In the period from the end of the Second World War to the end of the Cold War, most conflicts took place in the developing regions of the world, primarily in Africa, the Middle East, Asia and Latin America. The end of the Cold War, the break-up of the Soviet Union, and the pace and intensity of globalization, have contributed to major conflicts in Europe and the former Soviet Union, notably in Tajikistan, Chechnya, former Yugoslavia and Nagorno Karabakh.

Populations affected by armed conflict experience severe health and social consequences as a result of direct and indirect effects, including displacement, food insecurity, lack of access to basic services, and fear and distress.

Modern-day conflicts are increasingly internal, rather than between states, and often have as a prime objective the undermining of the lives and livelihoods of an opposing group. Up to 90 per cent of the casualties in current conflicts are civilians; not only young adult men but children, women and older people are all affected. Recent years have witnessed massive atrocities committed against social groups: use of chemical and biological weapons against the Kurds in Halabja, the genocide against Tutsis in Rwanda, systematic rape and ethnic repression in Bosnia, the latter also recently in Kosovo. Occurrence of conflicts in the heart of Europe has projected their effects onto television screens and front pages worldwide; this inequitable treatment of global conflicts has nevertheless served to highlight the terror, fear and anger present, alongside the immense destruction to the social and economic fabric of affected societies.

One consequence of the targeting of entire communities and their livelihoods has been the dramatic rise in numbers of forcibly displaced people. There are currently estimated to be around 30 million internally displaced people (IDPs) and 23 million refugees (those seeking refuge across international borders) – the vast majority fleeing conflict zones. Those displaced within countries have even less access to material and services support from the international community. Without crossing an international border, internal populations are assumed to be under the protection of the state; in many circumstances, however, it is the state itself, whether directly or indirectly, that is responsible for their forced movement.

Provision of resources and services to conflict-affected populations is increasingly coming under scrutiny and major gaps and limitations have been identified: the lack of attention to gender, to the needs of specific groups, to promoting equity within affected communities. Older people, as a specific population with differentiated needs, are largely invisible in discussions of priorities in relation to humanitarian assistance, as are issues of intergenerational equity. In earlier conflicts in Africa and Asia, affected populations had fewer older people. But as life expectancy improves generally, and as conflicts occur more frequently in areas of the world which have a greater proportion of older adults, they are likely to be more affected by conflict.

Older people have different exposures to situations that affect health and access to health care, and have differential power to influence decisions regarding the provision of health and other social services.

Although numbers have traditionally been assessed in order to plan and provide relief, little attention has been devoted to establishing the precise composition of refugee and IDP populations, whether in terms of age, sex, religion, local geographic origin or ethnicity. This imposes significant constraints given the differing needs and roles of groups within populations; while the elderly have particular age-related health needs, they simultaneously have the potential to contribute age-related social capital to their communities.

Addressing ageing issues in humanitarian assistance has to be done against a background of the changing patterns both of conflict and the delivery of humanitarian assistance. The number of agencies operating in these complex settings has increased hugely.[3] Despite meaning well, poorly trained service providers, and inexperienced organizations can at worst do more harm than good, with serious consequences. Furthermore, every conflict has winners and losers; the predators identify opportunities amidst the turmoil to further enrich themselves and entrench their political position.

In highly contested environments, humanitarian aid itself may become a resource over which groups compete. Recognition by the humanitarian community of these problems has led to measures to improve practice by developing codes of conduct, promoting minimum standards, and enhancing mechanisms of accountability to local populations. Promoting the derivation and uptake of good practice is always difficult; but all the more so in complex emergencies. Rapid staff turnover, failure to acknowledge the values underlying activities, lack of explicit criteria for prioritization, and underdeveloped mechanisms for involving local communities, all hamper the emergence of more effective and equitable responses. Populations which have not traditionally been prioritized, like the elderly, have to fight for visibility and attention.

The impact of conflict on the elderly

The health of older people is affected by factors which existed prior to the conflict as well as others arising more directly from the conflict environment. Both types of factor are exacerbated by forced migration and the disruption of health and social services. Conflict and non-conflict factors interact dynamically within humanitarian emergencies. The figure on page 115 conceptualizes the influences on older people's health and identifies some of their consequences.

The nature of the conflict greatly determines the extent and form of impact on health and well-being. Refugees and internally displaced persons typically experience high risk of mortality in the immediate phase following their migration; in children death results from malnutrition, diarrhoea and infectious diseases while in adults, communicable and non-communicable diseases, as well as injuries and violence, are the main causes of death.

The impact of conflict on older adults has been poorly researched and documented, but is, to some extent, predictable. Many older people, even in 'healthy' societies, will have health problems of varying degrees: non-communicable and chronic disorders, disabilities and frailty, and mental health decline. It is to be anticipated, therefore, that during periods of intense conflict and rapid forced migration, access to the services that form part of the social and health response to these conditions, will decline. Services may themselves be targeted or may collapse as a result of inadequate resources; personnel may flee to safer areas; people, especially the elderly, may be unable to get to health facilities in the absence of functioning transport support systems.

Older people may suffer particularly poor health, primarily from non-communicable diseases and disabilities. They are vulnerable not only to the direct stresses, strains and destruction of the conflict itself, but are also greatly affected by the conflict-influenced disruption, and in some cases, outright destruction, of health-related services. The supply of drugs, for example, will typically be adversely affected by conflict: their distribution will be hampered, the availability of trained personnel to diagnose and prescribe will decline, and gaining access to those services which do exist may be compromised. Older people who flee their homes are likely to lose their access to treatments necessary to maintain their state of health. A study supported by Help the Aged, UK, among Tigrean refugees in Sudan found also that many older people were unable to move with their families, and had remained behind despite the relative lack of social and service supports.

The usual institutions of social support, notably the family, may be severely disrupted, and the priorities of younger adults may be shifted to ensuring the survival and integrity of their children rather than older family members. Reduced access to medical care transforms treatable conditions, such as hypertension, diabetes, and chest disease, into potential killers. Among older people fleeing Kosovo, other problems such as dehydration occurred and hypothermia and confusion were frequent

given the poor conditions in which many people were initially housed. Food insecurity, overcrowding, poor access to water and sanitation, increase susceptibility to illness, while the provision of care in focused areas poses particular problems for those less mobile.

Despite the considerable experience of relief agencies in providing services to affected populations, there remains limited awareness and commitment to meeting the needs of specific sub-groups within the population. Older people are virtually invisible in priority setting – despite their presence among affected populations. Recently, however, some agencies have started to give serious attention to humanitarian assistance and older people. The European Commission Humanitarian Office (ECHO) is investing in the development of guidelines and the UNHCR are working on staff training on best practice in working with older refugees.

Current critiques of humanitarian aid point to significant weaknesses in the provision of emergency assistance: best practice is infrequently employed; clear policy objectives are often lacking; mechanisms for working with new players such as the military and the private sector remain inadequately developed.[2] The outcomes of poor quality services include increased morbidity, mortality, disability, further spread of communicable diseases, community dissatisfaction and breakdown and psychosocial distress.

Despite recognition that the accountability of relief efforts to affected populations should be enhanced, mechanisms to assure this are in their infancy. Efforts to promote good practice through the adoption of a Code of Conduct for agencies providing humanitarian services, and through the Sphere Project[4] offer important opportunities to focus attention on vulnerable sub-groups such as older people. An emerging problem among those promoting value-for-money responses is the implicit, and at times, explicit, assumption that the life of an older person is worth much less than that of the young.

As well as being criticized on human rights grounds, this valuation may fail to take account of the roles played by older people in caring for the family, in providing role models for the young, and in providing the cement with which communities maintain their structure. Older people may be seen as a burden, but they are also the receptacles for the community's history, culture and wisdom, and may offer much undervalued balm.

Ongoing humanitarian challenges include understanding how best to upgrade host population health services alongside efforts to improve those available to refugees, how to most humanely and efficiently provide good quality services, and how to maintain the role of communities in structuring both the determination of priorities and the pattern of service provision. Key elements of an ethical approach include maximizing benefit and minimizing harm, treating individuals with appropriate care and dignity, and recognizing the roles they play and have bestowed upon them by their communities.

Although older people may not specifically be targeted by opposing groups, they may suffer the stress and distress of seeing younger family members seized, tortured or shot. Not only the conflict but its aftermath may impinge upon older people; many older people who return after the conflict to areas in which they once lived, may be especially vulnerable. In Tete Province, Mozambique, older people were in some villages isolated and separated from their families. In situations where no family members were present it was particularly difficult to ensure local support. In Mozambique, even with food distribution points nearby, there were access difficulties for older and disabled people. In eastern Slavonia, an area handed to Croatia after the Dayton peace accords, Serb families in some cases left their elders behind to maintain their property and claims upon it, while younger members went to the Federal Republic of Yugoslavia to seek alternatives. Many elders remaining in Croatia had health needs that were not met due to their own isolation and fear, and because of discrimination by service providers.

Older people remain a key resource for communities: they are the repositories of stories, of culture, of knowledge and of history. These are essential elements necessary not only to maintain but also to rebuild societal structures. Especially in societies emerging from destructive and disruptive periods, elders and traditional structures can help re-establish a sense of community, necessary to rebuilding social capital and moving ahead.

The aid community generates an extremely valuable set of evaluations and critiques of current practice, but has yet to develop effective and efficient means of disseminating and generalizing from field experience. Knowledge of dealing with older people is extremely limited: all we have are a few cases of how different agencies have addressed these concerns. Improving opportunities and funding to facilitate academic–NGO linkages and to establish mechanisms for disseminating and debating key findings with donors, host governments, service providers, and representatives of affected communities, will increase the likelihood of benefits to other and future populations.

A persistent challenge to humanitarian workers is to learn lessons and identify good practice from the vast foundation of field experience present within agencies. In the sphere of complex emergencies and older adults, these issues are all the more urgent.

Responding to the needs of older people in emergencies

A recent HelpAge International workshop stated that:

> 'in an emergency situation, older people are frequently overlooked with regard to the provision of basic needs due to their lack of access (social, political, physical), invisibility and marginalization. Older people must

At the age of 58, Adera Karwirungu looked after ten orphans in Rwanda in the aftermath of the conflict.
© John Lowrie/ HelpAge International

be involved in planning, implementation, monitoring and evaluation of the provision of basic needs'.

This point is reiterated in the figure below (page 115), which highlights the central role of affected communities in analysing and influencing the humanitarian response to their needs. Taking this forward is complex, however, given that older people are not a homogeneous group and are divided by gender, ethnicity, class and level

Learning about older people in humanitarian emergencies

HelpAge International has been listening to and working with older people in different emergency situations for the past 15 years. Drawing on experiences, which range from natural disasters to complex political emergencies, they have identified a number of lessons about working with older people in emergencies.

Older people's vulnerability in emergencies

Isolation is possibly the most important factor in creating vulnerability. Older people find that the problems they face are compounded by the destruction of their families and communities and with them the support mechanisms on which they had relied. Isolated older people are often left to fend for themselves as those around them struggle to ensure their own survival and that of their families.

The capacity of the community to take on the care of its vulnerable members is seriously compromised by the lack of food, medical, material and human resources associated with emergencies. Many older people find themselves looking after young dependants whose parents are missing; others live alone or as vulnerable couples relying on hard-pressed neighbours and the support services for the essentials that they need. The very limited opportunities that the fittest find to supplement their incomes are rarely open to the more vulnerable.

While in principle older people may be recognized as a vulnerable group, in practice their particular needs are rarely met by the providers of emergency services. Chronic health, mobility and mental problems are not seen as a priority in most emergencies and yet it is these very factors that make it difficult for older people to support themselves through the emergency.

Reducing the vulnerability of older people is not primarily about creating special services for older people but about ensuring that older people have equal access to all mainstream services alongside other vulnerable groups. Ensuring this access for older people relies on raising the awareness of service providers to the particular problems and obstacles they face with a view to promoting relevant changes in policy and practice.

How older people characterize their problems

The key problems identified and prioritized by older people in the 21 emergency situations reviewed by HelpAge International, fall into five categories: Health; Family and social; Economic and legal; Mobility; Basic needs.

Health
- Access to health (mobility, distance to centralized services, absence of community health systems, loss of regular health facilities).
- Poor age-specific health services (absence of medication for chronic disorders, especially those disorders that will become acute without regular treatment).
- Food and nutrition (reluctance to include older people in supplementary feeding programmes; unsuitability of available food for older people; distance to centralized distribution points; insufficient strength to compete for limited food supplies).
- Water and sanitation (distance to water points; insufficient strength to compete for the limited water supplies; rapid debilitation caused by diarrhoea).
- Psychosocial needs (trauma and stress; disorientation caused by sudden changes; distress caused by sudden changes in social status).

Family and social
- Separation/loss of family (isolation, bereavement, loss of carer).
- Dependants (older people left with younger children or other dependants in the absence of middle generation adults).
- Destruction of social structures (loss of family and community, loss of social supports, changes in the role and status of older people).

- Protection/security (theft, dispossession, physical abuse, sexual abuse/prostitution).
- Loss of respect and social status as cultural and social norms break down.
- Abandonment.

Economic and legal
- Income (inflation, loss of employment, no pensions, loss of markets, lack of access to credit schemes).
- Land (displacement, dispossession).
- Advice and information (legal rights, health advice, information on credit, repatriation, trespass, inheritance).
- Loss of documentation (some older people have never had identity documentation, some have had their ID stolen, some older people do not understand the nature of and need for personal documentation and become excluded from systems that require it).
- Skills training (need for literacy, numeracy and new language skills in changed situations; need for new practical and income generating skills).

Mobility
- Incapacity (housebound older people are left behind or are unable to gain access to essential services).
- Population movement and transport (older people are unable to mount trucks; older people slower than others and get left behind; disadvantaged by distance to nearest essential services in the absence of regular transport facilities).

Older people and conflict: factors influencing health

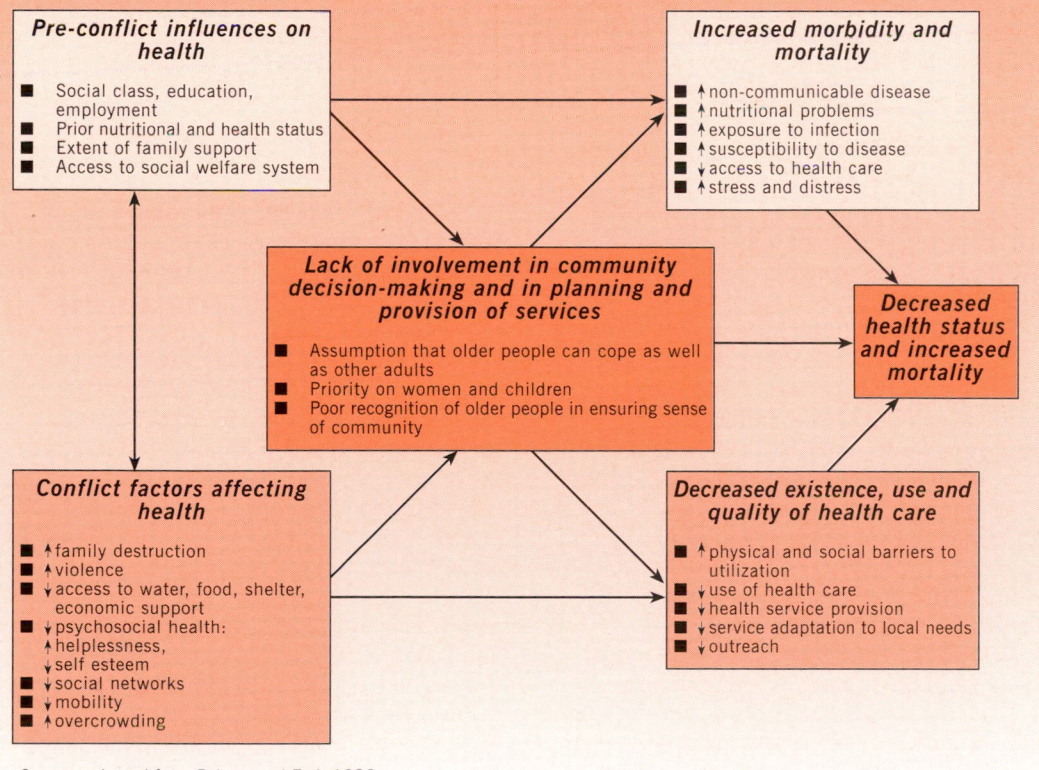

Source: adapted from Palmer and Zwi, 1998

- Disability (need for basic mobility aids, such as prosthesis or spectacles lost in the emergency; need for physiotherapy and other exercise opportunities to reduce joint and muscle pain).

Basic needs
- Shelter (materials and support with labour in rebuilding shelter).
- Fuel (assistance with fuel collection, linking older people with neighbours or other individuals for shared cooking arrangements).
- Basic need items (including clothing, blankets, pots, pans, other kitchen and household equipment; need for mattress or raised sleeping area to avoid acute joint and muscle pain caused by sleeping on the ground).

The capacities and contribution of all older people in emergencies

In emergencies where the regular leadership structures have been disrupted or destroyed older people are well-placed, given their length of experience and knowledge of the community, to step into leadership roles. Where older people still hold control of economic assets and decision-making, they may be able to play a leadership role in conflict resolution and problem solving.

Older people may bring knowledge of traditional coping strategies and alternative technologies and medicines to the emergency situation. They can help to preserve the cultural and social identity of communities in crisis and may be able to influence younger generations in peace building, community justice and other activities aimed at regenerating broken communities.

Older people are more likely to be givers than receivers of aid. They will often be carers for young and disabled family members in the absence of other able adults. Support for older people's basic needs such as health care, income generation, skills training, bring benefits to their family and immediate community.

Recognition of the special contribution of older people in emergencies should not result in devolution of yet more responsibilities to older people without a corresponding increase in the support they need to meet them.

Source: HelpAge International

---

of mental and physical capacity. Precisely how best to involve them is poorly explored and documented and warrants in-depth research.

It is also important to recognize that older people may play both positive and negative roles within their communities. While they may help rebuild the sense of community and of social support and networks (social capital), they may also at times contribute to the poisoning of relationships between people by dredging up biased perspectives of the past and promoting a particularly warped view of history. In such settings they may contribute to what has been termed 'anti-social capital' – a term which recognizes that not all social structures of networking and support are necessarily positive.

Agencies providing support to older people may face technical constraints. It is only recently that understanding has increased on how to measure nutritional status in older people in developing countries.[5] Furthermore, a population of older people embedded within a general population will include a wide range of states of health, of mental and physical capacity, of social support, and of need. Identifying and responding to the needs of those most vulnerable and those at greatest risk of death, disability and morbidity presents significant problems to humanitarian agencies. Relief agencies typically prioritize young children and women; responding appropriately to the needs of older people warrants debate and negotiation. Older people may exhibit particular needs which require redress: dealing with their chronic health problems, ensuring that available health services can be brought to where older people are located; and devoting attention to confusion and disorientation which exacerbate vulnerability, dependency and frailty.

For older people, and their families, the fear of death, dying and burial in a foreign land is of immense significance: responding to this fear must be a priority for any agencies working with affected populations and wishing to re-establish their sense of humanity and dignity despite adversity.

Notes

1   Anthony Zwi is head of the Health Policy Unit at the London School of Hygiene and Tropical Medicine (contact details: LSHTM, Keppel St, London, WC1E 7HT, UK; email a.zwi@lshtm.ac.uk).
2   There were over 240 NGOs working in and around Rwanda in the aftermath of the genocide; 100 agencies were providing humanitarian assistance to the Kosovar Albanians in mid 1999.
3   Key problems identified in the evaluation of the humanitarian response to Rwanda include lack of prior investment in disaster preparedness, lack of coordination between UN, humanitarian agencies, host-governments and the military, poor quality health care delivery, inadequate accountability of agencies, poor camp security, inadequate food distribution practices and poorly coordinated registration of refugees, delays in providing compensation to host-communities absorbing the costs of providing care to displaced populations.
4   The Sphere Project is a global initiative involving widespread collaboration of North American and European non-governmental agencies, as well as the International Federation of Red Cross and Red Crescent Societies, in seeking to develop and promote minimum standards for humanitarian assistance. Draft standards have recently been produced for pilot testing: these cover nutrition and food security, health services, water and sanitation, and shelter.
5   See HelpAge International and London School of Hygiene and Tropical Medicine, Gregory, K and Peachey, K (eds), 1997, 'Assessing the Nutritional Vulnerability of Older People in Developing Countries', report on symposium held on 23–24 September.

Part II

The State of the World's Older People

10

The Situation of Older People in Latin America and the Caribbean

Martha Pelaez and Alberto Palloni[1]

Introduction

When we speak of 'ageing societies', the images brought to mind differ sharply. In some cases, they revolve around nearly bankrupt pension or social security systems and around families physically and economically overburdened with the responsibility of simultaneously caring for their very young children as well as their very old family members. In others, we see societies overloaded with unsatisfied health care demands of the chronically ill, functionally disabled and the mentally and physically impaired. In yet others, references to ageing evoke rumblings about stagnant economies, snail-paced increases in productivity, heavy taxation burdens, conservative ideologies and dismal mobility prospects for younger generations. Each of these issues corresponds to a dimension of the ageing process. What societies choose to emphasize, what researchers identify as salient or interesting, and what policy makers conceive as strategic will vary across countries and time-periods.

These different conceptions about the ageing population's impact upon societies require an examination of the different dimensions of the ageing process in the context of developing countries. They also require a radical shift in the way that we think about investing in older persons. Developing nations need to carefully examine the contributions that older people make to the economic development of their societies and need to invest in the development of adequate health care and health promotion for older people. Without health the years gained through the miracle of longevity in the 20th century become a burden to individuals, family and societies. With adequate health, older people can and will become part of the development formula.

> '*Developing nations need to carefully examine the contributions that older people make to the economic development of their societies and need to invest in the development of adequate health care and health promotion for older people. Without health the years gained through the miracle of longevity in the 20th century become a burden to individuals, family and societies. With adequate health, older people can and will become part of the development formula.*'

The demographic dimension of ageing in Latin America and the Caribbean

Population ageing is, first of all, a demographic phenomenon. An 'aged' society is one whose population is skewed towards older age groups, or one where there is a smaller proportion of people below age 15. When the population aged 60 plus exceeds 10–12 per cent of the population in a particular society, we characterize this society as relatively old.

With a few exceptions (Argentina, Cuba, Puerto Rico and Uruguay), countries in Latin America and the Caribbean experienced high levels of fertility until around 1965–1970, when a precipitous decline in fertility began to take place in all but a handful of nations (mostly in Central America, Bolivia, Peru and Ecuador). But

mortality levels in many countries had begun to fall before 1950, although the bulk of the decline took place during the Post-Second World War era. As of 1990, most countries in Latin America and the Caribbean have experienced a combination of recent sharp fertility reductions and of less recent, but equally sharp, reductions in mortality.

In 1950, with the exception of Uruguay, the older population made up less than 10–12 per cent of the total population everywhere in Latin America and the Caribbean. However, this demographic make-up is rapidly changing. According to the latest observed statistics in 1990, Argentina, Cuba, Barbados and Puerto Rico joined the ranks with Uruguay, and projections suggest that only four countries in the region will have less than 10–12 per cent of their population in the 60 plus range by 2025.

The demographic momentum of ageing in the region is rooted in the history of demographic growth experienced during the past fifty years. The rate of increase of the older population will remain high or will increase, and so will the mean and median ages of the population. The fraction of the population represented by older persons could increase or decrease, depending on future trends in fertility. The most likely scenario is that this fraction will also undergo an upward swing as fertility levels plummet in an irreversible process. Neither of these driving forces can be manipulated, as they are the result of history or are a result of the larger macro process – a process that is unlikely to be easily tinkered with. Policymaking efforts need to concentrate on making the extra years of life worth living for the individual, for the family and for society.

To fully understand the trajectory of the population aged 60 plus during the period 1990–2025 we need to focus on three components:

- Changes in fertility from 1930–1965
- Changes in mortality under the age of 60 from 1930–1965
- Changes in mortality for the 60 plus population from 1990–2025

Two consequences of the trends for ageing in Latin America are worth noting. First, individuals who attain their sixtieth birthday between 2000 and 2025 were born during a surge of fertility during the years 1950–1965. Thus, the rate of increase of the group aged 60 plus will grow, partly as a result of past, though fleeting, higher fertility levels. Second, and most important, the older people who will hold their sixtieth birthday between 2000 and 2025 are the beneficiaries of unusually large improvements in survival, particularly during early childhood. Thus, individuals born, say, in 1960 experienced much lower levels of early child mortality than those born in 1955. This will increase the relative size of the cohort of people reaching age 60 in 2025 compared to those who will reach the age of 60 in the year 2020.

> *'Policymaking efforts need to concentrate on making the extra years of life worth living for the individual, for the family and for society.'*

However, the relative size of the ageing population does not tell us much about the potential social and economic consequences that lie ahead for an ageing population to deal with. The *composition* of the older population – its characteristics of age, gender, social class and rural–urban residence – has to be taken into account.

Age composition

Individuals of 60 years old and more form a heterogeneous population in terms of their health and functional status, their demand for health and care services and their social, economic and emotional needs.

While the majority of men aged 60–69 are at least partially-active in the labour force, participation rates decrease markedly thereafter, and the consequent increase in economic dependence that follows from withdrawal from labour force markets appears. In addition, the oldest-old are

more likely to have lost a spouse, less likely to have access to a social network of support and more likely to depend on their closest family member. By 2025, the fraction of the population aged 80 plus among those aged 60 plus will exceed 10 per cent in all Latin American and Caribbean countries, and in some of them, this increase will be substantial.

Gender composition

In countries of this region, ageing is, above all, a gender issue. This is because the populations aged 60 plus and 80 plus are disproportionately composed of females. Estimates for 1995 and projected values for 2025 indicate that fully two-thirds of the population older than 75 will be women.

The most vulnerable among the older population in the region are already women, particularly widowed women. Their vulnerability is first, and above all, a result of their lesser power to secure adequate economic resources. This is worsened by restrictions in pension programmes related to survivors' benefits. As a result, older populations in the region contain a sizeable component of women living near or below the poverty line.

Secondly, women's health status appears to be much worse than that of males at comparable ages. This suggests the existence of a larger potential demand for formal and informal sources of care. If the gender gap continues to widen as life expectancy increases, then ageing in the region will be associated with a large demand arising from special needs of older women.

Socio-economic class composition

To the extent that illiteracy among older persons reflects poverty, the following figures show the composition of the older population by literacy levels in a number of countries in the region around 1990.

Percentage of those aged 60 and over who are literate		
Country	Male (%)	Female (%)
Argentina	93	91
Bolivia	59	32
Brazil	59	54
Colombia	73	64
Guatemala	43	31
Honduras	39	33
Jamaica	62	73
Mexico	71	59

These figures are useful only to gauge the extent of the economic problem of older populations. They indicate that the prevalence of poverty among older persons will be very varied across countries in the region, thus requiring sharply different policy approaches.

Second, countries in Latin America and the Caribbean will experience rapid ageing under conditions that guarantee higher levels of poverty among older persons when compared with the experiences of developed countries at similar points in their transition to an older age-structure. This means that ageing in countries in the region will occur more quickly, during a time when the general level of well-being among the population has not yet reached the levels attained elsewhere. Again, this suggests the need for very different policies than those that were appropriate in developed societies.

Rural–urban residence

A unique characteristic of the ageing process in the region is the relatively high concentration of older persons in rural areas. Because it is those who are young and still active in the labour force who migrate from rural to urban areas, current age distributions in rural areas will be biased toward older people.

Most countries in the region are projected to have between 15 and 40 per cent of their total older population in rural areas. Rural populations form part of fragile labour markets, and individuals who live there will only receive marginal income support from public programmes and will not participate at all in existing private schemes. To the extent that younger groups continue the rural-to-urban migration, alternative sources of social, economic and emotional support for older persons will be less available in rural areas than they are in urban areas.

The health dimension of ageing

Ageing societies face important dilemmas, but none of them is as salient and consequential as the health conditions of the older population.

Because early life conditions influence health and disability in later life, there are likely to be important changes in the distribution of the older population's disability and health status. The most likely scenario is one where health and disability status will steadily worsen as those older people who were the first to experience the decline in mortality approach older ages.

'Because early life conditions influence health and disability in later life, there are likely to be important changes in the distribution of the older population's disability and health status. The most likely scenario is one where health and disability status will steadily worsen as those older people who were the first to experience the decline in mortality approach older ages.'

Improvements in survival during early life are often associated with medical innovations but not always accompanied by proportionate changes in standards of living. The already strong differentials between standards of health and disability among older people in poorer and better-off groups, men and women, people living in rural and urban areas, are likely to increase with the ageing process.

This calls for careful evaluation and monitoring of health care services to older persons and regular monitoring of their health and capabilities. Future increases in life expectancy at age 60 in Latin American and Caribbean countries must be accompanied by a corresponding strengthening of efforts as they concern other determinants of good health. Otherwise, a larger number of years of life gained by older persons will be spent in disability or ill health. This will correspond to a burden not only to the older persons themselves but also to their families, other generations and society.

An illustration may help to place these considerations in perspective. The prevalence of respiratory tuberculosis (TB) (latent) among adults in Latin America is fairly high. Due to the introduction of mass vaccination against TB the late 1940s and to improved exposure conditions, it is very likely that prevalence of latent TB increases with age. The highest prevalence is thus among the oldest people. Respiratory TB is very sensitive to changes in nutrition. Thus, if the older population experiences a reduced standard of living, there will be increases in active respiratory TB and, consequently, of its rate of transmission. It is obvious that increases in active TB will not *improve* health and functional status among the older persons afflicted by it. If an increase of one year of life after age 60 (that might be generated by improvements in the treatment of congestive heart disease, for instance) is unaccompanied by parallel improvements in nutrition among poor older people, this will not translate in a proportionate increase in healthy life.

Although an individual may not have control over early life experiences or other factors such as childhood diseases, poverty or educational level, actions taken during the remaining years of life greatly affect health in older age. Information about healthy lifestyles needs to be promoted; this includes the importance of a balanced and healthy diet, adequate exercise, the avoidance of smoking and the avoidance of excessive alcohol consumption. In addition, policy decisions that encourage healthy, active ageing must include the creation of supportive social and environmental conditions throughout life. Equitable and efficient provision of basic services and the participation and inclusion of all in society are essential components of realizing the opportunities and reaching the potential of a rapidly ageing world.

The family dimension

Most older persons' support in developing countries comes largely from exchanges between the older person and his/her family members. Indeed, it has been argued that high fertility levels are maintained in more traditional societies to insure that there are younger family members to support the older members after they are no longer able to work or perform activities in the interest of the family. Although the importance of this issue relative to other determinants of high fertility is unclear, it is believed by some to be a very important influence on fertility.

Marital patterns of older persons are an important feature of family life since the conjugal union is central to a family's structure. These patterns eventually determine what shape intergenerational relations, inheritance and residence patterns, expectations of responsibility and rights, independence, interdependence and gender roles will take. They are the key factors determining whether a family is extended or nuclear. Indeed, they are the foundation of all residential arrangements involving older persons.

A majority of older men tend to be married, while this is much less likely for women. In fact, as a rule, around 15 per cent of men and around 40 per cent of women or more tend to be widowed. Thus, residential arrangements which include older people are disproportionately composed of unmarried women or women not in a partnership. This imbalance increases with age and is likely to be continued in the near future.

How have living arrangements in the region changed over time? Using Brazil's censuses from 1960 and 1980, it is shown that, among men aged 55 and over, the proportion of men living alone only increases from 3.8 to 5.5 per cent, whereas the fraction of all females living alone increases from 5.1 to 8.8 per cent. The trend is even more marked in the unmarried population. Thus, the proportion of unmarried men aged 55 and over living alone increases from 18 to 29 per cent, whereas among females the increase is from 8.8 to 16.4 per cent. The bulk of the increase is attributed to a decrease in the fraction of older persons living in three-generation families. The case of Brazil is telling, since by 1980, the bulk of the fertility decline had not yet taken place, whereas the mortality decline had already made its major impact. This means that one cannot attribute these observed changes to demographic constraints alone. Availability of housing or changing preferences by older or younger people must also be part of the explanation.

'Each dimension of ageing demands an understanding of the multifaceted character of ageing. Single sector policy responses will be inadequate.'

In many countries in the region, joint co-residence is part of an exchange that provides material goods (costs of housing, food sharing etc) and emotional and psychological support (company, care and attention). Therefore, the trend towards older persons living alone may have negative consequences, and it will be even worse in light of inadequate pension systems.

Policy issues: health expenditures, social security and quality of life

What are the most relevant policy issues identified by our review of the demographic transition in Latin America and the Caribbean? Each dimension of ageing demands an understanding of the multifaceted character of ageing. Single sector policy responses will be inadequate. However, to properly take account of ageing in national policy, governments in Latin America and the Caribbean must:

- acknowledge the contributions of older persons and combat age discrimination in all sectors of society;
- promote policies and programmes that enable older persons to be active participants in the development process;
- promote lifelong learning opportunities;
- ensure access to health care and rehabilitation services for older persons;
- target the low-income older person and the rural elder who, due to conditions associated with health status and disability, access to health care services and labour market participation, are likely to suffer from more health problems than elders from higher socioeconomic strata;
- promote income security policies to provide adequate income protection for older persons through reliable public and private pension arrangements;
- target older women for income generating programmes and dedicate resources to the health promotion and protection of older women; and
- develop community-based interventions to support family caregivers.

Note

1   Dr Martha Pelaez is Regional Advisor on Aging and Health at the Pan American Health Organization, regional office of the World Health Organization in the Americas, based in Washington, DC. Dr Alberto Palloni is Professor of Demography at the Center for Demography and Ecology, University of Wisconsin-Madison. Martha Pelaez and Alberto Palloni are collaborating with a multidisciplinary team of researchers in a population study on the Health and Wellbeing of Older Persons in eight urban centres in Latin America and the Caribbean.

11

The Situation of Older People in Rural and Urban India

Shubha Soneja[1]

India is a country experiencing substantial migration from rural to urban areas. This is having a profound impact on the lives of many older people, whether they choose to move to the cities or remain in the countryside.

Together with declining fertility and mortality rates, population migration is the third critical determinant of the demographic transition currently underway. International migration has been a major feature of recent decades, but so too has the large-scale movement from rural to urban areas in many developing countries.

India has been in the past and remains today a predominantly agrarian society. According to the 1991 census, 76.3 per cent of the total population were living in rural areas. The concentration of older people in the countryside was even more striking, with over 80 per cent in rural areas.[2] However, the process of urbanization in India is accelerating, and the projection is that by 2001 the proportion of the rural

Dyeing sarees on racks, Pali, India. © Jeremy Horner/ Panos Pictures

population will be down to 66 per cent overall, with 72 per cent of older people still in the rural areas. It is therefore not surprising that the rural population is older than that of the urban areas.[3]

The social implications of this migration can be profound. The combined effects of changes at the level of the family and the community, gradual rural decline and the corresponding increase in urban areas (often slum environments on the edge of the growing cities) are presenting great challenges to India's 'grey population'.

At an individual level the process of migration usually begins with a single person, often a man, moving into the city. He is later joined by his wife and children, often leaving his parents behind. Thus a new household is formed, which grows into a joint household with the arrival of sons' wives. Meanwhile the elderly parents are left to fend for themselves without the social and emotional support of their children.

Older people in rural areas

The elderly who are left behind in the rural areas are largely landless labourers, surviving on day to day earnings, without any long-term savings. They are no longer physically strong because of their age, and hence their capacity for work is progressively reduced. In the unorganized sector there is no retirement age, and though the government recognizes old age poverty, the pension scheme for the destitute elderly reaches only 2.76 million out of an estimated 28 million below the poverty line.

Nor is earning a daily income just a matter of enough for food. Health care is relatively inaccessible; in some cases one Primary Health Centre covers up to 10 villages, making it unfeasible for an older patient to travel to consult a doctor and get free treatment.

For the majority living in the rural areas, inadequate income and poverty lead to dependency on breadwinning sons.[4] According to the 1991 census, the old age dependency ratio is higher in the rural areas, at 13.26 per cent, than it is in the urban areas at 9.68 per cent. Even though support of dependent parents is still considered the responsibility of the eldest son, this also depends on a number of factors, including the status of the children's employment, cost of urban living and the size of the son's own dependent family.[5]

Older people in rural areas thus report a poorer quality of life than those in the cities and towns.[6] They are severely disadvantaged by economic hardships, unresolved chronic health problems, functional impairment and illiteracy.[7]

> 'Older people in rural areas thus report a poorer quality of life than those in the cities and towns. They are severely disadvantaged by economic hardships, unresolved chronic health problems, functional impairment and illiteracy.'

Older people in urban settings

If older people move with their children into the urban areas, they face a new set of problems. The family unit typically settles in unplanned, congested areas in and around the cities. The first problem encountered by the family is the lack of space arising from the insufficiency of adequate housing facilities for the arriving migrants.[8]

A report on slums surrounding New Delhi describes the living conditions of elderly residents. Many dwellings consist of only one room, in which families of upwards of 4–6 people are living. The lack of space in the dwelling caused some older family members to sleep outside. Very few houses have yards or gardens. Water and sanitation consists of public taps and toilets, though many older people do not use the latter because of the charges. Environmental pollution, a hazard for urban dwellers of all generations, is especially problematic for the ageing.[9]

Loneliness and isolation are further difficulties to be faced by older people. The younger generation of the family goes to work every day, leaving older people at home. This is increasingly likely to include the female members of the family who, traditionally, have taken on the role of care giving for older relatives. The older people themselves are unlikely to be able to find work other than unskilled daily paid labour, which may be beyond their physical capacity. It is difficult to interact with other households in the neighbourhood, because of cultural and language barriers. People from all parts of India are settling around the large cities, and slum neighbourhoods are therefore extremely heterogeneous. Thus inaction and a lack of interaction produce a growing feeling of isolation.

> *'One urban survey found that younger family members attached high value to the presence of ageing parents in the family because of their childminding role.'*

The primary contribution which older people are able to make to their family is to act as caretakers of the home while younger family members are at work. Cooking, looking after grandchildren and bringing them from school are tasks which increasing age makes more difficult. Nevertheless older people continue to perform them out of a feeling that their very survival as valued family members depends on their ability to do so. One urban survey found that younger family members attached high value to the presence of ageing parents in the family because of their childminding role.[10]

> *'However, the (as yet fragmentary) evidence points to the major risks created by poverty, particularly for older people. While urbanization has not created old age poverty, its impact seems to have been a further erosion of the capacity of older and younger generations within poor families to offer each other adequate support.'*

Increasing frailty of older members is a major risk factor for the material survival of the family group. Although medical consultation may be free, the cost of medicines can be prohibitive, and health facilities are often remote from slum areas. Public transport is crowded and there are no fare exemptions for older people. Furthermore, the implication for younger relatives accompanying older people to get medical advice is the loss of a day's income, which is simply not sustainable for families below the poverty line.

It is therefore not surprising that high levels of depression are reported amongst older urban dwellers. One survey discovered that over half the respondents suffered from depression, while over two-thirds expressed feelings of material dependency on their families. A similar proportion felt anxious because of their health status and strained family relations. Another study found high levels of insecurity and acute fears of the possibility of abandonment. Some respondents reported physical and emotional abuse from their families.[11]

The urbanization and industrialization of India in recent decades have had a radical impact on all generations, and older people have not been exempt from the impact of these changes. Whether they have remained in the rural areas, migrated to urban areas, or indeed themselves grown old in India's expanding towns and cities the position of elderly people has not been improved by urbanization. For example, though family structures have been maintained in many urban settings, this continuity in itself tells us little about the roles and functions of different generations, and intergenerational support, within family units. However, the (as yet fragmentary) evidence points to the major risks created by poverty, particularly for older people. While urbanization has not created old age poverty, its impact seems to have been a further erosion of the capacity of older and younger generations within poor families to offer each other adequate support.

Notes

1   Dr Shubha Soneja is Head of Research and Development with HelpAge India.
2   Census of India, 1988, *Report of Expert Committee on Population Projections*, Occasional Paper 4. Office of Registrar General and Census

Commissioner, Government of India.

3 Sharma, S P and Xenos, P, 1992, *Ageing in India. Demographic Background and Analysis based on Census Materials*, Occasional Paper 2, Office of Registrar General and Census Commissioner, Government of India.

4 Kumar, V, 1998, 'Responses to the Issues of Ageing. The Indian Scenario', *Bold* 8(3).

5 Banerjee, S K, 1998, 'Modernisation and Ageing in the near future. A future of Asian Countries', *Ageing and Society* 6.

6 Laswarmoorthy, M and Chadha, N K, 1997, 'Quality of life of the aged in Tamil Nadu' in Chadha, N K (ed), *Ageing and the Aged. Challenges before Indian Gerontology*. New Delhi.

7 Prakash, J, 1994, 'Gender Ageing: Psychosocial Issues' in Ramachandran and Shah (eds), *Public Health Implications of Ageing in India*, ICMR, New Delhi.

8 Banerjee, 1996, op cit.

9 May, R, *Report on Older People's Living Conditions*, Institute of Public Administration, New York, forthcoming.

10 DeSouza, A, quoted in Ara, S, 1994, *Old Age among Slum Dwellers*, HelpAge India, New Delhi, p17.

11 May, forthcoming, op cit.

12 The Situation of Older People in Cambodia[1]

HelpAge International and the Cambodian Ministry of Social Affairs, Labour and Veteran Affairs

Despite the war and trauma of the past, Cambodian traditions of respecting older people, providing care, and using their special knowledge and skills have remained remarkably strong, especially in rural areas. Older people still work to support themselves and their families for as long as they are physically able to. Children (mainly daughters) and relatives are still the primary source of support for parents who are no longer able to work, and relationships with neighbours still form an informal network of support (although at a very low standard of living) for the most vulnerable. In turn, older people make an important contribution to the household in terms of income, childcare, housework, crafts and home gardening. Older people also play a crucial role in organizing and supervising religious events and village projects. Both old and young see older people as responsible for guiding the young people in the village to live moral and productive lives as members of the community, although older women are less likely to be recognized as productive members of the community.

The real threats to the livelihood and dignity of older people in Cambodia are not from the past but from the present and future. The two most serious problems at present are poverty and lack of competent and affordable healthcare.

Poverty

For the vast majority of older people in Cambodia who are not rich and who work for their living, declining physical strength means declining income and therefore a declining quality of life. Although in most cases children and relatives do try to provide support, many are too poor themselves to be able to give adequate support to their parents. In addition, a certain number of older people are childless or lost their children during the wars of the 1970s and 80s, and therefore have no one to support them as they become older. For these reasons, there are older people in Cambodia who are living in conditions of poverty, hardship, and fear of the future.

Lack of affordable healthcare

The huge expense of medical care very often puts poor older people in the position of having to choose between their own lives and the livelihoods of their families. The majority of older people in the rural areas have to go without the basic aids for sight and eating which would greatly improve their standard of living because they are too poor and such aids are not easily available in the countryside.

For the near future, unlike most other Southeast Asian countries, Cambodia is not facing the challenge of a rapidly increasing number of older people and a decreasing number of younger people who can support

them. However there are certain national trends which are already beginning to affect the situation of older people.

Rural poverty

As older people have divided their land among their children, the land holdings which were sufficient to support a family in the 1980s are no longer sufficient to support the families of their grown children and their parents. This is not a problem for those families who can afford fertilizer and pumps to increase the productivity of the land, or who can diversify into business. However for families without the necessary capital, the division of land may mean a fall in living standards for both children and parents.

Unequal geographic development

Although Cambodia is not yet experiencing the large scale rural to urban migration that many developing countries have, unequal geographic development is already apparent. In the two poorest villages studied (in Kampot and Battambang), poverty and lack of opportunity forces young people to abandon their children and parents to look for work elsewhere – generally logging in Koh Kong, or selling labour in Thailand. While some children come back or send money, others disappear, leaving ageing parents to care for small grandchildren.

AIDS

Cambodia is in the beginning stages of the AIDS epidemic. In the near future, a large number of young people will become sick and die from AIDS, and it is their parents who will have to care for them and the orphaned grandchildren. AIDS will also deprive many older people of children to support them in their old age.

A more subtle threat is to the social position of older people

New patterns of education and entertainment

Although older people are still regarded as sources of advice, primary education is making grandchildren more "educated" than their illiterate grandparents. Particularly in urban areas, older people have to compete with video and TV for their family's attention.

Out-dated skills

While younger people say they respect older people for their knowledge and skills, few young people want to learn *krama* weaving or basket making because there is no market for the products. Traditional midwifery and Khmer medicine cannot compete with modern medicine. While this change is inevitable, it means that young people have less reason to seek out older people than they used to.

Changing institutions

While older people (especially older men) hold unquestioned predominance in traditional community institutions such as wat committees, the new institutions (such as NGOs and government projects) for organizing development projects frequently ignore older people. This neglect undermines the traditional position of older people and excludes them from the development process. This neglect also deprives Cambodia of the unique resources that older people possess, such as experience and traditions of social relationships which could be used to encourage community cooperation and action. As one young man in the squatter settlement of Tonle Bassac (Phnom Penh) said, older people are a good role model because "Older people know how to help each other when they have hardships."

Recommendations

The recommendations from this study are divided into two sections: general recommendations which are important to improving the situation of all Cambodians, including older people; and recommendations which are specific to the situation of older people.

General recommendations

- In rural villages where poverty is high and economic opportunities are low, poor older people are in danger of being left without support because their children are forced to seek high-risk work in other provinces or countries. Therefore, government and NGOs should pursue programmes and policies that will reduce rural poverty, foster equitable and geographically dispersed economic development, and increase employment opportunities in the countryside.
- After poverty, illness and the cost of health care is the biggest problem facing older people. Healthcare reform – with the goal of ensuring competent, accessible, and affordable health care – would be an important step towards improving the lives of older people in Cambodia.
- Buying medicine without prescription is the most common form of medical treatment among older people. Therefore government and other organizations should consider how the standards and professionalism of pharmacies, especially in the rural areas, can be improved.

Recommendations specific to the situation of older people

Survival strategies

- A substantial number of older people, both men and women, continue to work and support themselves and other family members well into their 60s. Therefore, government and NGO programmes should encourage them and not discriminate against people in matters of credit, skills training and employment solely on the basis of age.

- Cambodia still has a tradition of individual and community assistance to older people who have no other means of support. Therefore, government and non-governmental assistance to older people should focus on community-based care rather than institutional care whenever possible.

Health

- Many older people have problems seeing and chewing, and lack basic aids such as glasses or dentures which could improve their productivity and quality of life. The lack of glasses and dentures is especially great in rural areas. Therefore older people's access to eye and dental care and prostheses should be improved.
- Older people in villages believe they have an obligation to visit other older people who are ill. Therefore, community health programmes should consider working with older people to spread information and provide follow-up care.
- Older people who are traditional healers (such as *Kru Khmer* or midwives) have considerable knowledge about healthcare practices in their communities and are respected by villagers. Therefore, government and NGOs should consider training traditional healers to be community educators on HIV/AIDS and other public health problems.
- In the near future, the number of people who have AIDS and who die from AIDS will increase rapidly. The burden of caring for ill children and raising orphaned grandchildren will fall heavily on older people. Therefore, government and other organizations should consider educating older people about the nature of AIDS and caring for people with AIDS; and also how to support (emotionally or materially) older people whose children have AIDS, or who have AIDS themselves.

The role of older people in society

- In many villages, older people continue to play a crucial role in mobilizing community interest, money, and labour for village projects. Therefore older people are a valuable resource which governments and other organizations should encourage and work with in the planning and management of development programmes. In particular, older people's role in guiding young people and settling disputes through reconciliation should be supported. However, since many traditional institutions are biased against women, government programmes, NGOs, and religious institutions that work with older people through traditional institutions also need to take positive steps to make sure that older women can be included in the process.
- While universal primary education is essential for the development of Cambodia, it is also (in conjunction with the influx of foreign entertainment and technology) overturning the traditional relations of knowledge between young and old. Therefore the school curriculum should include respect for older people and customs and traditions.
- Older people (especially older women) play a major role in growing and preparing food for the family, as well as having responsibility for educating grandchildren. Therefore home gardening and nutrition programmes should consider older people as allies for improving nutrition in the household.
- Gender issues do not diminish with age. Gender roles and expectations affect older women as much as younger women in terms of access to resources and respect. Therefore, government and NGO programmes must be both age and gender sensitive.

Note

1   This chapter is based on a detailed analysis of the situation of older people in Cambodia published in May 1998. It was led by HAI Research Officer Elisabeth Kato. The research team from the Ministry of Social Affairs, Labour and Veteran Affairs was Pheng Pheasa, Kaew Malee, Koy Pharin, Pok Sokravuth, Huon Atthea, Kong Sokhem, Svay Thonmunearin. The Research team from HAI was Ith Chouen, Mak Sangvan, Srey Sakhan, Hem Pisey, Nhiek Bun Touch, Vong Soyem.

13 The Situation of Older People in Tanzania[1]

HelpAge International

Poverty, vulnerability and change

'Towards a society for all ages' is the theme of the UN International Year of Older Persons. In Tanzania the family caregiving roles taken up by many older people need wider recognition.
© Mr Haji/HelpAge International

Tanzania is one of the world's poorest countries. The majority of the population are smallholders – largely subsistence farmers. Tanzanians have had to adjust to dramatic changes in the management of the economy and to an increasingly hostile natural environment in which severe droughts were followed by some of the worst flooding for decades. While life has become more difficult for ordinary people, such difficulties tend to be magnified for older people who are generally more vulnerable to change and armed with fewer coping strategies. At the same time, economic and religious changes have weakened the fabric of society and the traditions and customs with which older people grew up. The combination of all these factors has changed the world significantly for older people in recent years.

Earning a living

Most older people have productive land, but they are unable to use it to earn an income. Agricultural work is often out of the question because they lack capital either to maintain their shamba (smallholding) or to pay someone to work on it. Starting up any sort of income generating project runs into problems since crops fetch such a low price that they cannot even cover their costs, never mind earn any profit. Many older people no longer have the strength to engage in vigorous work, and the younger people are not staying in the village or available to help their parents. The problems of surviving through agriculture are exacerbated by the tradition of dividing land with children who have grown up and married and need a plot of their own to cultivate. Older people earn income by working on local handicrafts, and in urban areas work can be found as night watchmen or cooking in a small cafe.

Many older people plant coffee and tea bushes for security in their old age but they are not reaping the benefits they had anticipated. There are two ways of marketing these two crops – the old parastatals, and the newer private buyers. The private buyers pay cash on the spot, but at a fraction of the price paid by parastatals. However, parastatals buy on credit, and it can take years for the money to come through. Older people, strapped for cash, will have little choice but to sell to the private buyers and feel that they are often cheated.

Older people often have no choice but to engage in laborious and hazardous ways of earning a little money. Seaweed farming, for instance, is carried out by older women who plant the weed on the seashore and harvest it after three or four weeks. Because it must be planted at low tide, the women are forced to work day or night. It is very labour intensive. By necessity the work must be done submerged in salt water for hours on end. This affects their health and many women complain of chest pains, the strong sunlight reflecting from the water damages their eyes, and harmful sea creatures cause injury to legs and feet. In addition, the constant work in seawater wears clothes out very quickly. At the end of all this, the market for seaweed is unsatisfactory. It is monopolized by one person who keeps the price low, and any efforts to sell to another buyer or to get a better price are thwarted.

Some older people were found to be involved in small businesses, such as selling coconut husks, fish, tomatoes and running their own tailoring shops. Most emphasized that these businesses generate very little income, considering the amount of effort invested. Some make knitted palm leaves for sale, but they rely on picking up the palm leaves after they have been blown down by the wind. Marketing their produce is also difficult, since many of these older people are not mobile. Thus they are forced to sell to local middlemen for very low prices.

Mutual family support

The family is the most important and most likely source of support for older people. Many older people were found living happily and comfortably with their children but there is still a general opinion that support from the family has declined drastically. The chief reason given is poverty.

This has had many repercussions. Whereas in the past, children were happy to stay in the village and cultivate the family land, now they either find that they cannot make ends meet, or they have greater ambitions and wish to improve their standard of living and educate their children. Since there are few employment opportunities in the villages, they move away to another place, often to cities. Here they find that life is more difficult than they expected. They have nothing spare to send to their elderly parents and cannot afford the fare for regular visits. The physical absence of children is a particular hardship – many older people say they do not need money, but help on a regular basis, for instance for gathering firewood and water or for cultivating their shamba.

In many cases however the tables are turned and children are relying on their parents. Those who have moved to cities may send the grandchildren home to be looked after by their grandparents. In other cases the children themselves become ill, often with AIDS, and come home to be supported by their parents.

Older people parenting grandchildren

Bringing up grandchildren is arduous and creates problems, particularly the expense involved in education, added to the costs of medical treatment, food and clothes. This is a real financial burden of responsibility for older people. Nonetheless, grandchildren offer company and ease loneliness, and help with the household chores from a very early age – things which are talked of with much appreciation by their grandparents.

The presence of orphaned grandchildren often intensifies an already desperate situation for older people. Often very elderly, vulnerable widows will be bringing up children. A very frail woman who estimated her age at 98, for example, was struggling alone with two young orphans, and a woman of 80, who had been left with four orphans after the death of her daughter, said '*I know I am too old to depend upon, but what can I do except try to support them?*'

Teachers affirm that hard work, a poor diet and missing school are direct causes of poor academic performance among such children. One teacher said that in every class three out of four children with the lower grades were from poor families, particularly those headed by grandparents. Older people and their grandchildren are thus caught in a vicious circle: older people scrimp and save to educate their grandchildren in the hope that they will have a better life, and perhaps will later be able to help their grandparents more effectively, but the children remain severely disadvantaged.

Basic needs

The lack of the most basic needs is a pressing concern for older people in Tanzania. The only exception to this is water, since there have been many projects to bring piped water to villages. The lack of basic services is connected both to the decline in support and socio-economic changes. Older people receive less help in areas such as cultivation, water and firewood collection; many commodities are now much more expensive; traditions such as giving older people cattle as dowry payments are being eroded; health and education must be paid for; and environmental changes have also taken their toll. This has resulted in previously plentiful resources now being scarce and difficult to obtain. Coping strategies used in response to these difficulties involve begging, belt-tightening, enduring bad conditions, and working harder.

Older people's way of life in Tanzania is often detrimental to their health, but health care is problematic too. There is a widely recognized lack of commitment by health staff to treating the ailments of older people. This is magnified for very vulnerable older people – the housebound, the sick – who are forced to be highly dependent, but who are suffering more acutely from the withdrawal of especially family support.

Security

Lack of security can be a very big problem for older people, especially those living alone, or with small children. All 30 old men interviewed in one area had been the victims of robbery at least once. One old man of 80 explained the series of disasters which had befallen him and which left him destitute. The first time he was robbed, he lost 35 cows. In the second incident, 22 goats disappeared, and the final time, three hundred shillings was stolen. He said, through tears '*I reported the first and second incidents to the police, but when I saw that no action was taken, I didn't bother to go again, since I had already lost everything.*' Older people said that they are

Coping strategies in the face of age and poverty in Tanzania

In order to cope with the hardships of daily life, older people adopt a variety of strategies to meet their basic needs:

Water

Women go out in the middle of the night when water may be flowing from the taps. Those who are unable to collect water themselves either ask someone else to collect it for them or buy it. People do fewer water based tasks, like washing, washing clothes or cleaning.

Food

Those with some land maintain an area of bananas close to home to eat or to sell, and may also plant cassava or yams, which are very hardy and drought resistant. Many people beg for food from neighbours, mosques or churches. Several older people reduce the amount of food that they eat, and may only have one meal a day or less. Destitute older women in towns scrape around in the debris of the market looking for bits of maize and old vegetables.

Firewood

People who are unable to go and collect their own firewood either beg or buy it, depending on their resources. Some go without meals since they are unable to cook. Older women reported trying to steal a little firewood from the woodlots on the local tea estates.

Shelter

Older people with inadequate housing say that they just endure living in a house with broken down walls or a leaking roof. Homeless older people have a life of sleeping rough outside, moving around from house to house, sleeping in corridors, or taking refuge at the homes of relations or at missions.

Health

Many older people do not go to hospital when they become ill since they know they will not receive good service, nor will they be able to afford the treatment. They stay at home and hope they will recover. If the illness gets much worse then hospital treatment is likely to be even more expensive. Some sell crops, such as bananas, hens or other belongings to raise the money for medical treatment. Others economize on the cost of medicine and only buy half the prescribed dose. Where it is possible, many people travel up to the refugee camps where treatment and medicine are free. Many older people prefer to go to a traditional healer with whom they can negotiate over the price or pay in kind.

Many older people rely wholly on their children to support them, or on their grandchildren to carry out household and agricultural tasks, or even their neighbours. Some grandparents make arrangements with schools to relax the rules on wearing (expensive) uniform and to allow the children to miss school so that they can help on the shamba.

Others have started some sort of petty business in order to generate income, maybe weaving mats or collecting firewood for sale. A few find employment as watchmen.

Many older people say that nowadays they have to work harder in order to make ends meet, which adversely affects their health. Older people insist that coping strategies have changed over the years – in the past, there was more community support, families were less fragmented, and there was less necessity for money, particularly because health services were free.

Source: 'Older People in Tanzania: A Research Report from HelpAge International', prepared by Kate Forrester et al, HAI, Dar es Salaam, September 1998

Poverty and vulnerability in older people

In 1993 Bibi (62) left Shinyanga to visit Mwanza to see relatives, while Babu (54) came from nearby Magu to collect his wages. They met, and later set up house together in Luchelele. Now they are finding life very difficult.

Babu and Bibi live as caretakers of a cotton shamba. They have been housed in an old hut of grass and branches and have been apportioned a small cotton shamba from which, however, they have failed to harvest a crop. They have not cultivated any food crops either. Bibi collects sticks of firewood and makes clay pots, which she sells to buy flour. She also keeps hens and sheep to help with household expenses. They have no furniture and just a few clay cooking pots, and they sleep on the ground, huddled up to the fire. Just recently Babu's older sister has arrived with her grand-child to live with them, and she now depends on them. They are in the process of building another hut for this sister.

Babu suffers from numbness in his legs and needs fifteen thousand shillings – about US$350 – for an operation. His own children do not know about this situation. One of Bibi's children is aware, but has not offered to meet the costs. Bibi's children are better off than Babu's, but Babu cannot bear to ask for help from them for fear of scorn from his wife. They have no means of communicating with Babu's children, since they do not have an address, and anyway, they are not literate. The children themselves have not visited for over three years. Now they have another worry – the owner of the shamba has begun to show signs that he may be about to move away from the area, in which case, they would lose their employment.

no longer able to sleep inside their houses at night – they are forced to sleep lightly outside to guard against intrusion. In addition there are frequent incidents of crop theft from shambas. Oldest people have been hardest hit because they do not have the means to mount a guard against intruders.

Courts and the police are almost universally criticized for obstructing the rights of older people. Some of the reasons advanced were corruption and favouring the wrongdoer. Older people complained that bribery makes cases a foregone conclusion: the richer person will win, and older people do not have the means to compete.

Vulnerability

In every community there are many extremely old and frail people. The most vulnerable older people are those with no children and poor health, who are unable to work and dependent on neighbours or insti-tutions.

For instance in areas where water collection is not a problem for most of the population, it will still be difficult for a housebound elderly person. In areas where water is a problem for everyone else, it becomes an intolerable burden for the vulnerable older people, who have to wait for someone either to fetch some water for them, or to give them money to buy it. In the meantime, they cannot drink or cook or wash.

Similarly, in areas where older people do not suffer from food shortages there will still be some who are unable to produce any food, nor if they have food will they be able to prepare it. In every research area, the vulnerable older people complained of problems of clothing and bedding, and said that they were unable to repair their houses if they were damaged.

Vulnerable older people are often highly dependent, which brings its own problems, not least the fact that it is extremely disagreeable and frustrating to the older people themselves. Many depend on family support and it is those with no children who are in the most desperate situation, and whose survival basically depends on luck and on the kindness of neighbours.

Gender

Many gender inequalities reflect Tanzanian society in general. Women, whether old or young, tend to have more work than men and enjoy fewer benefits, although increasingly women are establishing their own businesses through necessity, and are found to control the profits themselves. However many other gender issues are age specific – many more women than men have been widowed and are now struggling alone, while those who have not been widowed may have been supplanted by a younger wife. Older women are also much more likely to be accused of being witches.

Roles of older people in their communities

In the past, villages were 'governed' by a council of elders. In many places these councils still exist, and still carry out their traditional functions: to settle disputes between people, and to teach young people the ways of the past, for instance about inheritance. Councils of elders must approve, for instance, clinics in a community and will organize participation in maintenance of health centres, draw up byelaws and facilitate collective village actions.

The role of these councils is diminishing. There are many reasons for this. It is partly because the elders themselves are no longer so willing to help – they have enough to do to scrape together enough money to live and eat and believe that they are less appreciated than in the past. But their function has also been usurped by the village governments, installed after independence. In the past some districts had a council of elders in every village, but now there is only one in every ward.

Older people are traditional healers and birth attendants – there seems to be no shortage of people wanting to consult traditional healers and there is a traditional midwife in every village – even though in urbanized areas there is an increasing trend for women to go to hospital to give birth.

In the past, traditional health attendants were appointed by the communities to handle health issues – for instance to cope with epidemics, supervise house cleanliness, organize the drive to construct pit latrines. However, now all these responsibilities have passed to the village government, who do not see this work as a priority, and are thus are seen as ineffective in this role.

Recommendations

These recommendations have been shaped by the feedback meetings with older people through a workshop to discuss the research findings involving HelpAge International staff and partners who had been involved in the project. Older people were delighted that anyone was interested in talking to them and that they were given a voice. They hoped that their views would be passed on.

The recommendations are aimed at all organizations working with older people directly or in communities that include older people.

Practical projects

Practical projects are needed to bring material improvements in the quality of life for older people in the following key areas:

- Health care – including training in healthy ageing for older people and in care of older people for health workers
- Access to income-generating skills through training and capital
- Low-cost and appropriate technology housing
- Water supply – appropriate technology projects to improve water harvesting and supply for older people, particularly those with mobility problems
- Fuel – introduction and dissemination of information about fuel-efficient stoves
- Education and training programmes for older people

Lobbying action and awareness raising

Advocacy is needed on the following specific areas:

- Development of a comprehensive government policy on older people in Tanzania.
- Changes in government policy to include universal pension, social security system, exemption for older people from the development levy.
- Wider awareness among the public, children and NGOs working with children of the roles of older people, particularly their new role as carers of grandchildren.
- Water supply: older people should be consulted by government and NGOs working in the water sector.

Capacity building

Structures providing support to older people need to be strengthened through:

- Civic and legal rights information and training for older people's organizations.
- Provision of support to specific organizations of older people.
- Training in age care to personnel of key structures, eg government and religious institutions and health care workers.

Note

1   This chapter is based on a research project involving 1,500 older people in Tanzania conducted by HelpAge International and partners. Participatory techniques were used and the study was undertaken in five regions of Tanzania: Dar es Salaam, Mwanza, Zanzibar, Kagera and Mbeya with a focus on one district in each region. The research was coordinated and the report was written by Kate Forrester, a Consultant to HelpAge International.

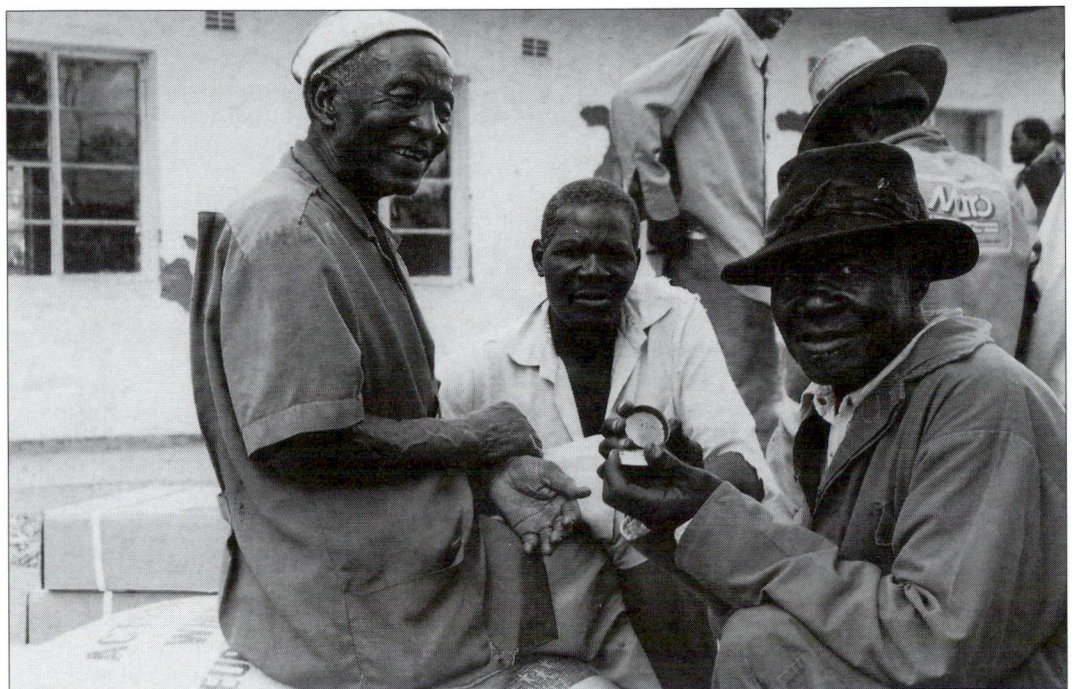

14 The Situation of Older People in Zimbabwe

Donald J Adamchak and Adrian O Wilson[1]

This analysis of the situation of older people in Zimbabwe is based on a study[2] sample of 150 men and women aged 55 and older. The mean age of the sample was 69; a third were 55–64 years, 43 per cent were 65–74 years, and a quarter were 75 and older.

Forty-eight per cent were married. Nearly 30 per cent of the men and 67 per cent of the women were not married. The two types of marriage are civil and traditional, and remarriage is common following divorce or widowhood for a man, and for a woman if she is still of reproductive age.

Fifty-six per cent of the sample had received no formal education at all. The mean for years of formal education was 2.4 years.

The mean number of living children for the total sample was five. Six per cent had no living children. Nine per cent of women but only 1.6 per cent of men had no living children.

Sixty-five per cent of female respondents, but only 20 per cent of male respondents, were widowed. Among the widowed respondents, 12 per cent of women had no living children, whereas all men had living children.

Sources of income and cash

Income is probably the most difficult characteristic to obtain for older Africans for several reasons. Income is not regular and is not recorded like pensions or social security. There may not be regular and complete census or survey information. Many old people participate in the informal economy as agriculturalists or in other sales or service activities. Often sample surveys are the sole source of information on income and cash generation.

Men received more income than women from the following sources: salary, children, rent, pension, and savings/interest. The largest difference was in salary where 28 per cent of males received a salary compared to only 1 per cent for women. Women generated more cash than men from agricultural production, the informal sector, their spouse, and public assistance. This is consistent with other research, which shows women are the primary subsistence agriculturalists and that they perform various production and sales activities in the informal economy including selling things like peanut butter, beer and vegetables.

Women face disadvantages financially in old age as they earn a living in fluctuating and perhaps marginal sectors such as agriculture and the informal economy. Elderly rural women have fewer sources of cash generation than any other group, and no rural woman earned a salary. Furthermore, fewer rural women received cash from their children than any other group. Forty-nine per cent of the men and nearly 43 per cent of the women received money from children. Most older people receive cash from multiple sources. This is most likely an important and necessary strategy to achieve relative economic security.

Men generated 42 per cent of their collective total cash generation from salary, followed by the informal sector and rent. For women, the informal sector, agricultural production and children generated 73 per cent of total income. Males obtain income from more formal mechanisms such as salary, rent, pensions, and saving/interest. Eighty-five per cent of cash received by rural women comes from informal sources.

There is a significant difference in the mean total annual income by gender. Women received only 44 per cent of what men received, and this was consistent for both rural and urban residents. However, all older people are at a disadvantage financially. The average income for the entire sample was only 34 per cent of the formal sector minimum wage, although men were better off than women. Men received 51 per cent of the minimum wage while elderly women only received 23 per cent of the minimum wage. And, rural elderly women were the most disadvantaged receiving only 21 per cent of the formal sector minimum wage.

Older people who are married received about twice as much income as those who are not married. Married men received about 55 per cent of the formal sector minimum wage and unmarried men about 46 per cent. However, unmarried women received less than a fifth (18 per cent) of the minimum wage in the year prior to the survey. When controlling on gender, marital status and residence, women had significantly lower incomes, particularly unmarried women (mostly widowed women). And, within this group, unmarried rural women received the lowest income, just ZW$289 (approximately US$145) in the year prior to the survey, which was only 16 per cent of the formal sector minimum wage. Rural elderly widowed women are clearly the most vulnerable group.

Non-cash support from children

Sixty-one per cent of the respondents received support from their children, 33 per cent received no support and 6 per cent had no living children. The main types of support were clothing (40 per cent), food or groceries (13 per cent), and 8 per cent received other types of support (general maintenance, medical care, or chores). Married men were least likely to receive non-cash support from children, and unmarried men and married women were more likely to receive support. Unmarried women were less likely to receive non-cash support than the previous two groups mentioned. These women mainly received clothing from their children.

Two-thirds of the women in the sample were not married (most were widowed) and 12 per cent of widowed women had no living children, thus older women are placed in an extremely vulnerable position. Their income was only 23 per cent of the formal sector minimum wage, and they earned less than half of what elderly men received. In addition, 61 per cent of older individuals received non-cash support from their children, including food, clothing, medical care, general maintenance and chores. It is important that older persons received cash from a number of sources as a survival strategy, since their cash generation during the year prior to the survey was only about a third of the formal sector minimum wage and about 60 per cent of commercial farm work or a domestic worker.

Furthermore, nearly 23 per cent of older people provided financial support to others. Most of this support went to children, nieces, nephews, and grandchildren and mainly included school fees, food, and money. These findings also show that intergenerational transfer from children to elderly parents is intact. Although the average amount of cash transfer was small, the fact that 45 per cent of older people received this transfer and that 61 per cent received in-kind support from their children indicates that the family is still a major support mechanism. The question for Zimbabwean policy makers is what will happen to older individuals if this support deteriorates in the future?

Living arrangements

Household composition is likely to have an important impact on the well-being of the elderly. A larger proportion of married women live in extended families, and a larger proportion of unmarried women in the complex family type. Overall, about 13 per cent of older people live alone, 21 per cent live in nuclear families, 26 per cent in extended families and 40 per cent – particularly unmarried men and women – reside in the complex family types including relatives and non relatives. This may represent another survival strategy with the elderly contributing cash and/or in kind to a complex household, perhaps to avoid living alone. Older, married rural men live nearly equally in nuclear families or extended families. Sixty per cent of urban married men live in extended families, while the remaining 40 per cent live in nuclear families. Two-thirds of rural unmarried men live alone; the remaining third reside in the complex family type. Two-thirds of the unmarried urban men live in complex families.

Conditions of unmarried rural elderly women

The poorest and most vulnerable group of elderly, unmarried rural women, live in two types of living arrangements, alone or in complex families. For both types, levels of illiteracy, widowhood and education are very similar. Those who live alone received or earned slightly more cash. Perhaps these women are forced to be more resourceful, given that they have fewer living children and have no one else to depend on within their households. Only 20 per cent of women living alone received money from their children, compared with nearly 38 per cent of those living in the complex family type.

Women living alone must travel far to their water source, and nearly twice the percentage use a bush toilet. These are important proxy indicators of personal hygiene, disease and health, and also demonstrate a struggle to maintain the household on a daily basis. A positive characteristic of rural women living alone is that 90 per cent own their home, and 70 per cent own land, usually a communal farm plot or smaller. Women living in complex families have similar percentages. Several additional items related to physical health indicate that 80 per cent of those living alone and 62 per cent living in the complex family report they eat enough food. What is more important is that 20 per cent and 38 per cent, respectively, indicate that they are not eating enough food. Only about 20 per cent of each group indicate that they 'feel healthy.' We can't go any further than this, but the issues of rural health care and geriatric health care need to be assessed.

Given the economic conditions of unmarried rural elderly women, it is somewhat surprising that they appear to be in good emotional spirits with 70 per cent of both groups reporting that they are either satisfied or somewhat satisfied with life. Seventy per cent of the women living alone, but only 48 per cent of the women living in the complex family, report they are satisfied or somewhat satisfied with their economic support.

Any decline in traditional family support could be devastating for older people, without a commensurate increase in systemic support (ie, social security). Furthermore, the potential decline of inter-generational transfer from children to parents could also negatively affect the transfer from parents and grandparents to younger generations, judging from the finding that nearly 23 per cent of elderly respondents provided financial support to younger generations. However, governmental policies should strive to maintain and strengthen the family as a source of elderly support. Even in the absence of economic incentives such as tax deductions for elderly dependants, media campaigns and community and village level volunteer programmes could assist the elderly.

These respondents received support, particularly income and cash, from multiple sources. Any contraction of the current resource base will be detrimental to their survival. As development and modernization produce structural changes in the family as an institution, the elderly, particularly rural widowed women, will be in an extremely vulnerable situation in Zimbabwe, and more generally, in sub-Saharan Africa.

Notes

1   Professor Donald J Adamchak, Professor of Sociology, Waters Hall, Kansas State University, Manhattan, Kansas 66506–4003, USA and Dr Adrian O Wilson, African Foundation for Research and Interdisciplinary Training in Ageing (AFRITA), PO Box 19, Harare, Zimbabwe.

2   This report is extracted from a study prepared for the ICPD + 5 Technical Meeting on Population Ageing held in Brussels in October 1998. HelpAge International is very grateful to Professor Adamchak, and Dr Wilson for permission to use this extract. Collaborators for the Zimbabwe research project were: Mr Andrew C Nyanguru and Father Joseph Hampson. The following organizations assisted in the Zimbabwe research: The University of Zimbabwe, HelpAge Zimbabwe, the Government of Zimbabwe Central Statistics Office and the Rockerfeller Foundation.

15 The Situation of Older People in the Transitional Economies of Eastern and Central Europe

Mark Gorman

There is no historical precedent for the challenges which have been faced by the countries of eastern and central Europe as they undergo the transition from centrally planned to pluralist and market-orientated economies. A decade on from the removal of communist governments, these countries still face enormous problems in trying to provide adequately for all their citizens. The problems of already failing social policy have been compounded by soaring inflation and unemployment against a background of sharply reduced state intervention in social welfare.[1] Though inflation levels have reduced significantly in many countries in the late 1990s, the earlier years of transition have left a legacy of poverty for many in the region.

Demographic change (falling fertility and rising longevity together with large-scale migration), combined with centrally directed economic and social development during the communist era has resulted in significant long-term impacts on older people. The family and community structures within which today's generation of older people grew up have been dramatically transformed in the past half-century, and the political transition of the last decade has reinforced such changes. For many older people, ties of kinship and locality remain strong, despite decades of efforts to break them down, and indeed provide critically important support structures. Throughout the region the priority issues for older people relate to income security, the potential growth in care needs, and means to maintain the roles and relationships of older people within their families and communities. While national and local situations vary widely in this very diverse region, these core questions provide a common theme.

The vulnerability of older people to rapid change

Even before 1989 the well-being of older people had relied on maintaining a combination of assets. These included notably, income from a state-provided pension, family support, and their own productive activities. Involvement with the family and intergenerational transfers has always been of critical importance.

In all the countries in transition higher proportions of older people live with their families than is the case in the European Union. In Hungary in 1984 nearly one-third of those over 65 lived with their children, compared to 6 per cent in Sweden.[2] A decade later economic hardship and lack of opportunities have meant that large numbers of older people still lived with their younger relatives. In Latvia in 1995, 29 per cent of those over retirement age (55 for women, 60 for men) lived in extended families.[3]

Despite the importance of family care for older people (not to mention the support offered by older people to younger generations), the policies of most

governments in the region have been focused predominantly on the needs of families with children. This is a continuation of the situation inherited from the communist states which, while giving recognition to the role of women caring for children, provided little practical support for the family care of older people. In some states legal codes required families to maintain dependant older relatives, but provided no support to facilitate such caregiving. Today such benefits as are available to carers are very difficult to obtain, and offer only limited financial assistance. Indeed it has been proposed that a major role for the NGOs in the region is to act as advocates for older people trying to obtain state benefits.[4]

Economic changes have brought increasing stress in family situations. High unemployment and inflation mean that many families are unable to provide adequate support to all their members, young or old. Migration in search of work may only increase problems, as those moving from rural areas to the cities to seek work face a struggle to sustain themselves, and are unable to send remittances to dependants who remain in the countryside. In the cities other problems may arise, notably acute housing shortages. The result is that many families share extremely overcrowded accommodation. In Albania for example, such has been the extent of urban migration that two-bedroom apartments in Tirana are often occupied by as many as 15 people.[5] In such circumstances pressures on family life and the capacity to care adequately are extreme. Sudden shocks such as the collapse in August 1998 of the rouble against the dollar have plunged families already facing profound hardship into an economic crisis. Pensions in Russia have remained unpaid since the summer of 1998 removing from many families their primary (or sole) source of income.

The importance of intergenerational relationships

In the light of these circumstances intergenerational relationships become the very basis of survival; nor are such relationships simply a matter of transfers from younger to older family members. There is clear evidence that older people make valuable contributions to family and other local economies but the extent is often difficult to gauge. Older people's work is often unrecognized and unrecorded. For example, older people often take on time-consuming tasks to free other family members for paid work. A survey in Russia in 1992 found that on average people over 60 spent 20 hours a week queuing in shops. Similar findings are reported for Romania, where informal household activities such as care of children or other older people were important tasks undertaken by older people.[6] Sharing accommodation is another survival strategy, which also facilitates pooling of tasks and income sources. A recent report on a small town in Poland notes cases of unemployed people in their thirties sharing housing with their parents.[7]

Earning an income

Informal employment has always been an important source of income for some older people, though it has been men who have tended to have more access to these opportunities. However, the competition for jobs of all kinds in recent years has meant that older people are increasingly marginalized from all employment opportunities, whether in the formal or informal sector. One exception to this is small-scale food production on allotments, which in the southern parts of the region and Russia especially provides older people with some additional resources. Indeed older people say that younger generations are losing the traditional skills of growing and preserving vegetables, which are now gaining a renewed importance.

There are also situations where even such limited self-help is impossible, and where the breakdown of external systems has created emergencies. In Russia in1998 for the first time the annual 'great delivery' of food and other essentials to the otherwise uninhabitable arctic areas failed to take place. This created the real possibility that these mineral rich areas, inhabited by millions of migrant workers in the former USSR, would be cut off. An emergency operation, mounted by the International Federation of the Red Cross during the winter of 1998/9, was necessary to prevent mass starvation. At an early stage the Red Cross food distributions identified older people as a particularly vulnerable target group.[8]

Pensions

Growing numbers of older people who are living alone are often reliant on an increasingly inadequate state pension to survive.

The pension system inherited from the communist states was in most cases earnings-related, with a safety net minimum. Typically, workers retired from state enterprises with 40–50 per cent of the average wage. This was much lower for workers in rural areas, and for women. Retirement ages tended to be early, with many workers leaving employment in their fifties. Low inflation, price stability and state provision of other health and welfare services protected older people's standards of living, (although this was somewhat offset by the fact that pensions, particularly in the Soviet Union, tended to reflect only past roles, with no attempt to match current needs).

During the last decade, the freeing of prices, rising inflation and lack of linkage between pensions and prices have rapidly eroded the value of pensions across the region. In Latvia a monthly pension equivalent to US$63 in 1996 was calculated to be less than half of the minimum necessary for basic existence.[9] A subsequent increase to US$100 still leaves a substantial shortfall, given rising inflation.

The situation is significantly worse for older women. Under the former state socialist systems women were disadvantaged in various ways which have had a long-term impact. Women were often in lower-paid occupations, had limited access to the informal economy, and undertook most domestic work and caregiving. Their lifetime earning potential was thus restricted, a major handicap under systems where pensions were generally based on length of employment. Premium pensions and other social benefits were concentrated in certain occupations such as mining and (in some countries such as Hungary) on the urban industrial sector, where jobs for women were limited. Earlier pensionable ages for women (often 55 as opposed to 60 for men) were another limitation on their earning potential.[10] A legacy of old age poverty is the result for the current generations of retirees, and the future looks no better for future generations.

The effect of transition on women

Many women have lost their jobs as a result of economic restructuring, and future opportunities for employment have been curtailed by the withdrawal of such employment benefits as child care and canteen meals. 'As pension reforms in Eastern Europe become established and the link between lifetime earnings and pensions is tightened, women's poorer employment record will bring wider inequality of pension income in the future'.[11] It is ironic that one unintended result of this situation may be the higher mortality rates of men who, forced into retirement with increasingly inadequate pensions, seem less able than women to cope with the abrupt change and loss of status involved.

For those older people living without family support other assistance is also scarce. Most governments in the region express a commitment to enabling older people to remain in their own homes and communities for as long as possible. However there is a dearth of support services available to facilitate this. Certainly the smaller proportion of older people living alone in the countries of transition as compared, for example, to the European

Union would presuppose a lower level of support services offered to this group. However, the evidence that exists implies that services are scanty in many countries. Community services (both those offered on a group basis and those in the individual's home) are insufficient, leading the World Bank to comment of Hungary that 'there is a vast unmet need for social welfare services, particularly for the elderly'.[12] Such services as do exist are fragile, especially those run by the NGO sector. The economic collapse in Russia has led to the closure of a number of NGO-run soup kitchens in the cities.

Health

The declining economic situation of older people in the transition countries has been reflected in their health status. During the 1990s, mortality rates rose dramatically in a number of countries in the region. By 1993, life expectancy in Estonia had fallen to 62.6 for men, compared to 74 for women.[13] In the Russian Federation mortality rates have been such that life expectancy for men fell from 65 to 58 between 1987 and 1994, with a substantial proportion of these excess deaths occurring in the late mid-life and older age groups. Mortality rates responded with great speed to declining economic welfare and the collapse of the Soviet health care system.[14]

Similar links between health status, poverty in old age and declining health systems have appeared elsewhere in the region. In Romania for example, the commune-based primary health care system, where each administrative district theoretically has a dispensary and a general practitioner, has not been functioning in some areas because of lack of staff. Many rural-based doctors have left for urban positions, and the demands of subsistence food production, the cost of transport and the distance to facilities makes health care effectively inaccessible for most rural old people.[15] Despite efforts towards decentralization in recent years, health facilities still remain unbalanced with an excess of hospital-based physicians, but a shortage of primary health workers, general practitioners and nurses.[16]

Family and community support

At the end of the first decade of the transition, the family and community situation of older people in the region is in crisis. It is therefore unsurprising that there are widespread reports of older people suffering from anxiety and depression, with feelings of alienation both from their families and wider societies. Reports that older people feel abandoned by their societies, that they do not want to burden their children, and that they feel there is a lack of interest in their plight from the younger generation, are common. So too are reports of a sense of loneliness and isolation, rising depression, and an increase in the number of suicides by older people.[17]

Physical and material, as well as emotional insecurity also threatens the well-being of older people. A rising incidence of robbery and assaults (including rape) on older people has been reported in rural Lithuania.[18] In many of the former Soviet republics the large numbers of ethnic Russians who migrated in the post-war years to work throughout the Soviet Union are now, in their retirement years, losing rights to property and even citizenship. For many in the age cohorts above 60 years, the current period of uncertainty is simply the culmination of lifetimes in which invasion, conflict, forced migration and deprivation have been common experiences.

However there is also evidence that governments are taking the issues of concern to older people increasingly seriously, and seeking new policy directions to respond to them. Several countries are drafting legislation – Slovenia's National Strategy for Social Protection for example

covers both principles and practice – but overall, the needs of older people still remain low on policy agendas of the countries in transition.

Notes

1   Laczko, F, 1994, *Older People in Eastern & Central Europe: The Price of Transition to a Market Economy*, HelpAge International, London, p9.
2   Ibid, p43.
3   UNDP, 1995, *Human Development Report 1995*, p34.
4   Proceedings of NGO conference, Slovenia, October 1998, American Association of Retired Persons/HelpAge International.
5   Information provided by Albanian Association of Gerontology, October 1998.
6   Laczko, 1994, op cit, p21.
7   Steele, J, 1999, 'A good time is not being had by all', *The Guardian*, 9 March, p11. Sharing accommodation can also result in 'catch 22' situations. Steele points out that in one instance sharing accommodation involved the loss of unemployment benefit, because the parents were both receiving disability pensions.
8   HelpAge International, 1998, 'East & Central Europe Region Report', February, HelpAge International, London.
9   Information provided by Latvia Pensioners' Federation, December 1998.
10 Ginn, J, 1998, 'Older Women in Europe: East Follows West in the Feminization of Poverty', *Ageing International* XXIV(4), Spring.
11 Ibid, p115.
12 Laczko, 1994, op cit, p44.
13 WHO Regional Office for Europe.
14 Wallace, P, 1999, *Agequake*, Nicholas Brealey, London, p202.
15 *Information Romania* 36, August 1997, p4.
16 WHO Regional Office for Europe, 1997, commenting on Romania.
17 Proceedings of NGO Conference, Slovenia, October 1998 (AARP/HelpAge International).
18 Ibid.

Part III

Ageing and Development Data

A member of the
Uganda Reach the
Aged Association –
URAA is currently
soliciting the views of
older people as part
of the strategy to
develop a national
policy on ageing.
© Gilbert Awekofwa/
HelpAge International

National Policies on Ageing and Older People: A Review of the Status of Policies in 46 Countries

The growing awareness of ageing issues and the disadvantaged situation of older people in many countries has yet to be translated into policy actions by national governments. However, the picture is changing, and a number of initiatives have been taken (or are developing) across the world.

The following table examines the development of policy on ageing in a cross-section of countries in Africa, Asia, the Caribbean and Latin America. What emerges is a view of work in progress, with important developments underway in a number of countries. However it is also clear that, in many cases, policy on ageing is still a low priority for governments. Where policies have been introduced, progress towards effective implementation is still very slow.

Note: many countries have limited social insurance or social security schemes, such as Provident Funds, for some older citizens. These are normally limited to former government employees, or to small numbers of employees in the private sector. Such policies have not been included in these tables, unless there are plans to extend such programmes to the majority of older people.

Country	Is there a national policy relating to older people? Which Ministry is responsible for policy?	What are the main features of the policy? If no policy exists are there plans to introduce one?	Comments	Has there been any involvement of Civil Society in establishing the policy?
ARGENTINA	No specific policy as yet. The 'Office of Policy and Projects' is the Ministry responsible for ageing issues and the development of a national policy.	There is a document developed by the National Government called 'Basis for a National Plan on Ageing 1996–2000'. The Plan deals with the situation of older people on the following themes: • Causes of population ageing; • Distribution by area and by sex; • Socio-economic situation; • Family and housing; • Education; • Health; • Autonomy; • Economic activity; • Social security. It aims to address problems such as: • Fragmented care (coexistence of several Official Agencies at National, Provincial and Municipal level and a lack of communication between them). • Dissipation of resources: inefficient use, lack of satisfactory impact on needs and demands of older people. • Lack of social and epidemiological planning: problems in identifying beneficiaries and their concerns in the distribution of loans, and lack of monitoring and evaluation. • Use of inadequate technologies and scarce cost studies. • Absence of quality control in loans. • Training and education in human resources are scarce. • Unequal geographical distribution. • Limited capacity for the beneficiary sector to manage, control and evaluate their programmes.	Programmes effectively developed by the Government are: ASOMA: a programme of complementary food, medical care and recreation for people over the age of 60 with no social security cover. Run by the Department for Social Development. PRO-HUERTA: Creation of home and community gardens. Run by the Department of Agriculture (INTA). PRO-BIENESTAR: Complementary feeding carried out by the Centres of Retired People and Pensioners. Run by the National Institute of Social Security for Retired People and Pensioners. The applied policies are incomplete, fragmented and welfare-based. It deals briefly with retired older people but does not take into account the situation of older people with no protection. Constitutional rights acquired through retirement and pensions are inadequately protected.	In addition to the 'Basis for a National Plan on Ageing 1996–2000', some NGOs and organizations of older people have carried out studies and proposals. There is a need to coordinate the public and private sectors and intermediary organizations in order to define a integrated social policy, which focuses on the social integration of older people at all levels and takes account of all aspects considered in social development. These efforts at coordination have not yet happened.

BANGLADESH	No National Policy as yet.	A national plan, prepared by the Bangladesh Association for the Aged in collaboration with the WHO, has been submitted to the government for approval. The government is reported to be keen to implement the 1982 UN International Plan of Action and its national plans are being formulated according to these principles. An old age allowance has recently been introduced, providing financial assistance to 400,000 of the poorest people over 57 years old. Under the annual development plan for 1998–99, the government will establish six regional shelter centres for older people. The government should soon approve a national health policy that includes a section on 'geriatric treatment'.	The government has set up a National Committee on Ageing headed by the Social Welfare Minister and with representation from the Department of Social Services and the Bangladesh Association for the Aged. A National Geriatric Council has also been established. These committees will work to plan, initiate and coordinate welfare programmes. A National Coordination Committee may be set up to liaise with NGOs.
BARBADOS	No National Policy as yet. The Ministry of Social Transformation has primary responsibility for ageing issues. The Ministry of Health also deals with some subjects related to older people.	The government has plans to adopt a national policy. Personnel from the Ministry of Health who attended the Caribbean Forum on Ageing will spearhead these efforts after May 1998. The policy is currently at draft stage. Current programmes for older people include: • The Urban Development Committee poverty alleviation programme builds housing for needy older people. • The National Assistance Board (NAB) provides a Home Help Service to needy older people. • The NAB will be constructing a Senior Citizens Complex in 1999 as part of its plans to recognize the International Year of Older Persons. • Free bus passes are provided to older people using public transport. • Non-contributory pension of Bds$80.00 (US$40) per week. • Contributory pension of Bds$98.00 (US$50) per week.	A National Consultation on Health and Ageing was held in November 1998. 30 representatives of government ministries and departments, NGOs and elderly persons participated in the Consultation, which resulted in the development of a draft policy to address Health and Ageing. The Consultation also identified the need to involve older people in planning and policy formation related to older persons.

Country	Is there a national policy relating to older people? Which Ministry is responsible for policy? If no policy exists are there plans to introduce one?	Comments	Has there been any involvement of Civil Society in establishing the policy?
		Financial assistance to private operators, Nursing Homes, etc, providing care for older people. Private Homes for older people have to be licensed with the Ministry of Health and the Government. Homes are inspected to ensure that physical standards are met, and care standards are in place.	
BELIZE	No National Policy as yet. The Ministry of Human Development, Youth and Women has responsibility for ageing issues.	No information available.	HelpAge Belize has prepared a draft document. The National Council on Ageing, which should be operative soon, will take this forward.
BOLIVIA	In 1996 the Government issued a Supreme Decree relating to older people.	The decree included key entitlements such as the 'Bonosol', an annual single payment to those older people not entitled to join pension programmes. Free health care was also extended to older people. The government has reviewed all services offered to older persons to ensure maximum coverage and utilization of resources. Provisions for older people include housing, social assistance and medical care. Organizations working with older people also receive financial contributions. Although the Decree remains in law, a subsequent government rescinded the payment of the Bonosol in 1997. Free health care remains on the statute book, but lack of funding has meant that it has not been implemented.	The original draft decree was prepared by a working group of more than 20 older people's organizations. They organized a campaign, which included both a mass petition and enlisting the support of influential members of the government. The working group ('Defensa del Anciano') remains an active network.
CAMBODIA	No National Policy as yet. The Ministry of Social Affairs, Labour and Veterans' Affairs (MSALVA) will be the lead	Expected to be drafted soon. The creation of a National Committee for the International Year of Older Persons and Help to the Aged was approved and signed by Prime Minister Hun	WHO will provide support for the development of a healthcare policy for older people. The National Committee for the Elderly (which has yet to be convened) will consist of representatives from the Ministries

agency. They are currently building up their staff and do not yet have the capacity to be fully functional.

Sen in October 1998, but this only exists on paper at present as the members have not yet been named. The Committee is expected to draft the national policy for older people.

Cambodia's political instability and consequent changing administrations has made long-term planning for older people difficult. Government programmes focus on those with special needs resulting from the conflict. Cambodian tradition expects children and grandchildren, especially females, to care for and support the older generation, although there is no legislation to cover this.

of Health, Women's Affairs, Culture and Religion, Finance, Rural Development, Planning, Education and the Interior. HelpAge International and the Cambodian Association for the Elderly will sit as Advisers.

CHILE

Yes, it was agreed by the Committee of Social Ministers in May 1996.
At present the Ministry of Interior through its Older Adult Programme is responsible for ageing issues. In January 1999 The President of the Chilean Republic sent a bill to Congress which will create a 'National Department for Older People'

The general objective of this policy is 'To bring about a cultural change leading to better treatment and understanding of older people in society, which implies a different perception of ageing, and to achieve a better quality of life for all older people'. The principles which direct the work in the different areas are:
• Equity;
• Intergenerational solidarity;
• Self-worth and Active Ageing;
• Prevention;
• Flexibility in the design of sectoral policies;
• Decentralization;
• Subordination of the State and regulatory role.

At present specific sectoral programmes exist with different levels of progress. Better coordination and integration is needed between them. The project to create a National Service for Older People as well as the 13 regional committees will optimize the application of the policy.
Training/education with regard to this policy has also been one of the priorities of the regional committees. There is still a huge gap between needs and benefits offered.

Representatives of NGOs participated in the development of the policy. This was done through 4 working groups who dealt with 'sociocultural and demographic aspects of ageing', 'security and social welfare', 'health and the older person', and 'organizations caring for older people and support networks'.
Full participation of older people is lacking. There is a tendency to focus on the needs of older people rather than enhancing their skills and abilities.

CHINA

Yes, it was agreed in 1994. China Ministry of Civil Affairs and the China National Committee on Ageing are involved in implementation.

• To address the impact of ageing on China's socio-economic development.
• To alleviate the pressures on the family which have arisen due to the increase in numbers of older people.
• To adopt a holistic approach to improving healthcare for older people and their carers.

China National Committee on Ageing started a programme for the older person in 1996. This work primarily focuses on the consequences of natural disasters on older people, those older people living in poor areas and suffering from particular hardships.

The Plan for Action was worked out by the China National Committee on Ageing in keeping with the UN Plan of Action on Ageing based on a survey of the general situation on ageing conducted by the China Research Centre on Ageing. The China Fund for the Elderly, China Association of the Universities for the Aged and the Gerontological Society of China were also part of the process.

Country	Is there a national policy relating to older people? Which Ministry is responsible for policy?	What are the main features of the policy? If no policy exists are there plans to introduce one?	Comments	Has there been any involvement of Civil Society in establishing the policy?
COLOMBIA	No unified policy. The national development plan (Salto Social – 'Social Jump') 1994–98 includes measures relating to older people. Ministries relating to health, social security, housing and recreation and culture share responsibility for policies relating to older people.	'To improve living conditions in old age, and to enhance the quality of life of the whole population so as to reach a healthy and satisfactory old age' (from Ageing and Old Age, Social & Economic Policies Council, 1995). A key element of the 'Salto Social' plan is the 'Revivir' programme, aiming to ensure basic services to older people without access to social security benefits.	Government policy emphasizes the joint responsibility of government, the family and older people themselves in policy implementation. Although Article 46 of the Constitution makes it a legal obligation of families to look after elderly parents, abandonment and family abuse were among the five main complaints to Public Defenders Offices in Colombia in 1994/5.	
CUBA	Yes. The first national policy on older people was agreed in 1974. This was redrafted after the 1982 UN meeting in Vienna. Three years ago an integral programme for older people was created. The lead government agency is the National Directorate for Older People. Policy is coordinated between the Ministries of Health & Labour.	The policy provides for a comprehensive programme of community support and institutional care. House repairs and home help/meals services are offered to those still in their own homes. Community centres provide social activities and health services run by 'gerontological teams' of health and social workers.		Older people now participate in 'circulos de abuelos' (grandparents groups') run by councils elected by older people themselves.
DOMINICA	No national policy yet. Currently the Ministry of Community Development and Women's Affairs has primary responsibility for dealing with ageing issues. The Ministry of Health and Social Security also deals with related issues.	The Dominica Council on Ageing has submitted a draft set of policy recommendations to government in 1998. There are strong indications that this will be adopted as a policy in 1999. The main goal of the draft policy is to ensure that older people are provided with protection, care and opportunities to participate in the development of Dominica. It is guided by the United Nations Principles of Independence, Dignity, Care, Participation	There are limitations on government's ability to provide the necessary resources to implement the policy, though the collaborative approach stressed and the emphasis on using available community resources demonstrate awareness of this problem.	The development of the draft national policy was largely a civil society initiative, taken by the Dominica Council on Ageing. A series of national consultations were held throughout the island where broad cross-sections of people were able to make their input. Government representatives and representatives of different interest groups were also invited to

ECUADOR	and Self-fulfilment. The document calls particular attention to the needs of older people in the areas of housing, health, transport and social services.	To achieve the social well-being of the older and ageing population, through preventive and protective measures, , as well as service provision, in the domains of healthcare, housing, environment, social services, education, personal development, culture, recreation, participation and social activities.	Yes. The Ministry of Welfare, through the State Gerontological Office has responsibility for policies affecting older people. On a national level there are 20 civil servants that are responsible for the implementation of policies affecting older people.	Public and private entities, national and international NGOs develop their activities in coordination with the Secretary of State, demonstrating the positive participation of civil society and all these organizations, not only defining policies but also in their implementation.
EL SALVADOR	Organizational and management guidance and intervention.		Yes, it was agreed in December 1998. The National Secretariat for the Family and the Social Ministries are responsible for older people's issues.	A consultative process was developed at a national level with all organizations involved with the care of older people and a consensus between all the different actors was reached. This led to the consolidation of the document.
ETHIOPIA	• Developmental: in which participatory developmental social welfare programmes and services will be expanded. • Preventive: in which the causes of social problems are studied and preventive measures are taken, based on the studies. • Rehabilitative: in which members of the society who are already suffering from various social problems and require special treatment and attention are rehabilitated.		Yes a National Policy does exist; it is the 'Developmental Social Welfare Policy' and was agreed in 1996. There are four staff members in the Elderly Affairs Department.	Although the policy was formulated in 1996, the strategy for implementing it was issued very late in January 1999. This inevitably delayed actions that needed to be taken. The strategy focused on community participation, partnership and coordination between government and non-government organizations, research, capacity building, and advocacy and awareness creation as the main vehicles of implementing the policy. Though the policy emphasizes building the capacity of regions in implementing the policy, the technical and financial capacity	The strategies were developed by academics from Addis Ababa University. There has so far been little wider involvement of civil society both in the formulation of the policy and the strategies of implementation.

review and comment on the initial set of recommendations.

Country	Is there a national policy relating to older people? Which Ministry is responsible for policy?	What are the main features of the policy? If no policy exists are there plans to introduce one?	Comments	Has there been any involvement of Civil Society in establishing the policy?
FIJI	No, however there are plans to begin drawing up a policy which, it is hoped, will be completed in 1999. The Fiji Council of Social Services through the National Advisory Committee on Ageing and Elderly (NACEA) and the Ministry of Health are taking the lead. There are 2 part-time staff working on ageing issues at the Ministry of Health.	Currently in development.	The development of a national policy needs full time fully committed persons and funds. These do not currently exist at NGO or government level. The National Advisory Committee on Ageing and the Elderly has been working with the Ministry of Health in developing a wider policy for older people.	within the lead ministry (the Ministry of Labour and Social Affairs (MoLSA) is very limited. Civil society organizations involved include Fiji Council of Social Services, Fiji Employers Federation, Private Sector Group and Fiji Trade Union Congress.
GRENADA	None at present. There are no immediate plans or expressed intentions of developing such a policy. The Ministry of Housing, Women's Affairs and Social Services has responsibility for dealing with issues concerning older people.	No information available.	The Grenada government provides an annual subvention to thirteen residential homes for older people as well as to the NGO ECHO (an organization working with older people). Other forms of support to older people include pension payments, public assistance, a pauper's burial scheme and medical assistance.	
INDIA	Yes, it was initiated in January 1999.	• The national policy aims to strengthen the legitimate place of older people in society. • It also aims to help older people live the last phase of their lives with purpose, dignity, and in peace. • The State will support older persons, provide protection against abuse and exploitation, seek their participation and provide care services to improve the quality of their lives.		Extensive consultation took place across India over 18 months. NGOs, academic institutions, the private sector and the general public were all part of the process.

INDONESIA	A specific policy concerning older persons was inserted in the 'Broad Outlines of State Policy', in 1998. A National Committee on Ageing comprising the Ministry of Social Affairs and the Indonesian Forum for Older People are the lead agencies on issues affecting older people.	• Through the upgrading of the quality of life of the elderly population, their welfare condition, capabilities and community care to establish their integration with their social environment through an organized community effort between the government and communities. • Better services and social welfare support for those who have physical or mental disabilities. • Dignifying older people by giving them the respect they deserve.	In 1994 the National Committee for the Institutionalisation of the Elderly within the Nation's Life was set up by Decision no. 15 of the Co-ordinating Minister for People's Welfare. It maintains that the elderly constitute one of the nation's assets whose well-being should be promoted. This process is the responsibility of the government and the community.	The Indonesian Forum for Older People is coordinating with the government on older people's issues.
JAMAICA	Yes, it was agreed in March 1997. The National Council on Ageing that comes under the Ministry of Labour, National Security and Sports is given responsibility for implementing the national policy. There are two staff members in the Ministry who work on ageing issues.	• To ensure that senior citizens are able to meet their basic needs. • To ensure that those in need are assisted and protected from abuse and violence and are treated as a resource and not a burden. • To enhance the self-reliance and functional independence of senior citizens.	The National policy emphasizes the integration of ageing issues into national development plans, the expansion and establishment of inter-generational policies and programmes, and that due recognition be paid to the productive roles of older people in national develop-ment, not only from an economic standpoint, but in their social roles as leaders, counsellors, caregivers and cultural ambassadors.	Some elements of civil society were involved in the development of the National Policy for Older People. A committee was set up to draft the National Policy. The committee developed a questionnaire, which was administered throughout several communities in Jamaica to solicit the views and inputs of many older persons.
JORDAN	Yes, it was agreed in October 1998. The Ministry for Social Development is the lead agency with 5 members of staff working on issues affecting older people.	• To protect the homeless and poor who have no one else to look after them, through the homes of the elderly. • To provide services so that the elderly can remain in their own homes.		
LAO PDR	No, but the Elderly Assistance Division of the Ministry of Labour and Social Welfare is committed to gathering data in order to identify issues and formulate strategy.	The government is committed to policies that: • ensure the elderly can take part fully in socio-economic life; • strengthen the family system; • educate and mobilize public support.	The capacity of the State is very limited. Issues of ageing must compete with other urgent problems for limited resources. There is also a lack of expertise. The	The government recognizes the need for a close partnership between themselves, NGOs and other institutions for the benefit of the elderly.

Country	Is there a national policy relating to older people? Which Ministry is responsible for policy?	What are the main features of the policy? If no policy exists are there plans to introduce one?	Comments	Has there been any involvement of Civil Society in establishing the policy?
	The National Committee for Elderly Persons and the Ministry of Labour and Social Welfare are taking the lead. There are currently 15 staff members working on ageing issues.		population at large is less sensitized to the issues of older people. With different cultures in Lao there is a need to have a multi-faceted approach to accommodate the needs of all. The Lao government is getting international assistance to develop a social security system. This does not include an old age pension, as it is feared that the additional costs will affect Lao's competitiveness in the labour market.	
MALAWI	No. However, a draft policy has been referred to parliament and is expected to be debated fully.	No information as yet.	A senior parliamentarian has been assigned to lead the debate in parliament.	Not known of as yet.
MALAYSIA	Yes. It was agreed in 1996 under the aegis of the Ministry of National Unity and Community Development.	• The creation of an enabling environment which allows for the elderly to live with full respect and self-worth. • To ensure sufficient economic independence for the fulfilment of basic needs through income sources, family and societal support, self-effort and flexible social safety net programmes. • Ensuring access to health, recreation, social welfare and finance which will support and sustain their optimum physical, mental and emotional well-being. • Easy access to social and legal services to advance and sustain their rights. • The creation of a comprehensive social	A Health Council for the Elderly was created in 1997 to work on the expansion of curative, rehabilitative and preventive health care services. A review study is being undertaken by the Employees Provident Fund and the Pension Fund to consider the extension of benefits to the self-employed and those working in the informal sector.	

	security system to produce a stable income for the welfare of the elderly. • Comprehensive data and information collection with the cooperation of both public and private agencies for planning purposes.			
MALDIVES	No. However, the new Population Section of the Ministry of Planning is gathering data relevant to ageing issues.	No information available.	Although there is no specific national policy on ageing, ageing issues are integrated within other social sector development plans. There is a need to sensitize service providers, the government and policy makers to ageing. The government's intention is to a) achieve sustainability, b) increase the involvement of NGOs in the planning process. The objectives of the planning process are to: 1 Identify the country's needs by the year 2003. 2 Establish an effective coordinating body. 3 To conduct a survey on ageing and use census data to create a database by the year 2004. 4 Integrate ageing issues into planning by the year 2005.	There is a lack of input by non-professionals and non-governmental sources.
MALI	Yes. It was agreed in 1993. The Ministry of Health, Older People and Solidarity is responsible for older people's issues. All cabinet members in the Ministry deal with older people's issues.	• Reduce the inequalities and injustices towards older people. • Ensure better health and social welfare for them. • Ensure their socio-economic development. • Encourage them to have a dynamic community life. • Help them to participate in an active city life.		This policy was drawn up during a national seminar, which took place in April 1992. Social work professionals, NGO staff, Pensioners' Associations, Health and Social Service professionals were all part of the seminar and contributed to the policy.

Country	Is there a national policy relating to older people? Which Ministry is responsible for policy?	What are the main features of the policy? If no policy exists are there plans to introduce one?	Comments	Has there been any involvement of Civil Society in establishing the policy?
MAURITIUS	Yes. The Ministry of Social Security and National Solidarity is the body which normally deals with older people.	Government policy is based on an active solidarity towards aged persons through the provision of added and adequate protection with a view to ensuring that they have the necessary social, economic, and psychological support. Focus of the policy is to: • provide direct assistance (universal pensions and other allowances and facilities); • empower senior citizens; • provide welfare/recreational facilities; • provide homes for the elderly.	The elderly population is the fastest growing in Mauritius and their need for a healthy ageing has been recognized and factorized in social policy planning.	
MONGOLIA	The 1996 law on relief and assistance for the Elderly defines services for older people. The Ministry of Health and Social Welfare has been designated as the national body. There are currently 40+ staff working on ageing issues.	• Provide older people with opportunities to benefit from the contributions they have made to the development of the country. • Develop an infrastructure that will guarantee all older people a livelihood, provide them with medical, social and cultural services and expand the range of subsidized services. • Enable older people to continue an active life and contribute to the country's development. • Promote and sustain the traditional love and respect of the elderly and the bonds between the generations.	The move towards a free market economy has entailed financial restrictions that have restricted the implementation of programmes. In sparsely populated rural areas older people have little access to information or services.	The Ministries of Population Policy and Labour, Health and others along with NGOs were involved.
MOZAMBIQUE	No. However the government of Mozambique hopes to develop a national policy before the next elections in October 1999. The Ministry of Social Welfare is responsible for developing the policy and has 2 members of staff focusing on the policy.	In the process of being drafted.		The University is putting together plans for research into the needs of older people, which will form the basis of developing the policy.

MYANMAR	No policy at present. The Ministry of Social Welfare, Relief and Resettlement is the lead agency. There are approximately 50 permanent staff working on ageing issues nationally.	No information available.	The government is focusing on health provision for older people. A national health policy was introduced to raise the level of health in the country and promote physical and mental well-being using primary health care to achieve 'Health for all by the Year 2000'. Training in healthcare for the elderly will be given to 300 doctors and nurses and 11,000 basic health workers. There is a lack of technical and financial assistance.
NEPAL	No national policy as yet. However, the Nepalese Commission has issued a 'Concept Paper' which has incorporated some elements of the ageing agenda.	• To establish geriatric wards in regional hospitals. • To establish residential homes for older people in each region and encourage NGOs to manage them. • Implement income generation schemes for those in residential care. • Utilize older people's experiences for the benefit of national development.	Ageing is not standardized as a concept across ministries, nor are they aware of ageing problems or issues. Coordination is lacking between ministries. The National Planning Commission's role is to define policy and not to implement it.
PAKISTAN	Yes. It was agreed in October 1998. A National Committee on Ageing under the Federal Ministry of Social Welfare and Special Education was set up to look at ageing issues.	To promote the social and economic security of senior citizens while enabling them to contribute to national development.	Traditional family support has meant that hitherto ageing issues have had low priority.
PANAMA	Yes. The Ministry for Youth, Women, Children and the Family (MYWCF) is responsible for older people. There are 6 civil servants focusing on ageing issues.	• At a national level the policy aims at developing programmes and services which are beneficial for the public. • It tends to tackle the ageing phenomenon and the problems of old age by creating, empowering and improving new and existing administrative resources in the country.	The Society for the Welfare of Elderly Persons (SWEP) drafted a concept paper in consultation with other organizations. It is looking at sector policies and acting as a motivator. SWEP is planning to hold national consultative meetings. . The National Council on Older People will have representatives from the government ministries, municipal and civic authorities as well as religious and public sector bodies. This organization will be responsible for planning, revising and formulating policy as regards older people and monitor their performance/fulfilment. It is

Country	*Is there a national policy relating to older people? Which Ministry is responsible for policy?*	*What are the main features of the policy? If no policy exists are there plans to introduce one?*	*Comments*	*Has there been any involvement of Civil Society in establishing the policy?*
				through this agency that civil society will have the maximum active participation in terms of social policy.
PAPUA NEW GUINEA	No. The national policy is part of the government's agenda and will be discussed after the launch of the IYOP. The Ministry of Family Affairs will be the lead agency, with Health and Education also involved.	No information available.	The major problem in developing a national policy is that of funding. There also appears to be a lack of cooperation between the different agencies that might be involved ie government, NGOs, private sector and donors. This is particularly worrying.	
PERU	No. The Ministry for the Promotion of Women and Human Development (PROMUDEH) has responsibility for ageing issues. There is only one member of staff who is in charge of ageing issues.	PROMUDEH has convened a team of experts to work on Policy Procedures on Older People. The aim is to have a first draft ready for October 1999. However, ageing remains low on the government's priorities.	As no policy on older people exists, the needs and abilities of this sector of the population are not cared for nor developed.	
PHILIPPINES	Currently in draft form. The Bills are pending in both the Congress and Senate of the Philippines' legislature. The act has been called a 'Magna Carta for Older People'.	*'the State shall give full support to the improvement of the total well-being of the elderly and their full participation in society.* • Toward this end the State shall adopt policies ensuring the health, rehabilitation and self-reliance of older persons. • Older persons have the same rights as other people to take their proper place in society. They should be empowered to be self-reliant and live freely and as independently as possible. This must be the concern of the family, community and government. • The health care and rehabilitation of the	A number of laws have already highlighted issues of ageing but have been rather misguided. The Senior Citizens' Act (1996) gave older people 20 per cent discounts on medicine, transport, entertainment and restaurants, some of which were of little use to the rural poor. RA 7876 (1997) provided for the establishment of Senior Citizens' centres in every municipality but the	The Philippines Congress provides for sectoral representation and in the last two congresses there has been representation from the elderly sector. The latest representative is 86 years old. The act will establish a National Council for the Welfare of Older Persons that will comprise government, non-government and people's organizations. The council will appoint two older people and two representatives from the

		disabled older persons shall be the concern of the government. • The State recognizes the important role of the private sector in the improvement of the welfare of older persons and actively seeks their partnership.'	land on which they are to be built must be donated which is unlikely to happen in urban areas.	private sector.
RWANDA	No national policy as yet. However, the government is planning to develop a national policy for older people in the country. Currently the Ministry of Social Affairs is responsible for work on ageing.	No information available.	HAI are presently talking with the government and identifying ways of taking this initiative forward.	
SINGAPORE	A number of laws relate to the well-being of older citizens, although there is no national policy. The Inter-Ministerial Committee on Ageing Population is the lead agency. The Elderly Development Division of the Ministry of Community Development has 12 members of staff working on ageing issues. Staff from other ministries also deal with relevant issues as they arise.	• The welfare of the elderly person is the collective responsibility of the individual, the family, the community and the government. • The integration of the older person, as an active and contributory member, into the mainstream of economic and community life. • The family must provide the care, respect and emotional as well as financial support for the elderly person. • The community including employers, neighbours, voluntary organizations etc is an important source of support enriching lives and providing services for those who cannot cope. • The individual should strive to remain physically and socially active. • The government in its turn will put in place the necessary infrastructure, resources and programmes.		The Inter-Ministerial Committee on Ageing Population comprises representatives from government ministries, statutory boards and non-government agencies. They have drawn on the expertise of experts in civil society, academics and NGOs and will continue to do so.
SOUTH AFRICA	Yes.	The guiding principle for the policy is that 'older persons should be enabled to live active, healthy and independent lives for as long as possible' (discussion document on ageing, 1995). Main features of the policy include: • Responsibility for older people divided	The policy aims to increase the focus on community-based care and support, rather than the pre-existing emphasis on residential care. There has been a strong impetus towards replacing prior imbalances	The policy was drafted by a Discussion Group on Ageing consisting of government and representatives of NGOs, community organizations and older people.

Country	Is there a national policy relating to older people? Which Ministry is responsible for policy?	What are the main features of the policy? If no policy exists are there plans to introduce one?	Comments	Has there been any involvement of Civil Society in establishing the policy?
		between individuals, civil society and the state. • Appropriate, affordable community-based care should include adequate housing as a cornerstone. • Adequate primary health care is also critically important. • 'The protection of the rights of older persons requires special attention in view of the prevalence of age discrimination and abuse' (discussion document on ageing, 1995).	of provision by racially integrated services. South Africa is almost unique in sub-Saharan Africa in having made pension provision universal. The old age pension now provides a major source of income for South Africa's poorest families.	
SOUTH KOREA	Yes, 'The Mid and Long Term Plan of Health and Social Welfare for the Elderly'. It was agreed in January 1999. The Older Persons' Welfare Division of the Ministry of Health and Welfare is the lead agency. There are approximately 12 staff members working in the above division on older people's issues.	The policy proposes four areas of development until the year 2003: • Building an infrastructure for economic independence. • Securing a healthy life. • Promoting an active life. • Promoting social welfare.	The major constraints are budget and manpower to implement the new plan. The welfare budget for older people is only 0.24 per cent of total government expenditure.	The Older Persons' Welfare Division of the Ministry of Health and Welfare, The Korea Institute for Health and Social Affairs and NGOs, including associations for the elderly, have worked together on policy development.
SRI LANKA	Yes. The National policy and Action Plan on the Welfare of Elders was drawn up in 1992. It is in the process of being implemented. The Sri Lanka National Committee on Ageing is responsible for issues concerning older people. There are currently 15 members of staff working in the Department of Social Services on ageing issues.	• To enable all Sri Lankans on entering old age to lead socially, economically, physically, mentally and spiritually useful lives. • The National Plan aims to plan the welfare of the older person in Sri Lanka in accordance with traditional custom while strengthening the family unit and making society aware of ageing issues.	There are inadequately trained staff and a lack of financial resources, which make it difficult to implement the plan.	The policy was prepared by the Ministry of Social Services through the Sri Lanka National Committee on Ageing. Workshops and seminars were held in 1992 with academics, social service and institutional representatives.

ST LUCIA	No National Policy as yet. Policy recommendations were presented to the government some years ago; these are presently being reviewed. The Ministry of Health, Human Services, Family Affairs and Women has responsibility for matters dealing with older people.	Currently under review.	There are a number of policies and programmes in place which impact on older people. These are: • The Public Assistance Act, No 17 of 1967, which states that any old age person who is unable to maintain him or herself, is entitled to public assistance. Older persons on public assistance are assisted with glasses and burial services. • Operation of one residential home for older people, and subsidies to five privately run homes. • Government recently approved an Annual Subvention to the National Council of and for Older Persons. • Free medical attention to very needy older persons.	The St Lucia National Council of and for Older Persons has been lobbying the government to develop a comprehensive National Policy for Older Persons. A study of the situation of older people is planned for 1999, which will involve civil society organizations, and which will form the basis of policy development.
ST VINCENT AND THE GRENADINES	None as yet. The Ministry of Health is responsible for coordination of activity relating to older people.	A plan of action is being developed, for completion by the end of 1999.		A national consultation was held in 1998. This meeting developed a basis for establishing national policy guidelines. A committee was formed to draw up the guidelines, and to continue the work of raising public awareness regarding older people's issues.
TANZANIA	No National Policy as yet. There are plans to develop a policy as part of the national targets for 1999 IYOP. The Department of Social Welfare, Ministry of Labour and Youth Development, is	No information available.	There are few organizations concerned with ageing in Tanzania. Also, there are no geriatric medical specialists, no mention of older people in either social work training course or any specific	

Country	Is there a national policy relating to older people? Which Ministry is responsible for policy?	What are the main features of the policy? If no policy exists are there plans to introduce one?	Comments	Has there been any involvement of Civil Society in establishing the policy?
	responsible for ageing issues.		academics looking at ageing issues. The Ministry responsible has approved in principle the creation of an office for older persons and an officer but there are no further details.	
THAILAND	Yes. Until 1997 the National Committee on Ageing was responsible for developing national policies concerning older persons. Currently the committee is undergoing restructuring.	The Long Term Plan for the Elderly outlines strategies in five areas: • health; • education; • income and employment; • social and cultural issues; • social welfare. It aims to make the older person self-reliant and enable the family to give care and support.	There is concern that the current economic crisis in Thailand may make the government reconsider the feasibility of free health care. It may also delay if not curtail the implementation of other sector policies. The government's policy to limit numbers of governmental staff in all agencies will have an impact on expansion of services especially in state-run residential centres where the numbers of residents are increasing each year.	
UGANDA	None as yet. The Ministry of Gender, Labour & Social Development is responsible for older people's policy issues. Since 1998 there has been a Minister for the Elderly and Disability.	The government is currently developing a proposal for a research programme leading to the development of a policy proposal for Cabinet to recommend to Parliament.	Article 32 of the Constitution guarantees the social protection of older people, but currently welfare services and social insurance are very limited.	NGOs (led by the Uganda Reach the Aged Association) and the academic community have been involved in the development of the strategy so far. The planned research aims to target the views of older people as a priority.
VIETNAM	No, however the Department of Social Welfare, Ministry of Labour, Invalids and Social Affairs (MOLISA), Ministry of Health and Social Insurance	In 1991 the government approved the 'Strategy for Socio-economic Stabilisation and Development to the year 2000' which included various safeguards for sections of society as Vietnam developed into a market	There is as yet no coherent policy. The Central Committee of the Communist Party at the 1996 Eighth National Congress had only passing reference to	

Agency are the lead agencies coordinating a policy on ageing issues.

economy.
The main features of the policies for older people are:

- The integration of the elderly into the community and enabling the family to implement its responsibilities of care for parents and grandparents.
- Amendments to the pension system to make it more effective.
- The establishment of a network of care and social centres.

pensioners and the destitute. There is no mention of the elderly in the current five-year plan (1996–2000).
Traditions of filial piety and respect lead some to fear that a social welfare programme may damage the tradition of family and community support.

Taking Account of Older People in Development Cooperation: A Review of the Status of Ageing in Major Bilateral and Multilateral Aid Agencies

In 1996, aid donors signed up to an ambitious set of targets for development cooperation drawn from the UN Summits of the previous decade. The first and most important of these targets is to halve the number of people living in extreme poverty by 2015.

Taking account of the contribution and needs of older people living in developing countries is critical to the reduction of poverty and the achievement of this target but ageing as an issue is virtually invisible in most aid programmes. There are signs of change but a major shift in attitude needs to take place in recognition of both the rights and the contribution of older people.

Bilateral donors

Bilateral Donor	The Status of Ageing in Development Cooperation
AUSTRALIA	Australia's aid programme is addressing the International Year of Older Persons, allocating A$50,000 to support an activity which benefits policy makers in Care of the Elderly in the Pacific Region. This will involve collaboration between the United Nations International Institute on Ageing (INIA), the Pacific Community and Australia's aid programme and provides a short course for regional policy makers. Australia's aid programme is also focusing on health issues for the elderly under two large projects: 'Fiji: Taveuni Community Based Health Project' (A$12 million over 5 years) and 'Philippines: Integrated Community Health Services Project'. This will be co-financed with the Asian Development Bank (ADB) and is part of a larger $71.9 million Integrated Community Health Services Project. This larger project comprises a loan of $34.9 million from the ADB, grant funds of around $23.5 million from the Australian Government and $13.5 million from the Government of the Philippines and participating local government units.
AUSTRIA	Austria does not exclude older people, but they are not a target group in their own right. While there are programmes that benefit older people along with other sectors of society there are none that are specifically aimed at them. Older people are not mentioned as a separate group that needs to be taken into account under the Austrian Three Year Programme for Development. A number of programmes that support disabled people may include older people with disabilities.
BELGIUM	Ageing is seen as a relatively new issue and there do not appear to be any specific projects focused on older people. However, with increased awareness of ageing as an issue for both developing and industrial countries, future activities are possible. In 1998 the Government of Belgium supported a meeting on 'Population Ageing: Improving the Lives of Older Persons' hosted by UNFPA in collaboration with the Population and Family Study Centre in Belgium, as part of the five-year follow up to the International Conference on Population and Development.

CANADA

There are no specific programmes relating to ageing and development and no policy statements on the subject but there is some responsive project funding to NGOs concerned with older people. Aspects of existing policies on health and development or basic human needs, by implication, would apply to the situation facing older people.

DENMARK

Danish development cooperation has no activities that specifically target older people. However, the health sector is a major focus in around seven of the 20 programme countries in which Danish aid is concentrated. Within the health programmes there are activities that benefit the older person. When preparing health programmes, DANIDA (the Danish official development agency) makes a point of discussing with governments and beneficiaries the degree to which health services are available to the poorest of the poor, and this would include older people. There may also be small projects funded by Danish embassies that would be of benefit to the older person.

The Health Sector Guidelines mention older people very infrequently, concentrating mainly on children and reproductive health, as well as curative policies. The Guidelines do however discuss the vulnerable in society. Under HIV/AIDS they mention the demographic impact of increasing the ratio of older people and children to those of productive age, and also 'support the development of appropriate orphan care systems that focus on family or family like structures'. The guidelines also acknowledge that there is likely to be a shift in emphasis as 'an increasing proportion of the population in developing countries will be elderly, and, as in industrialized countries, chronic and degenerative health problems will assume greater epidemiological significance'.

FINLAND

The older person has not up to now been a specific focus of the Finnish aid programme, however, there have been a few activities funded that do focus on older people in developing countries:

1   Through the UNFPA follow up to the International Conference on Population and Development of which one focus is population ageing.
2   NGOs working with older people have been funded. Discussions were taking place at the time of writing on Finnish support for funding of a fact-finding mission to improve welfare services for older people in a number of African countries.

FRANCE

There are no projects specifically targeting older people. Older people would be included within projects concerned with traditional medicine, where their knowledge is crucial to understanding. Similarly, older people would be included in projects aimed at strengthening local democracy, where older people's groups and councils would be consulted as part of the process.

GERMANY

There is no official policy targeting the older person. There are projects which include the older person amongst their beneficiaries, but the German aid programme is more focused on youth and children as a specific target group. There is an awareness of the fact that ageing and the older person are being addressed in international discussions.

IRELAND

Ireland was, at the time of writing, at an advanced stage of revision of their Health Sector Strategy in which there is an explicit component for people with disabilities and for older people. This is a major change. Older people had been acknowledged, but implicitly, under the 'vulnerable in society'. The HIV/AIDS support programme also takes account of the needs of older people. There is likely to be increased scope for presenting the needs of older people under the Irish programme of Health Sector Development. This may provide a platform to put forward Ireland's perspective on health policies, which would include the component on ageing.

JAPAN

There are a number of projects whose beneficiaries include older people. Currently, there are two initiatives specifically aimed at benefiting older people:

1   Acceptance of Trainers for the Ageing Society and Welfare Policy Seminar. The purpose of the seminar is to provide participants with knowledge and experience for planning measures to promote welfare policies and related activities through information exchange and discussions on achievements in social welfare services for the older person.
2   Japan International Co-operation Agency (JICA) has despatched four overseas co-operation volunteers (OCVs) to developing countries to work specifically with older

people. Two are teaching massage and handicraft skills to older people's groups at the Christianity Institution in Chile. One is a care worker for elderly people and people with disabilities at the governmental organization in Sarawak, Malaysia and another volunteer is providing medical service skills for older people to Indonesian counterparts at the national hospital.

THE NETHERLANDS
The Ministry of Foreign Affairs held a seminar in January 1999 on 'Older Persons in Developing Countries' with the Ministry of Health and the Netherlands Committee for the International Year of Older Persons. An outcome of this seminar will be the development of a policy statement as to how the Dutch Government can make a positive contribution to the specific problems arising from the rapid increase in the numbers of older persons in developing countries. The policy is scheduled for completion later in 1999 and it is intended that activities resulting from the policy will dovetail into existing programmes.

NEW ZEALAND
The New Zealand Overseas Development Agency (NZODA) has no plans for the International Year of Older Persons. The only activity notified by NZODA concerning the older person was providing support for a student under the Postgraduate Scholarship Scheme to undertake a Master of Health Sciences Programme which will include a study of nursing care for the elderly in Sarawak, Malaysia.

NORWAY
The bilateral position is that there are no specific programmes for the older person because Norway's development cooperation is focused on work at the sectoral level. Smaller projects are dealt with through the NGO Unit and there is currently no specific dialogue with NGOs on the subject, however, there may be certain elements by which older people benefit.

SPAIN
Between 1995 and 1997 a number of initiatives have been funded by the Spanish Agency for International Co-operation (AECI), the Spanish Institute for Migration and Social Services (IMERSO), incorporated within the Spanish Ministry of Labour and Social Affairs and via the local governments. The projects have either been carried out by the institutions themselves or via NGOs and are targeting communities primarily in Latin America, although projects have been funded during this period in Bosnia, Croatia, Romania, Poland, India and Mozambique. Those projects funded by local authorities tend to focus their activities on basic infrastructure – primarily the rehabilitation and building of centres for older people and the supply of equipment. IMERSO's activities have focused more on capacity building and policy advice. IMERSO has been substantially involved in policy formulation for older people in Latin American countries. The total value of projects aimed specifically at older people during the period 1995–1997 amounted to just over 341million pesetas (roughly US$2.7 million), with NGO implemented projects accounting for 62 per cent of the funds.

SWEDEN
Sweden has not yet brought ageing onto the development agenda, however, a position paper on public health in general is being developed and scheduled to be released after mid 2000. Ageing may be a 'sub' subject within this paper. Currently the Swedish health sector programme focuses on women and children. There is a programme for the rehabilitation of people with disabilities and older people may be benefiting under this, but there is nothing that specifically targets the older person.

SWITZERLAND
There is nothing specifically aimed at the older person within SDC funding. However, this does not mean that senior citizens are not benefiting in some instances from SDC supported activities.

UK
The UK is working towards raising awareness of the issues facing the older person in developing countries within the Department for International Development (DFID). DFID have funded project work in the past, including both development and emergency programmes. The Department is currently involved in discussions with NGOs on the formulation of a concept paper to build awareness of ageing issues. DFID is also looking to develop an integrated strategy on ageing and the UK is a leading member of the informal Support Group on Ageing at the United Nations. The UK will be represented at the UN Expert Meeting on Ageing in early 2000.

USA
The United States Agency for International Development (USAID) does not fund programmes specifically aimed at older persons, however there are a number of projects that include the older person in their target groups. For the past two years they have had an infectious diseases initiative focusing on Malaria and TB in which older people benefit from

the programmes that aim to control and prevent these diseases. There are also a number of projects within central and eastern Europe, primarily under the Food Aid Initiative and the Bureau for Humanitarian Response – in Bosnia and Bulgaria, Georgia, Slovakia, the Ukraine. The Office of Food for Peace in the Bureau for Humanitarian Response operates programmes on food security targeted at the most vulnerable, which includes older people – in Sudan the programme always ensured that food rations were provided for the elderly, even when other segments of society were cut out.

Multilateral agencies

Multilateral Agency	The Status of Ageing in Development Cooperation
EUROPEAN UNION	The Commission of the European Communities does not have an overall policy relating to older people in developing countries. Nevertheless, through a number of sectoral and geographical budget lines it is among the leading multilateral donors for ageing and development issues.

Multilateral Agency — *The Status of Ageing in Development Cooperation*

EUROPEAN UNION

The Commission of the European Communities does not have an overall policy relating to older people in developing countries. Nevertheless, through a number of sectoral and geographical budget lines it is among the leading multilateral donors for ageing and development issues.

The Directorate-General for Development (Co-operation with Africa, Caribbean and Pacific Countries) funds projects aiding older people through co-financing, rehabilitation, human rights, food aid and health budgets. Funding for programmes in East and Central Europe has been made available by the Directorate for External Relations, although again this does not reflect specific policies relating to older people.

The European Community Humanitarian Office (ECHO) includes older people among vulnerable groups, although it does not have specific programmes for them. However ECHO funding has been given for humanitarian programmes in a number of emergencies in recent years. In recognition of the International Year of Older Persons ECHO is co-financing a research project on the issue of older people in emergencies, with a report and guidelines to be disseminated later this year.

The European Parliament Development and Aid Committee recently received a presentation on older people in developing countries.

ORGANISATION FOR ECONOMIC CO-OPERATION AND DEVELOPMENT (OECD)

The OECD interest in ageing in developing countries has been limited to pension reform in developing countries.

PAN AMERICAN HEALTH ORGANIZATION (PAHO)

PAHO has a specific unit on Aging and Health incorporated within the Family Health and Population Program of the Division of Health Promotion and Protection. The mission of the unit is to promote the health of older persons; however, its main focus is on developing the infrastructure and capability within the countries to address the needs of older persons and their families. The Programme Initiatives are as follows:

- Information Base Strengthening and Research.
- Dissemination of Information.
- Development of Social Communication and Advocacy.
- Human Resources Development.
- Formulation of policies, plans and programmes in the Region.

UNITED NATIONS DEVELOPMENT PROGRAMME (UNDP)

Ageing as such has not been a stated priority for UNDP, however, it is increasingly coming to the fore, with UNDP trying to incorporate it as much as possible, considering factors such as the specific contributory capabilities of older members in communities, within its participatory development strategies. There are some examples of programmes actually being focused towards older people (for instance, developing/refining social security systems) but most of the programming during the 1990s has looked at broader participative engagement of civil society.

In 1996 the Population Division organized a Working Group on Projecting Old-Age Mortality and its Consequences. The UN Population Division (UNPD) was given the responsibility of monitoring ageing research in various countries. A report was produced from the workshop, with recommendations for more longitudinal work that followed cohorts through transitions over time and for some form of international standardization of definitions to ease comparability.

UNITED NATIONS POPULATION FUND (UNFPA)

1994 saw the International Conference for Population and Development (ICPD) which produced a Programme of Action for Older Persons in which UNFPA took an active role. In 1997 UNFPA carried out a survey in many developing countries to see what developments had occurred since the ICPD. One of the issues explored was the degree to which governments and NGOs had taken action since ICPD to strengthen the provision of health care for older persons given the greater risk of their suffering a poor quality of health.

Responses from the African region were sparse, but the general theme was that the issue of the aged and provision for their health care has not yet assumed the proportions that would necessitate the mobilization of scarce resources.

Most Latin American and Caribbean countries noted that there was little or no explicit provision for the health care of older people.

Because of the wide variation in demographic status and degree of economic development, responses from Asian countries were wide ranging, reflecting substantially different priorities in recognition and action for the health of the elderly. Most countries tend to group the disadvantaged and marginalized sectors of society together.

WORLD BANK

The World Bank is actively promoting pension reform in many countries around the world. In 1994 it published *Averting the Old Age Crisis*. Current research is examining the issue of poor people who are uninsured or underinsured, administrative costs in individual account systems and the gender impact of pension reforms and the policy measures that should be considered to avoid gender disparity. Another project is looking at the economic impact of ageing populations on healthcare systems using data from Chile, Mexico, Brazil, Vietnam and Indonesia. There is little attention to projects focusing on more social and cultural issues around ageing.

WORLD HEALTH ORGANIZATION (WHO)

WHO has been interested in the health of older people since 1955 but it was only in 1974 that a first Expert Committee's report on the subject was published and in 1979 the World Health Assembly adopted its first Resolution targeted to health care of the elderly. This led to the establishment of a global Programme for Health of the Elderly (HEE) which was replaced in 1995 by a new programme on Ageing and Health. The programme incorporates the following perspectives:

- life course (elderly people are not to be compartmentalized but are part of the life cycle);
- health promotion (with a focus on healthy ageing/ageing well);
- cultural (the settings in which individuals' age determines their health status in older age);
- gender (differences in health as well as behavioural and societal attitudes);
- inter-generational (with emphasis on strategies to maintain cohesion between generations);
- ethical.

Facts, Figures and Trends in Ageing: Basic Data on Ageing and Development

Ageing is poorly documented and poorly understood. Few statistics show data disaggregated by age, let alone by different age groups among those over 60. Too few studies take the time to listen to and understand the experience of older people in developing countries. In Part II, six studies explored the situation of older people in a selection of geographical areas. Here, *The Ageing and Development Report* draws together the most significant figures on global ageing and ageing trends in developing countries.

Global ageing

Each of us alive now is living in an era of unprecedented global ageing – a worldwide process of change which is happening rapidly and inexorably. Ageing will become an almost universal feature of every society in the 21st century.

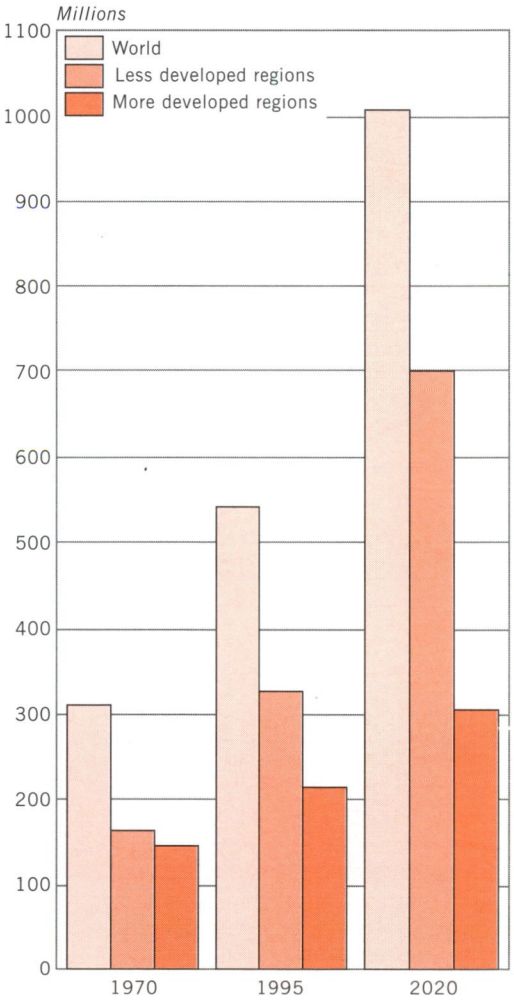

The numbers of people over 60

Millions

Legend:
- World
- Less developed regions
- More developed regions

(x-axis: 1970, 1995, 2020)

Source: UN Population Division, 1996

The share of older people in the world population

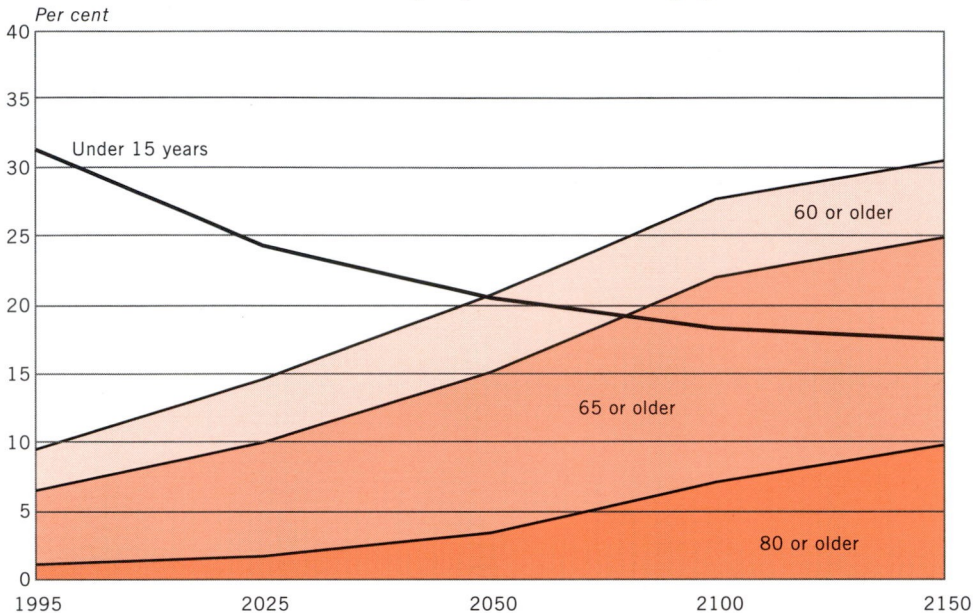

The share of older people in the population of developing regions

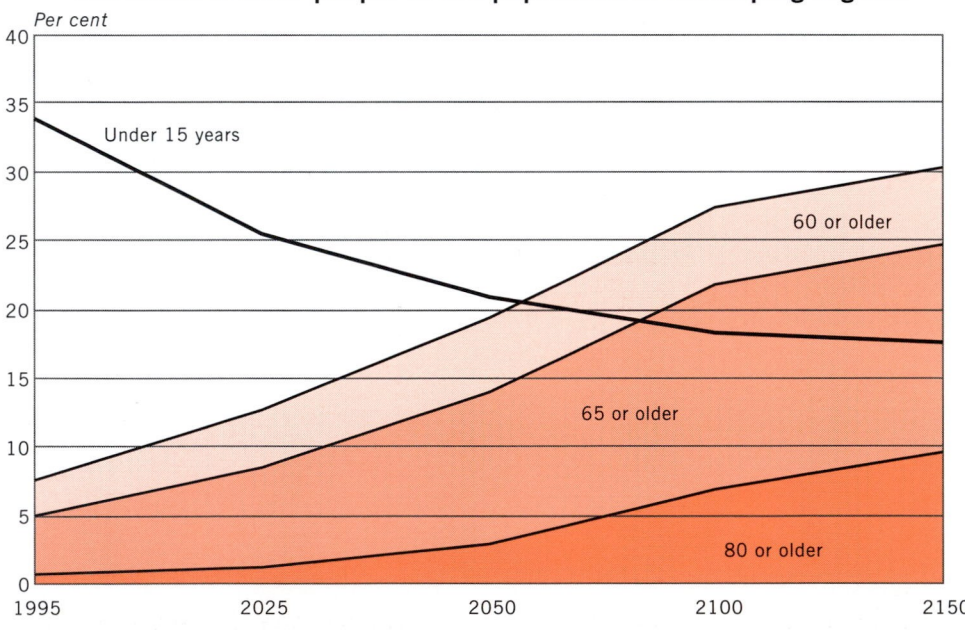

Source: UN Population Division, 1996

Globally, the proportion of the population that is over 60 is growing twice as fast as the population as a whole. In 2050, the percentage of people over 60 will exceed those under 15 and the gap will continue to widen for the next 100 years.

The world is getting older... and more quickly

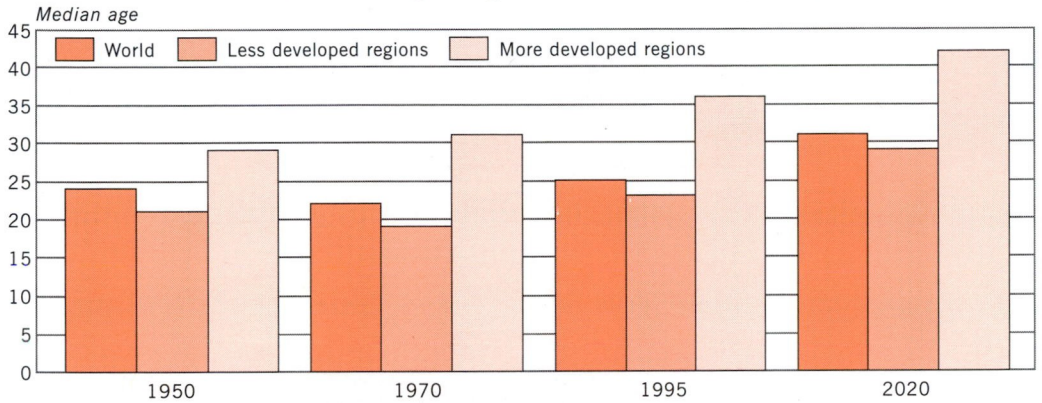

Source: UN Population Division, 1996

Annual growth rates in the populations of older people, 1995–2020

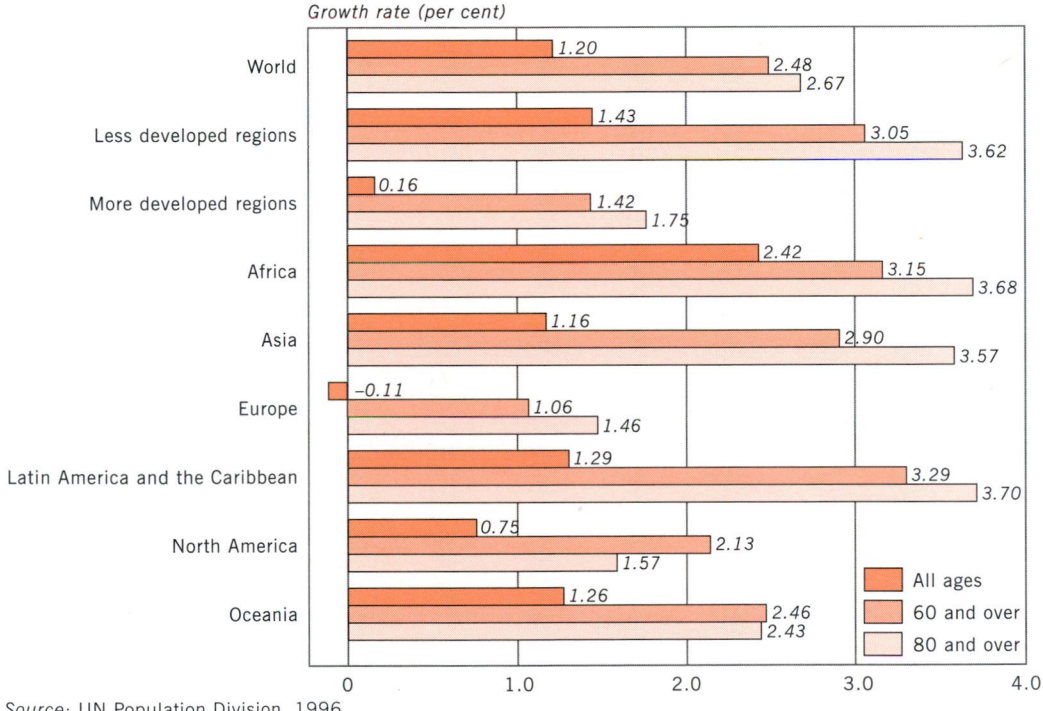

Source: UN Population Division, 1996

The world is getting older and at a rapidly increasing rate. During the 1960s and 1970s the world was characterized by increased youthful populations, especially in low income countries. But in the 1980s and 1990s the median age of the population has been rising almost everywhere and will grow more rapidly in the early part of the next century.[1]

Life expectancy at birth – estimates for 1990–1995 and assumptions to 2150

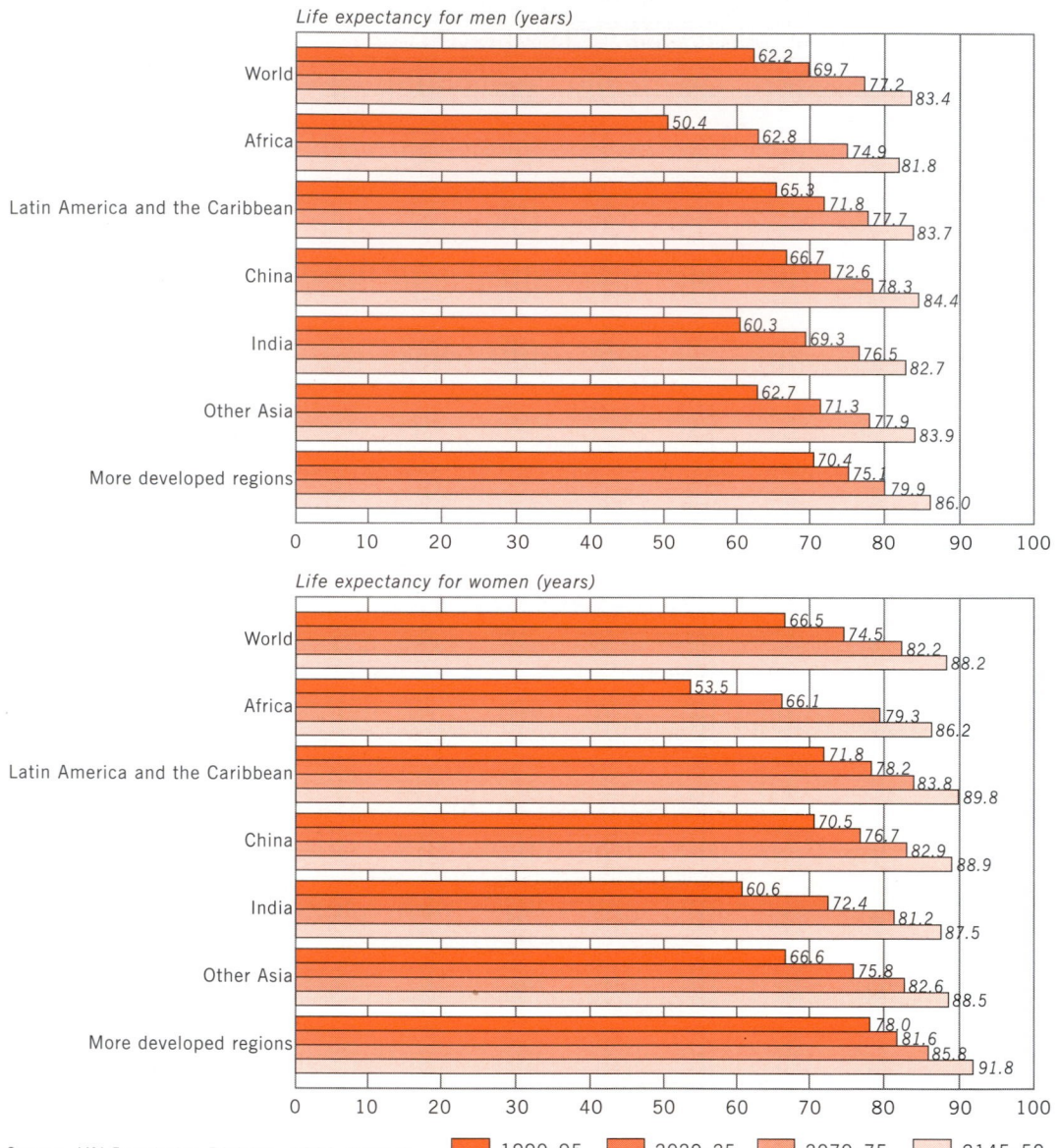

Source: UN Population Division, 1996, Table 3 · 1990–95 · 2020–25 · 2070–75 · 2145–50

Life expectancy

Old age is the public health success story of the 20th century. Increasing numbers of people born throughout the world will survive the childhood diseases and disabilities that ravaged their predecessors. They can look forward to life expectancies that no one dreamed about centuries ago.[2]

Life expectancy at 65 for selected countries in Asia

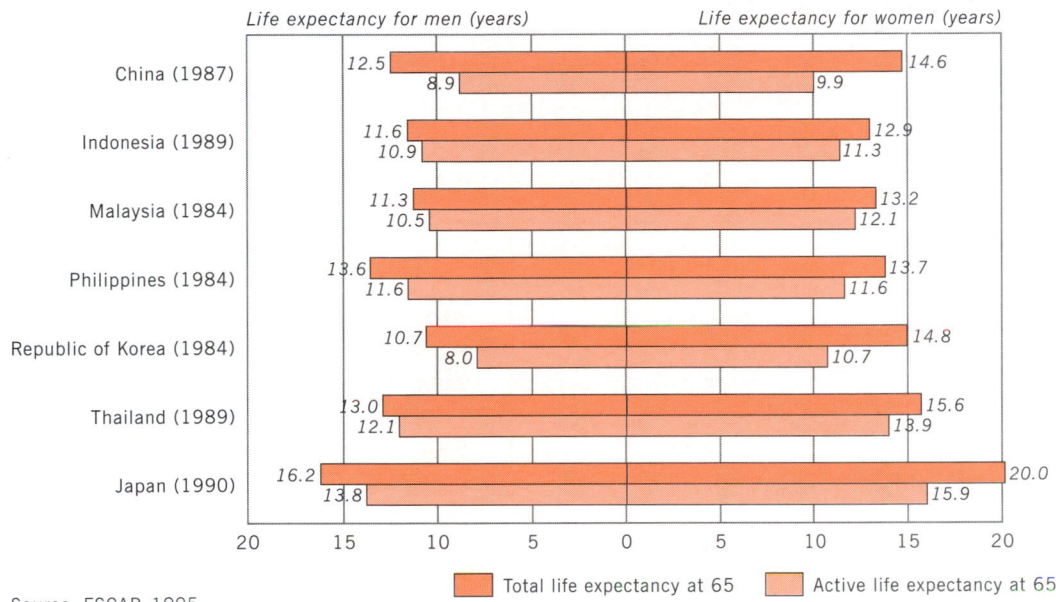

Source: ESCAP, 1995

There has long been a myth that ageing is not an issue for developing countries because overall life expectancy is low. But for those who reach 60, the prospects for additional years of life are good.

The proportion and number of people over 60 in selected developing countries

	Percentage of people over 60 in 1996	Percentage of people over 60 in 2025	Numbers of people over 60 in 1996 (millions)	Numbers of people over 60 in 2025 (millions)
China	9	20	115	290
India	7	12	62	165
Mexico	7	13	6	18
Egypt	6	10	4	10
South Africa	7	10	3	6
Brazil	7	16	11	31

Source: US Bureau of the Census, 1996a

This longer life expectancy translates into startling numbers. On a low mortality scenario, the over 65 year old population of China will grow from 63 million in 1990 to more than 400 million in 2050. The number of people over 85 could increase from under 3 million to 80 million.

A growing majority of the world's older people live in developing countries

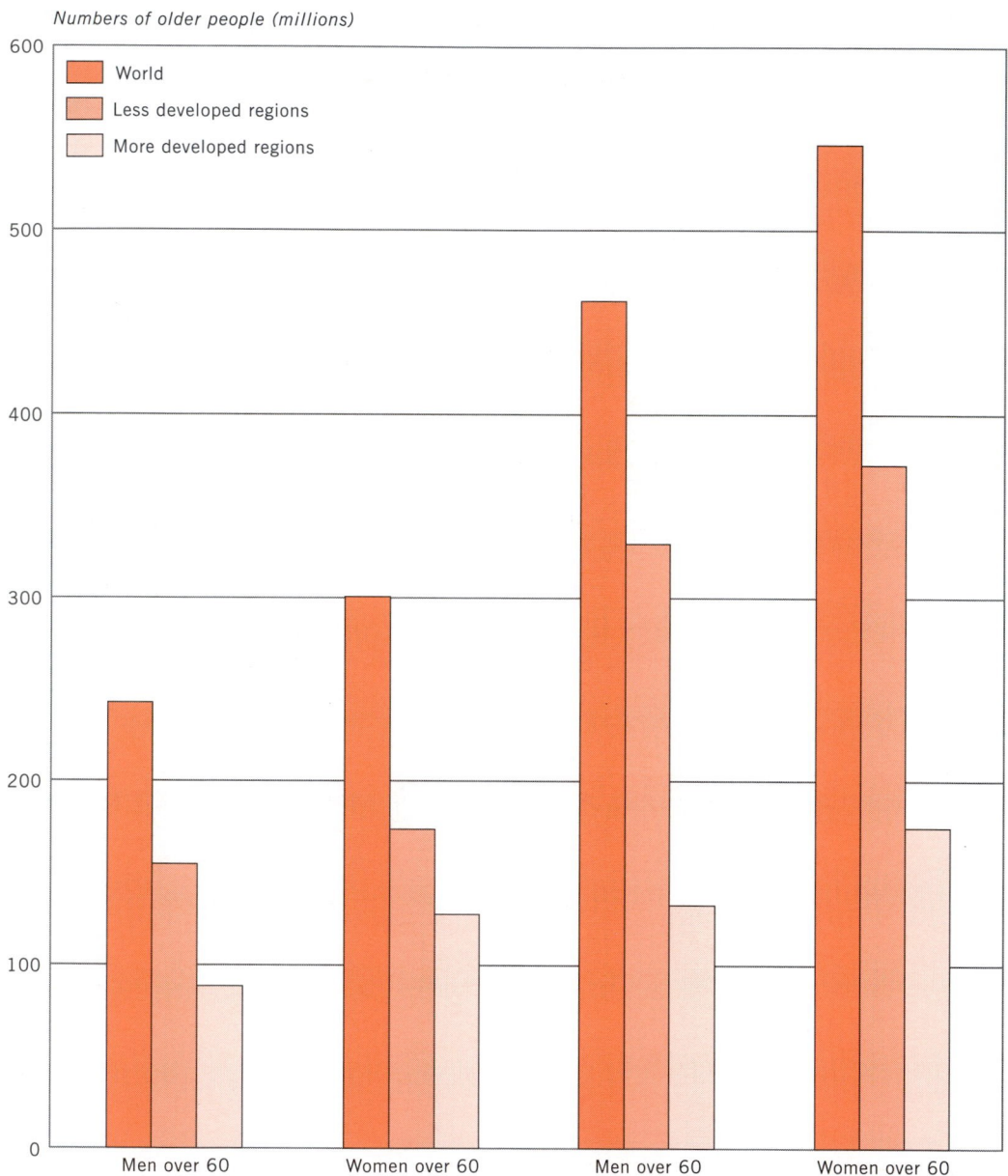

Numbers of older people (millions)

Legend:
- World
- Less developed regions
- More developed regions

Categories:
- Men over 60 in 1995
- Women over 60 in 1995
- Men over 60 in 2020
- Women over 60 in 2020

Source: UN Population Division, 1996

Ageing in developing countries

The majority of the world's older people live in developing countries:

Of the billion people over 60 in 2020, 700 million will live in developing countries.

Annual growth rates of older populations, 1970–1995 and 1995–2020

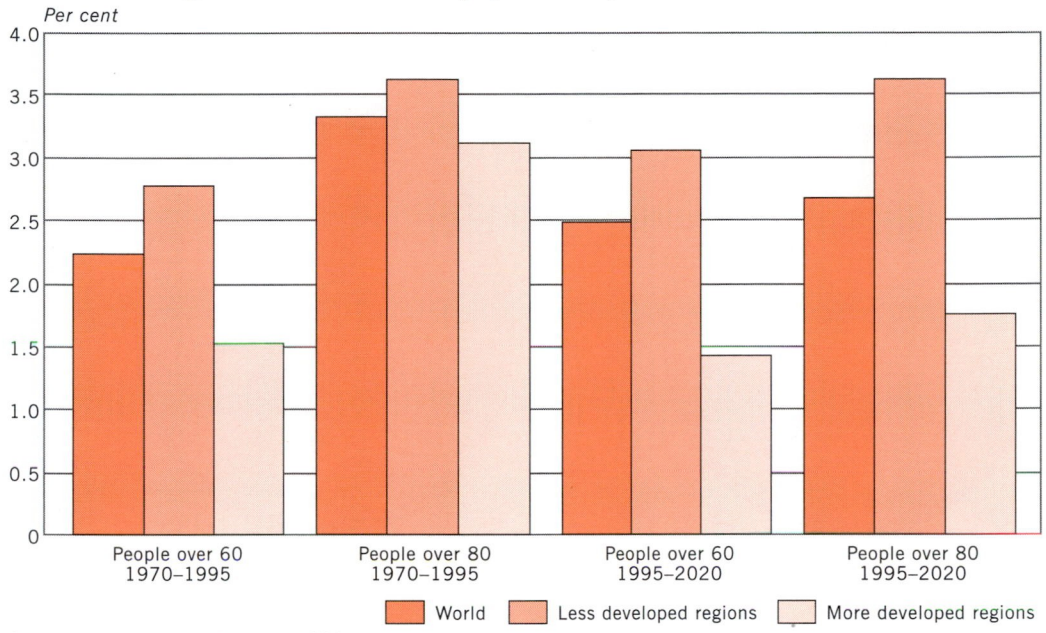

Source: UN Population Division, 1996

Growth of population over 60, 1970–1995 and 1995–2020

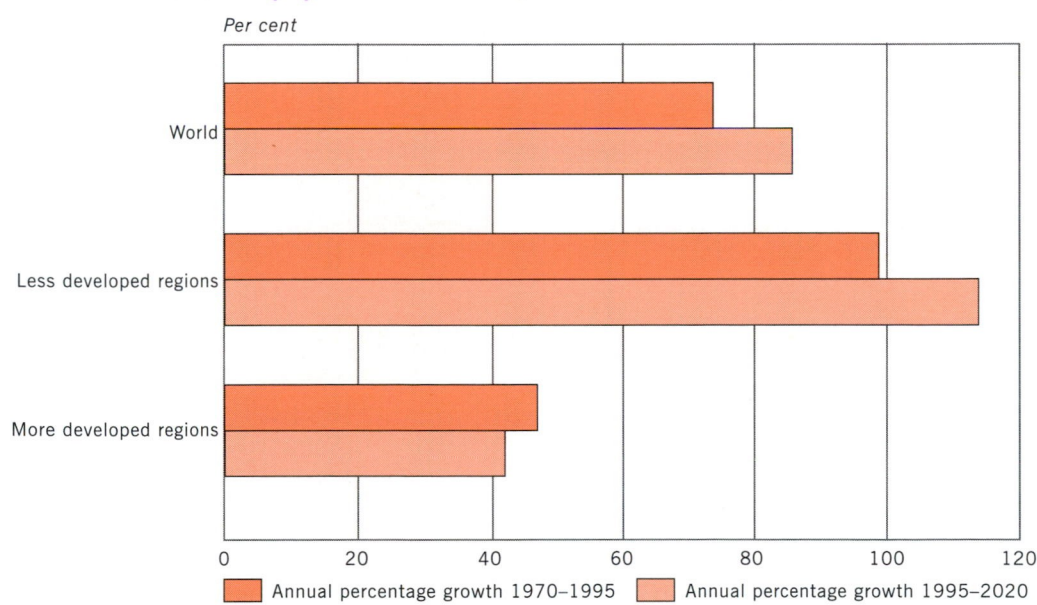

Source: UN Population Division, 1996

The rate of growth of older populations is highest in developing countries. The world population of people over 60 increased by more than 12 million in 1995. 80 per cent of the increase occurred in developing countries.

Distribution of world population over 60 and over 80 by region

Population over 60 (millions)

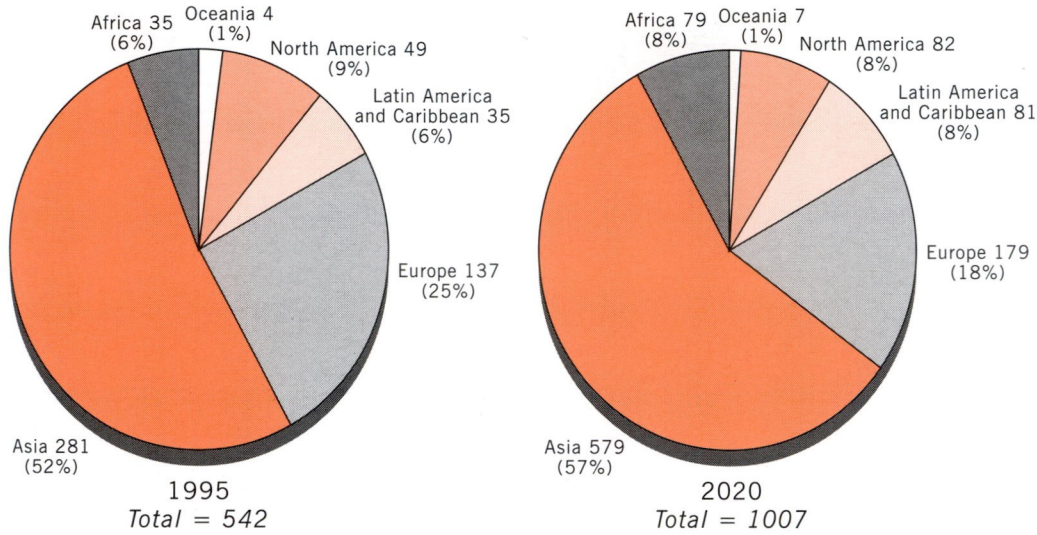

Population over 80 (millions)

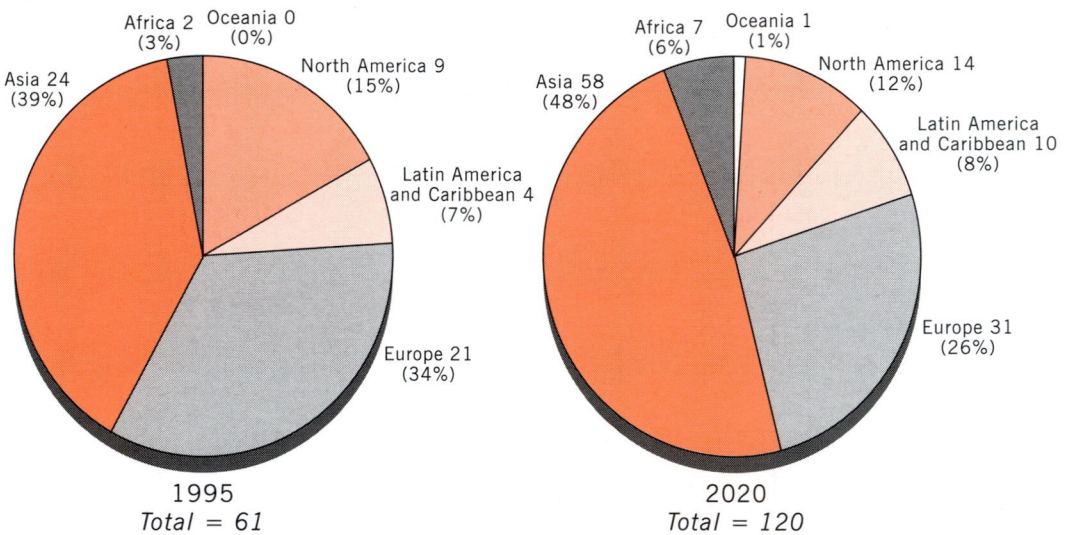

Source: UN Population Division, 1996

Older populations are concentrated in Asia. Currently, over half of the world's population over 60 are living in Asia. By 2020, 48 per cent of people over 80 will be living in Asia.

The number of people over 60 in Africa will more than double by 2020 and its share of people over 80 will increase from 3 per cent to 6 per cent of the global population.

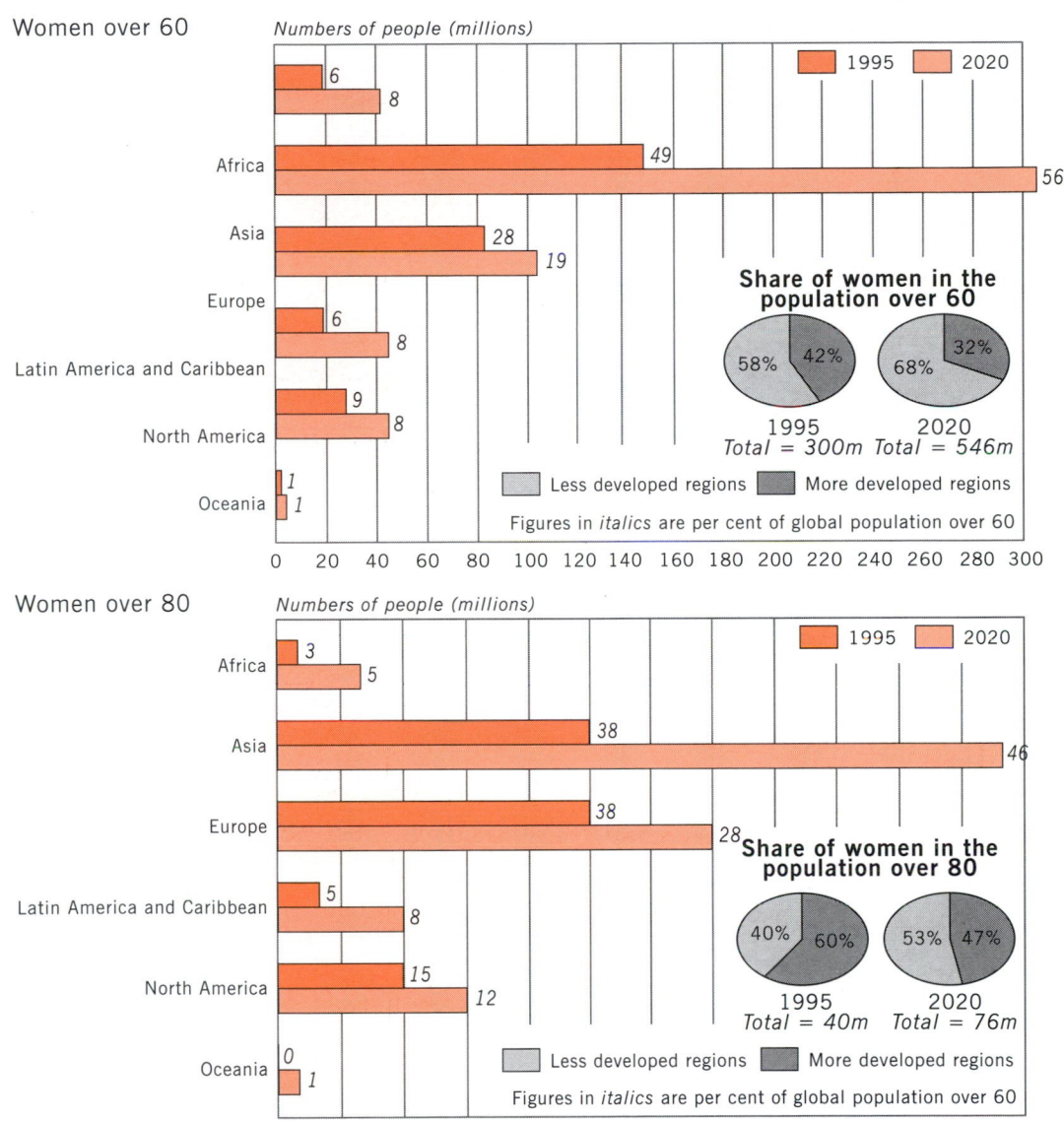

World distribution of women over 60 and over 80 by region

Women over 60

Women over 80

Source: UN Population Division, 1996, quoted in Leete

Gender

The majority of the world's older people are women. Of the 542 million people over 60 in 1995, 55 per cent were women. While the share remains roughly the same, those numbers will almost double by 2020.

For the over 80s, women currently outnumber men by approximately two to one.

Currently 58 per cent of women over 60 live in developing countries. That will grow to 70 per cent by 2020.

The gender gap between older men and women

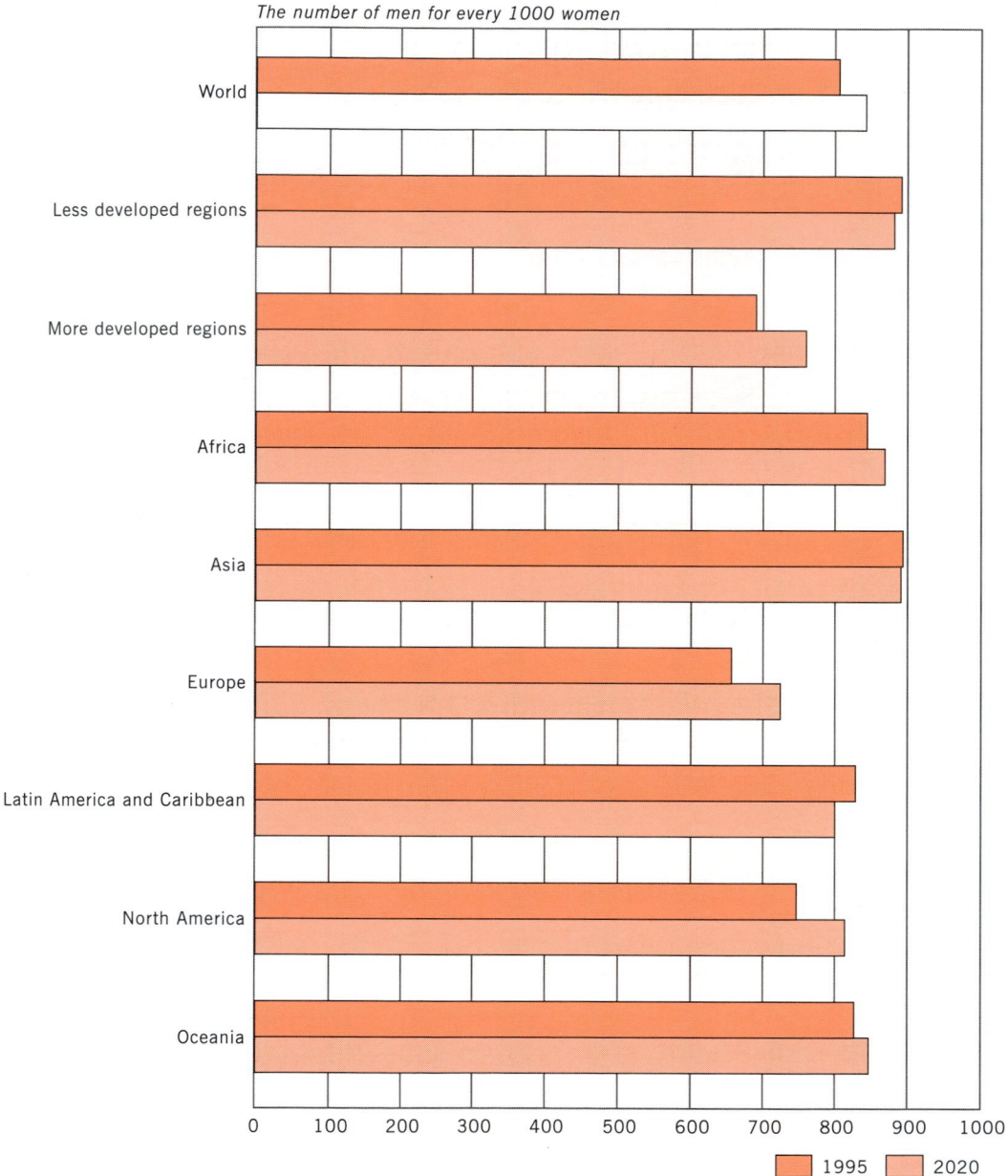

The number of men for every 1000 women

Source: UN Population Division, 1996

In almost all countries women enjoy longer life expectancy than men. But the gender gap is much smaller in developing countries where women live around three years longer than men, compared with seven years in developed countries. This is largely due to much higher rates of maternal mortality.

Percentage of men and women over 60 who are widowed

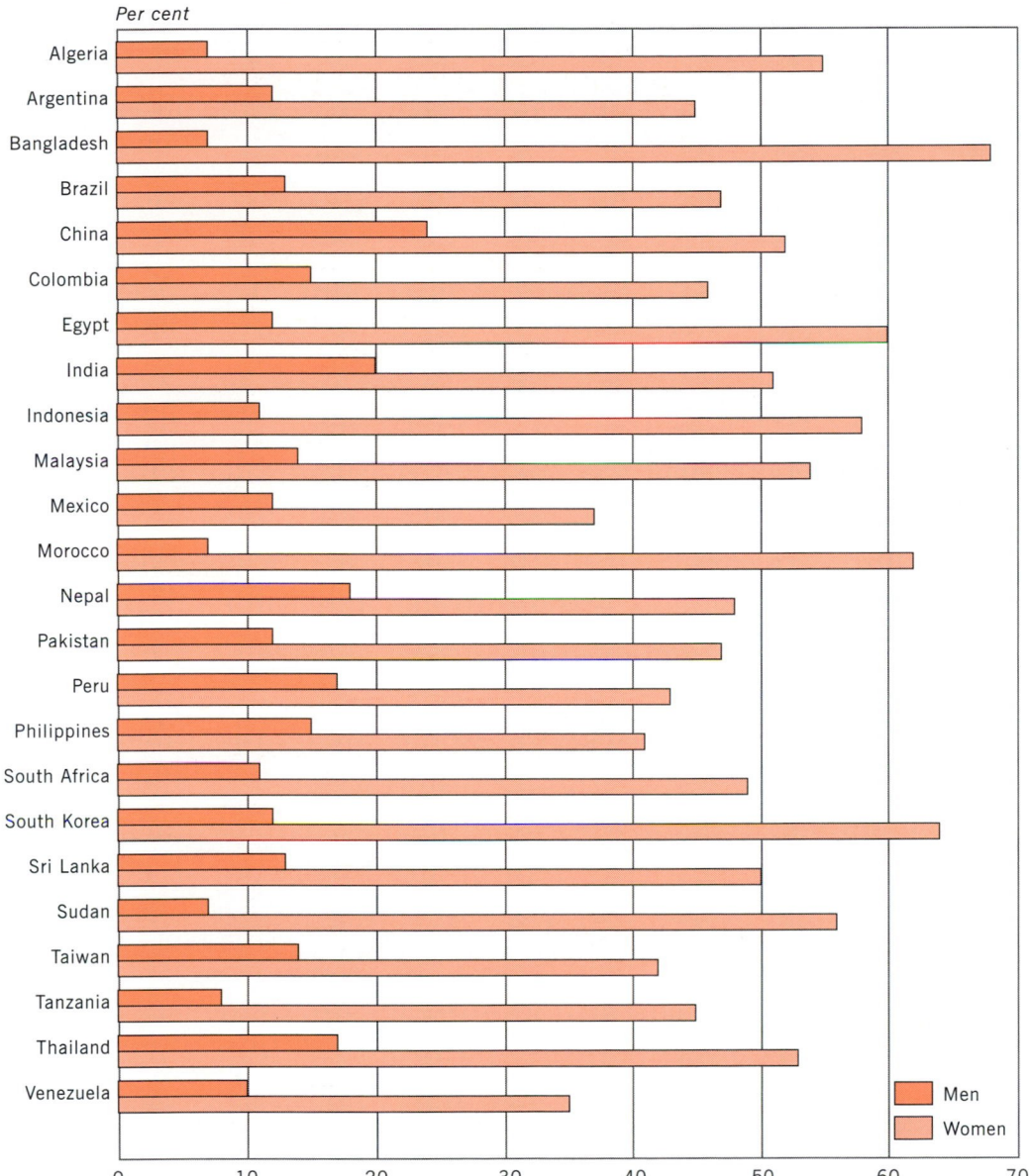

Per cent

Source: US Bureau of the Census, 1996b

Greater longevity for women is accompanied by more years of disability.

Women are much more likely to be widowed than men because they live longer, because younger women often marry older men and because men are more likely to remarry. Typically less than 20 per cent of men over 60 in developing countries are widowed compared with more than half of women.

Profile of older men and women in Zimbabwe

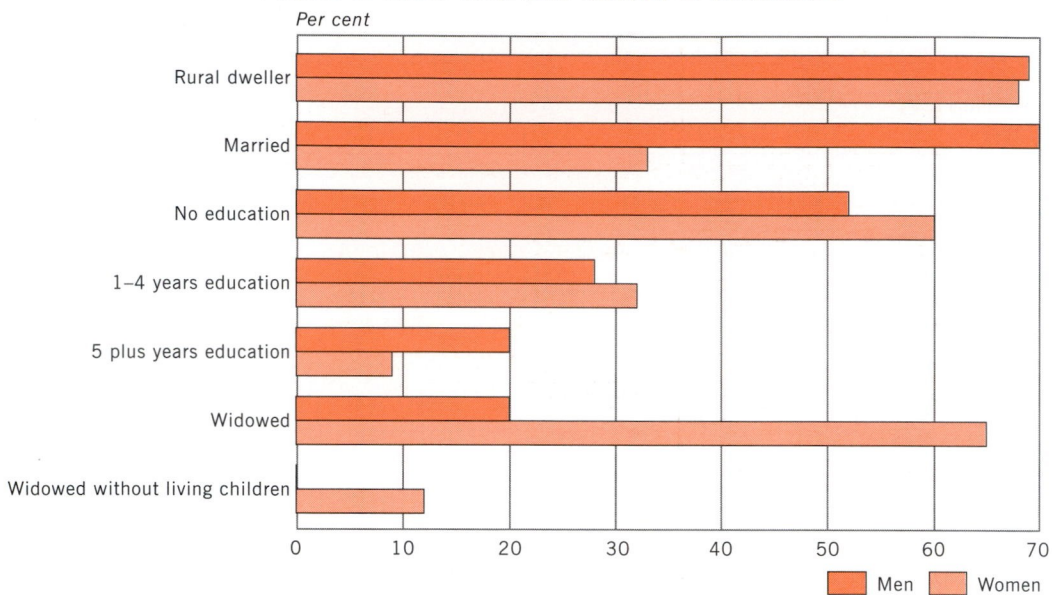

Source: Adamchak, 1998, Table 3

Older people are economically active

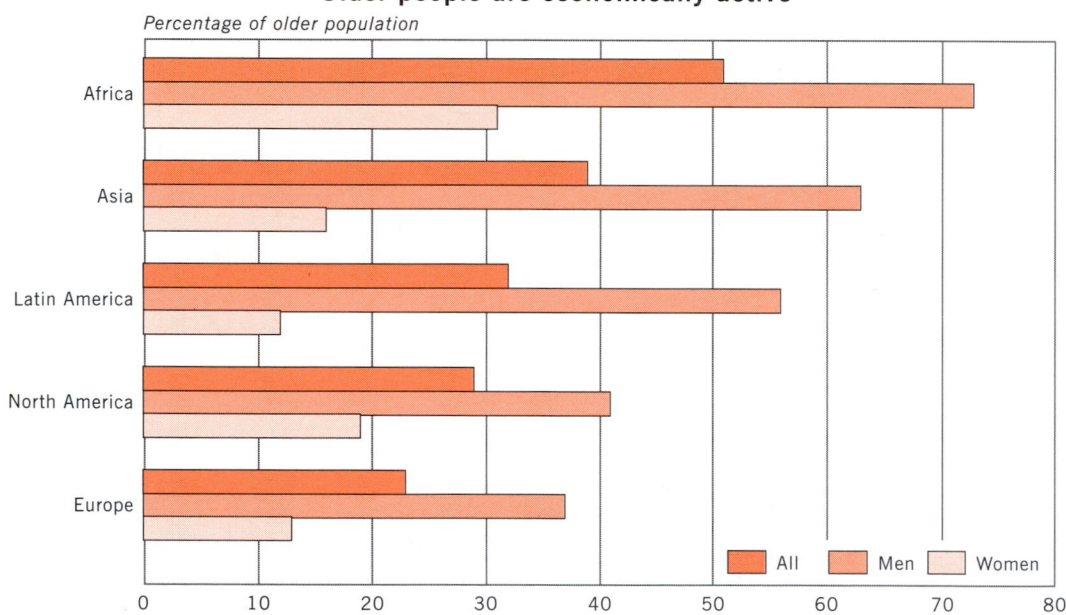

Source: UN, 1991

Livelihoods and Poverty

Older people are economically active. Even in the formal sector, labour force participation rates are high.

Percentage of the population which is economically active over the age of 60

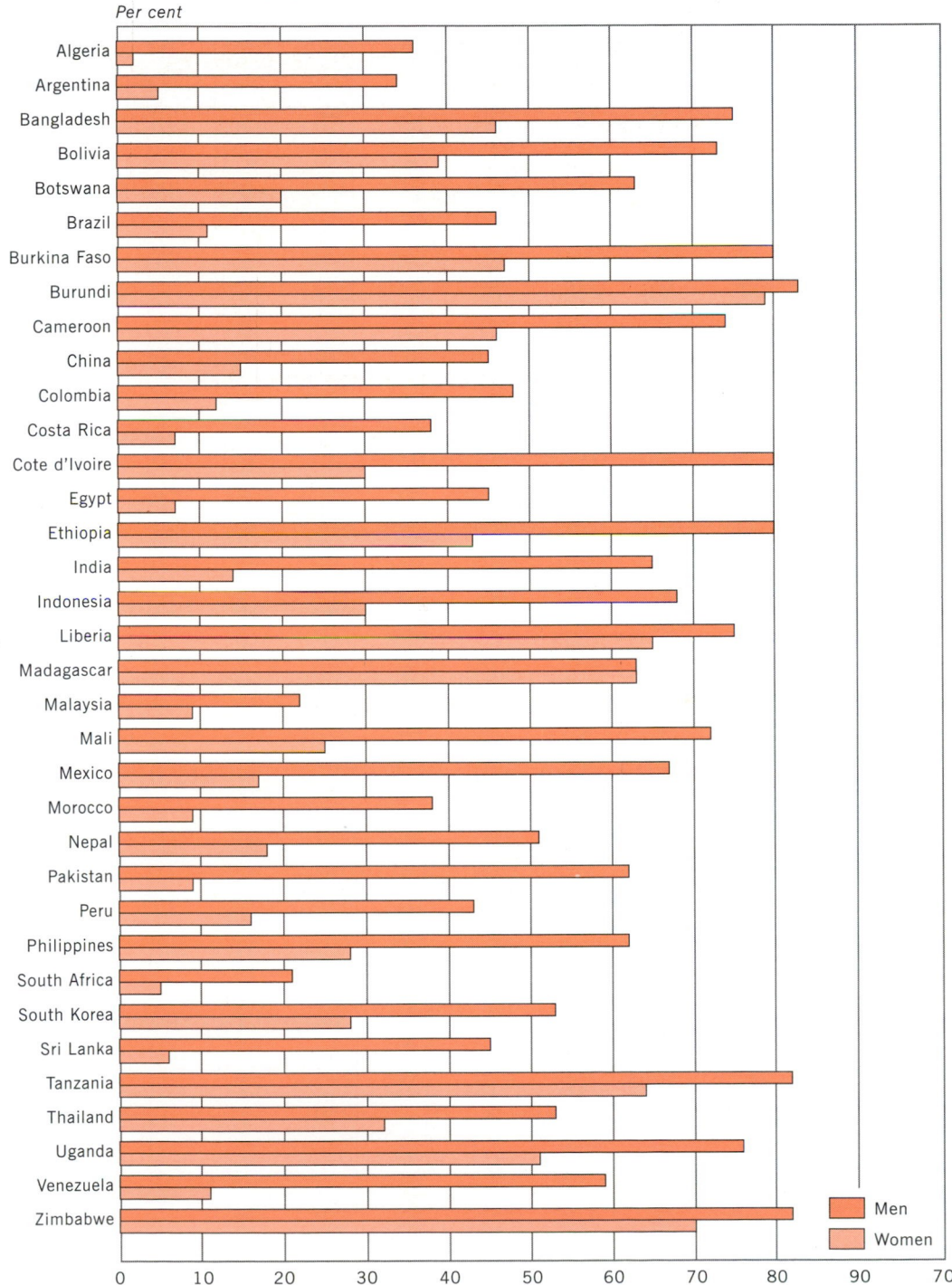

Per cent

Source: US Bureau of the Census, 1996b

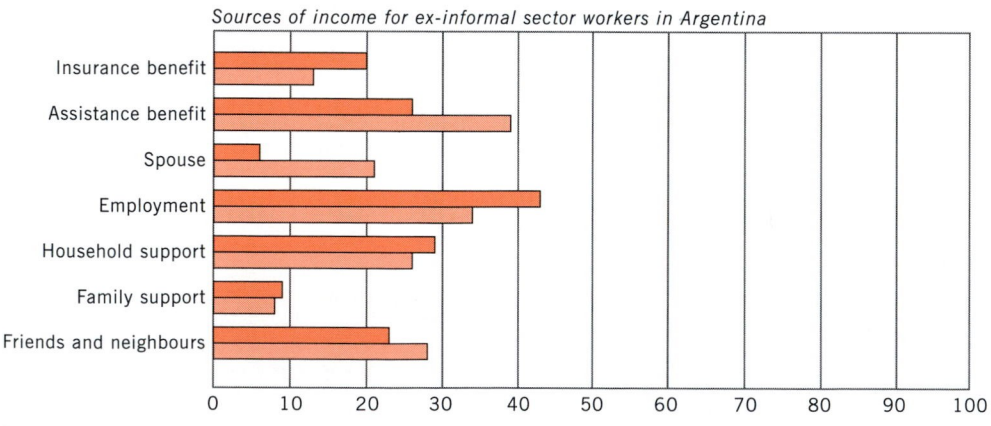

Sources of income and support for older people

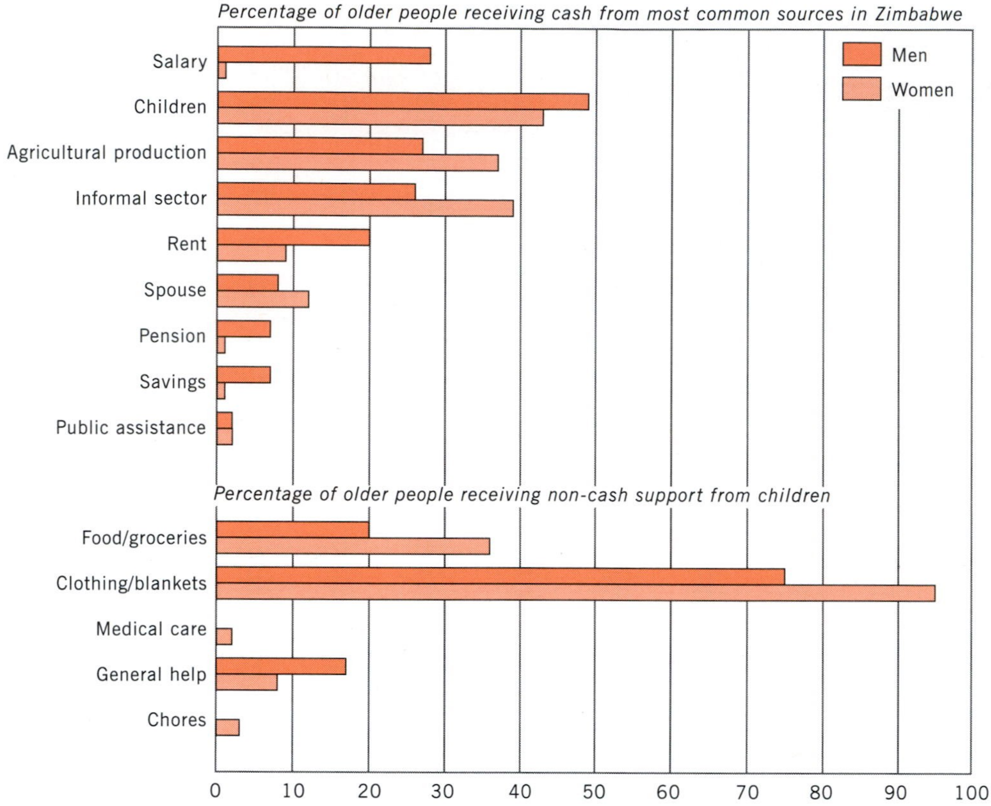

Percentage of older people receiving cash from most common sources in Zimbabwe

Source: Adamchak, 1998

Sources of income for ex-informal sector workers in Argentina

Source: Lloyd-Sherlock, P, 1997

Older people depend on a variety of economic and social livelihood sources.

Pensioners as a percentage of people over 60 for selected developing countries

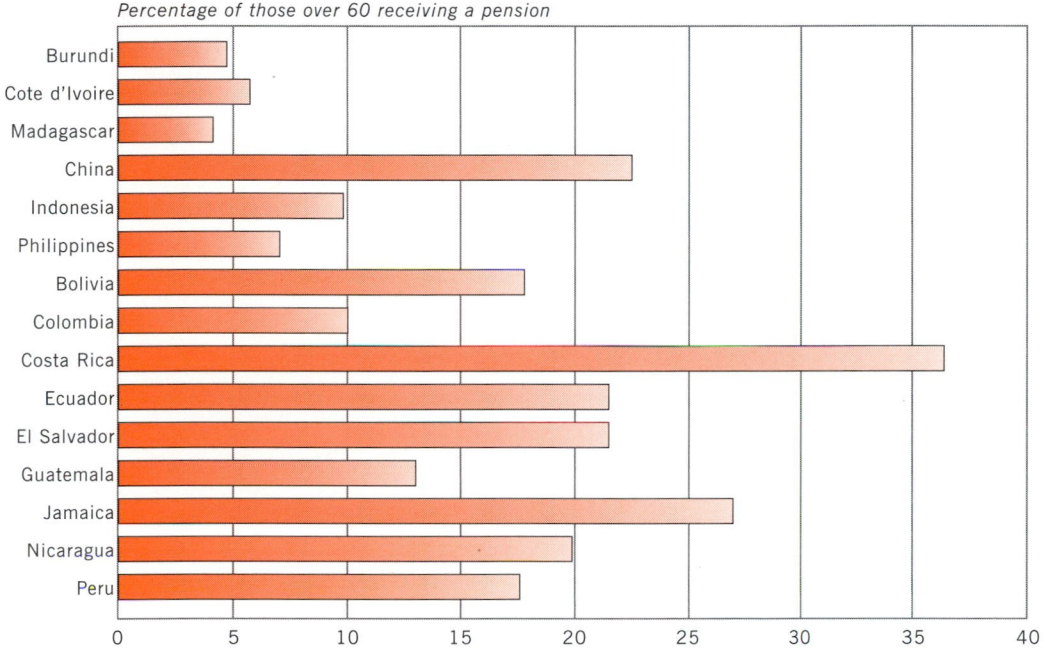

Percentage of those over 60 receiving a pension

Source: World Bank, 1994, Table A4

Pensions provision affects only very modest proportions of the population in developing countries and is skewed away from poorer groups, rural areas, the informal sector and women.

Annual cash income of older people in Zimbabwe, 1997

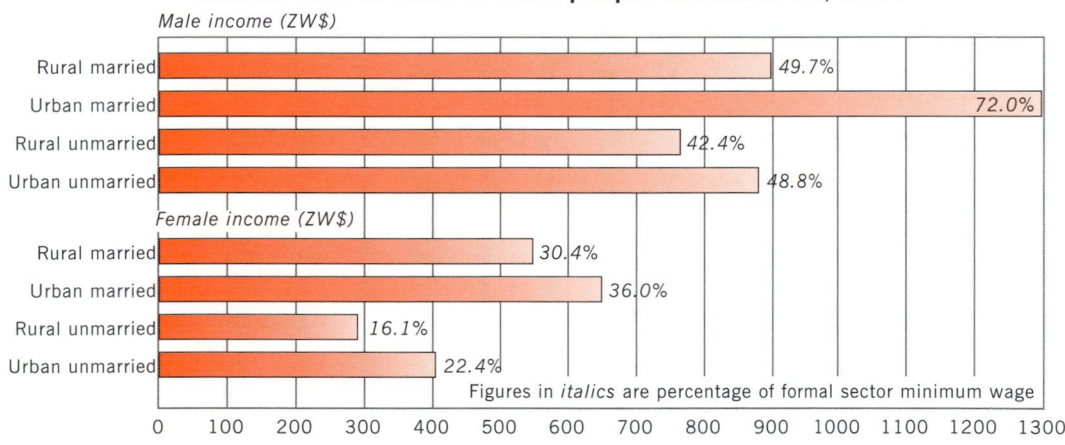

Male income (ZW$)

Rural married	49.7%
Urban married	72.0%
Rural unmarried	42.4%
Urban unmarried	48.8%

Female income (ZW$)

Rural married	30.4%
Urban married	36.0%
Rural unmarried	16.1%
Urban unmarried	22.4%

Figures in *italics* are percentage of formal sector minimum wage

Source: Adamchak, 1998, Table 6

Poverty appears greater among older people than among the population as a whole. Older women tend to be poorer than older men and widowhood is accompanied by poverty. Poorer, older women are among the most vulnerable.

In urban areas of China, 41 per cent of older women but only 4 per cent of older men live below an extreme poverty line.[3]

In India, households headed by widows are by far the poorest group, with an average expenditure per person 70 per cent below the national average.[4]

Notes

1   Leete, R, 1998, *Population Ageing: Background Review*, Technical and Policy Division, UNFPA, prepared for ICPD+5 Technical Meeting on Population Aging, Brussels, 6–9 October, p2.
2   Schulz, J, 1997, *Ageing in Asia*, ILO, Geneva.
3   Wu, Cang-ping, 1991, *The Aging of Population in China*, Institute on Ageing, Malta.
4   Dreze, 1990.

Sources for data

Adamchak, D J, 1998, *Meeting the Needs of the Poor Elderly in Zimbabwe and Namibia*. Paper prepared for the ICPD+5 Technical Meeting on Population Aging, Brussels, 6–9 October.

ESCAP, 1995, *Population Ageing and Development*, Asian Population Studies Series number 140, United Nations, Bangkok. Quoted in paper for Regional Seminar on Promoting a Society for All Ages, 1–4 December 1998.

Lloyd-Sherlock, P, 1997, *Old Age and Urban Poverty in the Developing World*, Macmillan Press, London.

UN, 1991, *The World Ageing situation 1991*, United Nations, NY, based on ILO, 1986, *Economically active population estimates and projections 1950–2025* vol V, ILO, Geneva. Quoted in ILO, 1997, Ageing in Asia, ILO, Geneva.

UN Population Division, 1996, *Sex and Age Distribution of the World Populations: The 1996 Revision and World Population Projections to 2150*, Department of Economic and Social Affairs, United Nations, New York. Some of the data used was originally analysed and quoted in Leete, R, *Population Ageing: Background Review*. Technical and Policy Division, UNFPA, prepared for ICPD+5 Technical Meeting on Population Aging, Brussels, 6–9 October 1998. This paper gives an excellent overview of the demographic changes currently underway and of their implications.

US Bureau of the Census, 1996a, quoted in *The Remarkable Improvements in Survival and Older Ages*, Vaupel, J W, Max Planck Institute for Demographic Research, Paper prepared for the Royal Society/British Academy Meeting, London, 7 May 1997

US Bureau of the Census, 1996b, Wallchart: *Global Aging in the 21st Century*, December. The US Bureau of the Census provides an invaluable global data base and in its *Aging World* reports and its series of international briefing papers highlight significant demographic changes and their implications. It provides good coverage of developing countries. The US Bureau of the Census will publish *An Aging World III* in 1999. The previous edition was published in 1993.

World Bank, 1994, *Averting the Old Age Crisis*, World Bank Policy Research Report, World Bank, Washington, DC.

Part IV

Reference Section

Fundraising volunteers, Helping Hand
Hong Kong.
© COSE

United Nations Principles for Older Persons

To add life to the years that have been added to life

The UN Principles aim to ensure that priority attention will be given to the situation of older persons. The UN Principles address the independence, participation, care, self-fulfilment and dignity of older persons.

United Nations principles for older persons

The General Assembly:

- Appreciating the contribution that older persons make to their societies,
- Recognizing that, in the Charter of the United Nations, the peoples of the United Nations declare, *inter alia*, their determination to reaffirm faith in fundamental human rights, in the dignity and worth of the human person, in the equal rights of men and women and of nations large and small and to promote social progress and better standards of life in larger freedom,
- Noting the elaboration of those rights in the Universal Declaration of Human Rights, the International Covenant on Economic, Social and Cultural Rights and the International Covenant on Civil and Political Rights and other declarations to ensure the application of universal standards to particular groups,
- In pursuance of the International Plan of Action on Ageing, adopted by the World Assembly on Ageing and endorsed by the General Assembly in its resolution 37/51 of 3 December 1982,
- Appreciating the tremendous diversity in the situation of older persons, not only between countries but within countries and between individuals, which requires a variety of policy responses,
- Aware that in all countries, individuals are reaching an advanced age in greater numbers and in better health than ever before,
- Aware of the scientific research disproving many stereotypes about inevitable and irreversible declines with age,
- Convinced that in a world characterized by an increasing number and proportion of older persons, opportunities must be provided for willing and capable older persons to participate in and contribute to the ongoing activities of society,
- Mindful that the strains on family life in both developed and developing countries require support for those providing care to frail older persons,
- Bearing in mind the standards already set by the International Plan of Action on Ageing and the conventions, recommendations and resolutions of the International Labour Organization, the World Health Organization and other United Nations entities,

Encourages Governments to incorporate the following principles into their national programmes whenever possible:

Independence

1   Older persons should have access to adequate food, water, shelter, clothing and health care through the provision of income, family and community support and self-help.

2   Older persons should have the opportunity to work or to have access to other income-generating opportunities.
3   Older persons should be able to participate in determining when and at what pace withdrawal from the labour force takes place.
4   Older persons should have access to appropriate educational and training programmes.
5   Older persons should be able to live in environments that are safe and adaptable to personal preferences and changing capacities.
6   Older persons should be able to reside at home for as long as possible.

Participation

1   Older persons should remain integrated in society, participate actively in the formulation and implementation of policies that directly affect their well-being and share their knowledge and skills with younger generations.
2   Older persons should be able to seek and develop opportunities for service to the community and to serve as volunteers in positions appropriate to their interests and capabilities.
3   Older persons should be able to form movements or associations of older persons.

Care

1   Older persons should benefit from family and community care and protection in accordance with each society's system of cultural values.
2   Older persons should have access to health care to help them to maintain or

regain the optimum level of physical, mental and emotional well-being and to prevent or delay the onset of illness.
3   Older persons should have access to social and legal services to enhance their autonomy, protection and care.
4   Older persons should be able to utilize appropriate levels of institutional care providing protection, rehabilitation and social and mental stimulation in a humane and secure environment.
5   Older persons should be able to enjoy human rights and fundamental freedoms when residing in any shelter, care or treatment facility, including full respect for their dignity, beliefs, needs and privacy and for the right to make decisions about their care and the quality of their lives.

Self-fulfilment

1   Older persons should be able to pursue opportunities for the full development of their potential.
2   Older persons should have access to the educational, cultural, spiritual and recreational resources of society.

Dignity

1   Older persons should be able to live in dignity and security and be free of exploitation and physical or mental abuse.
2   Older persons should be treated fairly regardless of age, gender, racial or ethnic background, disability or other status, and be valued independently of their economic contribution.

HelpAge International

HelpAge International is a unique development agency. It works via a network of development, research, community based and social service organizations that share a common mission to improve the lives of disadvantaged older people.

HelpAge International's innovative approach combines support for partners and members, direct programme implementation, research and advocacy. Increasingly, HelpAge International is involved in the formulation of national and international strategies on ageing.

The organization was founded in 1983 as an independent charity by HelpAge India, Help the Aged Canada, Pro Vida Colombia, HelpAge Kenya and Help the Aged UK. From five agencies it has grown to the present membership of 62 organizations world-wide.

Through its membership, HelpAge International has established a presence in areas ranging from remote rural villages to some of the poorest slums in Asia, Latin America, Africa, eastern and central Europe and the Caribbean. The organization currently works with over 200 partners in 70 countries targeting the most vulnerable older people.

HelpAge International is governed by a Board of Directors drawn from its membership who presently come from Canada, Dominica, Ghana, India, Kenya, Singapore, UK, USA and Zimbabwe. The secretariat is based in London and there are four regional development centres in Asia (Thailand), Africa (Kenya), Caribbean (Jamaica) and Latin America (Bolivia). HelpAge International also works in East and Central Europe and has representation in Brussels.

HelpAge International was the first organization to receive the United Nations award for services to the United Nations Programme on Ageing, and has consultative status (Category 1) with the Economic and Social Council of the United Nations.

How does HelpAge International work?

- Practically – through projects which address the basic needs of older people particularly economic insecurity and poor health and which tackle social issues such as isolation, fear, discrimination, disability and abuse.
- At policy level – challenging the poverty, inequality and discrimination which prevent many older people achieving their potential and realizing their rights. By strengthening older people's involvement in development programmes and in local and national policy making processes. And by creating awareness of the rights, needs and problems facing older people and the role they play in solving these challenges.
- In emergencies – responding to the specific needs of older people affected by civil conflict, economic collapse or natural disasters.
- Through its membership which includes national organizations; community based groups and regional networks. Support is provided to facilitate members learning from one another's experience, through funding, training, resource mobilization, capacity building and project management.

Member organizations[1]

Africa

- HelpAge Ghana
- HelpAge Kenya
- Mauritius Family Planning Association
- Senior Citizens Council, Mauritius
- Associação dos Aposentados de Moçambique (APOSEMO), Mozambique
- Sierra Leone Society for the Welfare of the Aged
- Elim Hlanganani Society for the Care of the Aged, South Africa
- The Muthande Society for the Aged (MUSA), South Africa
- Sudanese Society in Care of Older People (SSCOP)
- Uganda Reach the Aged Association
- HelpAge Zimbabwe

Asia/Pacific

- Council on the Ageing (Australia)
- Office of Seniors Interests, Australia
- Resource Integration Centre (RIC), Bangladesh
- Fiji Council of Social Services
- Helping Hand Hong Kong
- HelpAge India
- HelpAge Korea
- Instituto de Acção Social de Macau
- NACSCOM, Malaysia
- USIAMAS, Malaysia
- Pakistan Medico International
- Coalition of Services of the Elderly (COSE), Philippines
- Singapore Action Group of Elders
- Tsao Foundation, Singapore
- HelpAge Sri Lanka
- Senior Citizen Association of Thailand
- Senior Citizens Council of Thailand

Caribbean

- Society of St Vincent de Paul (SVP), Antigua
- HelpAge Barbados/Barbados National Council on Aging
- HelpAge Belize
- REACH Dominica
- ANAYA, Dominican Republic
- Extended Care Through Hope and Optimism (ECHO), Grenada
- Action Ageing Jamaica
- Old People's Welfare Association (OPWA), Montserrat
- National Council of and for Older Persons/HelpAge St Lucia

Europe

- Zivot 90, Czech Republic
- DaneAge Association, Denmark
- Age Action Ireland
- Elderly Woman's Activities Centre (EWAC), Lithuania
- Caritas Malta HelpAge
- Stichting Mensen in Nood / Caritas Nederland, The Netherlands
- Slovene Foundation (Slovenska Fondacija), Slovenia
- Centre for Policy on Ageing, United Kingdom
- Eurolink Age, United Kingdom
- Help the Aged (UK)
- London School of Hygiene and Tropical Medicine (LSHTM), United Kingdom

Latin America

- FAIAF, Argentina
- Pro Vida Bolivia
- Caritas Chile
- Pro Vida Colombia
- Asociación Gerontológica Costarricense (AGECO), Costa Rica
- Pro Vida Ecuador
- CooperAcción, Peru
- Mesa de Trabajo de ONGs Sobre Ancianidad, Peru
- Pro Vida Perú

North America

- Help the Aged (Canada)
- American Association of Retired Persons (AARP), USA
- National Council on the Aging, USA
- West Virginia University Center on Aging, USA

Note

1 As at 30 April 1999.

Acronyms and Abbreviations

ADB	Asian Development Bank
AECI	Spanish Agency for International Cooperation
AIDS	acquired immune deficiency syndrome
CIPE	Centre for Educational Research Promotion (Bolivia)
COSE	Coalition of Services of the Elderly (Philippines)
DANIDA	Danish International Development Agency
DFID	Department for International Development (United Kingdom)
ECHO	European Commission Humanitarian Office
ESCAP	Economic and Social Commission for Asia and the Pacific (UN)
FAO	Food and Agriculture Organization (UN)
GDP	gross domestic product
HAI	HelpAge International
HEE	Programme for Health of the Elderly (WHO)
HIV	human immunodeficiency virus
ICPD	International Conference for Population Development
IDP	internally displaced person
ILO	International Labour Organization
IMERSO	Spanish Ministry of Labour and Social Affairs
INIA	United Nations International Institute on Ageing
INTA	Department of Agriculture (Argentina)
IOL	intra-ocular lens
IYOP	International Year of Older Persons
JICA	Japan International Co-operation Agency
MOLISA	Ministry of Health and Social Insurance Agency (Vietnam)
MSALVA	Ministry of Social Affairs, Labour and Veterans Affairs (Cambodia)
MYWCF	Ministry for Youth, Women, Children and Family (Panama)
NAB	National Assistance Board (Barbados)
NACEA	National Advisory Committee on Ageing and Elderly (Fiji)
NGO	non-governmental organization
NZODA	New Zealand Overseas Development Agency
OCV	overseas cooperation volunteer
OECD	Organisation for Economic Co-operation and Development
OPA	Older People's Association (Bangladesh)
PAHO	Pan American Health Organization
PROMUDEH	Ministry for the Promotion of Women and Human Development (Peru)
SWEP	Society for the Welfare of Elderly Persons (Nepal)
TAMWA	Tananzia Media Women's Association
TB	tuberculosis
UN	United Nations
UNDP	United Nations Development Programme
UNFPA	United Nations Population Fund
UNHCR	United Nations High Commission for Refugees
USAID	United States Agency for International Development
WHO	World Health Organization